Teaching with technologies:
The essential guide

Teaching with technologies: The essential guide

Sarah Younie and Marilyn Leask

McGraw Hill Education

Open University Press

Open University Press
McGraw-Hill Education
McGraw-Hill House
Shoppenhangers Road
Maidenhead
Berkshire
England
SL6 2QL

email: enquiries@openup.co.uk
world wide web: www.openup.co.uk

and Two Penn Plaza, New York, NY 10121-2289, USA

First published 2013

A catalogue record of this book is available from the British Library

ISBN-13: 978-0-335246-18-2 (pb)
ISBN-10: 0-335246-18-4 (pb)
eISBN: 978-0-335246-19-9

Library of Congress Cataloging-in-Publication Data
CIP data applied for

Typeset by Aptara, Inc.
Printed and bound by CPI Group (UK) Ltd, Croydon, CR0 4YY

Contents

Acknowledgements

The authors would like to thank all of the teachers and other colleagues who have contributed over the past twenty-five years to the research projects listed in Appendix 2. They would also like to thank particularly: their families for their support and forbearance. Karen Cameron for her support throughout the preparation of the book and her attention to detail in bringing all the chapters together and her encouragement throughout. Annika Coughlin for her ongoing support in the production of the manuscript and cheerfulness in the face of pressure. Professor Christina Preston for her partnership in the Becta-funded ICT Tools for Future Teachers research. Tafadzwa Gwarinda for his insights on theories of motivation. To Doug Dickinson and Barry Dufour for feedback and encouragement.

List of tables

List of figures

Introduction

The purpose of this book

This book focuses on the current state of play with the integration of digital technologies into school-based teaching and learning. As well as providing a comprehensive analysis of developments to date, it identifies 'what works' with technology and education.

The study of ways in which technologies can be used to support learning is a relatively new field in education with work beginning in earnest in the 1980s. This book records this history and is written for those who are interested in technology and education: academics, practitioners, policy-makers, researchers, students, teachers and trainees across ages and stages.

The intention of the book is to provide an outline for effective practice for individual educators and school management teams together with policy-makers in countries and regional authorities to aspire to.

To achieve these goals, the book includes information on pedagogic approaches and learning theories, together with examples, which will inform teachers and, most important, will allow them to develop their practice in order to incorporate and exploit the affordances of digital technologies. Also, given the increased international focus on the quality of the teaching workforce (OECD 2007a, b; 2009), there is a growing awareness that teachers need to be regularly up-skilled and updated with new knowledge to ensure the profession keeps pace with changes and technological developments.

The book provides an overview of research in the field of technology and its application to educational practice. It brings together the findings from a range of research projects as well as highlighting effective practice. It provides an understanding of how digital technologies can and should impact upon the processes of learning and inform pedagogical approaches.

It also examines the challenges facing education in the light of technological advancements. Meeting the challenges to integrate digital technology requires changes in the ways teachers are trained to use new technologies; changes in curriculum content; organization of curriculum time to accommodate personalized learning; teachers' professional development and reflection on pedagogic practices.

The book also addresses the fact that there has been a failure of technology to impact at the level that policy-makers envisaged and investigates the question: why should teachers use technology?

It offers further knowledge and understanding about digital technology for learning and teaching, which is a relatively new field of inquiry that is diverse, complex and contested. The book provides a synthesis of research and application to practice and aims to provoke discussion and debate.

It also covers technology-supported learning and teaching and does so through the lens of educational research. The areas of theories of learning, technology *and* practical, pedagogic applications of technologies in the classroom are not well catered for, with books tending to be too specialist – for example, on computing and technology, or too generalist – for example, on generic classroom teaching.

This book provides an outline for effective technology practice, offering comprehensive coverage of the field as well as a critically informed overview of the research, which informs practice. In short, this book addresses the following issues:

- The field of digital technology and education is complex and diverse and there is an increasing expectation that policy and practice should be informed by research (OECD 2002; 2003; 2007a, b; 2009).
- There is misunderstanding of the purposes and role of technology in school-based education between teachers and policy-makers. For example, there are tensions between the vocational and pedagogical purposes and, as a consequence, there is a confused picture of the value of digital technologies in education.
- A weakness of the field is that it is hard for teachers as practitioners to gain an overview of theory, research and practice in the field. The major part of research in education and technology is contained in diverse academic journal articles and research reports for government agencies.
- The need for a coherent account of the developments in this field over the past three decades, which captures the story to date of a relatively recent and exciting field in education, is one which practitioners know they cannot afford to ignore.

Digital technology is not static and is a constantly developing and rapidly changing field. It will be many decades before practice in the poorest schools equals that of the best. At issue is the patchiness of technology provision and practices in schools.

The research base and theoretical framework for this book

There are many practical guides on how teachers are using technology in classrooms. However, the pedagogical approaches are under-theorized. This book therefore examines in detail links between known learning theories and practices and raises questions about the pedagogical approaches appropriate for different forms of technology. The book also gives an overview of the state of play with the use of digital technologies in classrooms in schools in the UK.

Table 0.1 Theories and approaches to learning

Relevant learning theories	Key ideas	Learning is conceptualized as:
1.1 Constructivism Piaget (1963)	Constructive – individual focus Concerned with how knowledge and skills are internalized Cognitivist Developmental	Learning is conceptualized as individuals actively exploring the world and receiving feedback. Constructivity – is the integration of new concepts and skills into the learner's existing conceptual/competency structures. Pedagogical applications: knowledge building requires interactive environments. Need activities to encourage experimentation and discovery of principles. Need support for reflection and evaluation.
1.2 Social Constructivism Vygotsky (1978)	Constructive – social focus Zone of proximal development Understand learner and scaffolders roles in collaborative activities	Individual learning is scaffolded by the social environment. Teachers/more knowledgeable peers have a key role in dialogue and interaction with the learner; how learners can progress beyond their immediate capability by supportive others scaffolding the learning experience. Pedagogical applications: knowledge building requires interactive environments. Need activities to encourage collaboration and shared expression of ideas/dialogic approach. Need support for reflection, peer-review and evaluation.
1.3 Communal Constructivism (Leask and Younie 2001) Holmes et al. (2001)	Social constructivism – dialogic learning **with** technology Situated learning and distributed cognition, using digital technologies for social/professional online networking for knowledge management	Social theories of learning (peer-to-peer knowledge construction) and the affordances of digital technologies (to create, share and build new knowledge online together; **with** and **for** each other) Learning is conceptualized as collaboratively co-creating knowledge, through cooperative, peer-to-peer, informal learning and interaction, using digital technology.
1.4 Situated Learning Lave and Wenger (1991)	Communities of Practice Situative CPD Work-based learning Situated learning	Learning is conceptualized as participating in communities of practice. Developing from novice to expert, focus on situativity attends to the social context of learning. Authenticity of the environment and support for peer-to-peer learning are highlighted.

(continued)

Table 0.1 *(Continued)*

Relevant learning theories	Key ideas	Learning is conceptualized as:
1.5 Multiple Intelligences Gardner (1983)	Individuals have multiple cognitive abilities Identifying multiple intelligences in the breakdown of intellectual capacities	Individuals have different and multiple ways of learning and processing information. To date, 8 intelligences have been identified, these are relatively distinct and separate: linguistic, logic-mathematical, spatial, musical, bodily/kinaesthetic, inter-personal, intra-personal, naturalistic; and a possible ninth intelligence, spiritual/existential. Influenced by Piaget and Bruner.
1.6 Emotional Intelligence Salovey and Mayer (1990) Goleman (1996)	Individuals have different emotional abilities/intelligence levels	Learning is conceptualized as the ability to perceive emotions; to integrate emotions to facilitate thought; to navigate social environments and process information of an emotional nature. Whether this is strictly 'intelligence' is contested. However, educationalists acknowledge the link between cognition and emotion, which both affect learning.
1.7 Experiential Learning Dewey (1938) Lewin (1951) Kolb (1984) Beard and Wilson (2006)	Experience is the foundation of learning Learning is holistic, socially and culturally constructed Learning is shaped and influenced by the socio-economic context in which it occurs	Learning is conceptualized as – learning from experience. Experiential learning is the process of making meaning from direct experience, upon which, reflection is encouraged to increase knowledge, skills, values and beliefs. Emphasis on learning by doing. Pedagogical applications: action learning; problem-based learning; emphasis on critical thinking and problem solving. Experimentation/experiential learning are constructivist; focus on how learning opportunities allow progressive discovery of concepts and skills.
1.8 Behaviourism Watson (1924) Pavlov (1927) Skinner (1953)	Classical and operant conditioning Antecedents, behaviour, consequences Stimulus-response Reward and reinforcement Trial and error learning	Learning is conceptualized as association between stimulus-response. Focus is on measureable behavioural outcomes of learning, rather than knowledge, understanding, values, attitudes and beliefs. Associative concern with external behaviours (not with how concepts/skills are represented internally) Pedagogical applications: instrumental teaching, drill and practice, rote learning.

Each chapter includes references to relevant learning theories. In this chapter Table 0.1 summarizes the major theories referred to throughout the text. These are provided to give the reader an overview of these fields and provides the theoretical framework to analyse the potential influence of various digital technologies on the teaching and learning process.

The text is underpinned by research funded by a number of European Union and UK government agencies over a 25-year period including Becta, DFID, TDA, DfE and the EU, which was conducted by the authors (see Appendix 2 for a list of projects). In addition, some of the last pieces of research commissioned in the UK, by what was the government agency responsible for this area (Becta), on teachers' uses of technology, underpin this book (Leask and Preston 2010; Younie and Leask 2009). Leask (2011) provides an overview of many of the key issues, which are particularly relevant to policy-makers.

Applications to practice

The vast majority of research in education and technology is contained in academic journal articles and research reports for government agencies and rarely is translation of research into practice undertaken, although it is recommended practice by the British Educational Research Association that researchers publish for academic, policy-maker and practitioner audiences.

There is an emerging tradition of 'translational research' to which the authors subscribe and, therefore, the reader will find that each chapter contains applications to practice, which are an outcome of the translation of research into practice. In this text, examples are used which are applicable across a range of contexts to aid the readers' reflection on the application of research and theory to practice in their specific context. Further information can be found in texts which provide specific advice for particular subject areas and for particular age groups.

For technologies which have not, as yet, a proven track record in classroom application, teachers will find a helpful synopsis of the potential uses and the important debates surrounding these. This information is intended to support teachers in reaching professional judgements about appropriate pedagogical approaches to use in their subject area. The first part of the book addresses in depth the theory and research related to the adoption and use of technology in schools by teachers and pupils. The 'futures' part of the book, picks up these theories and research and shows the application to practice in more depth and draws on a sample of innovative practitioners in the UK.

Change in the field of digital technologies is constant. However, the principles underlying education (learning and teaching) are relatively stable and these theories have remained largely unchanged in the past 40 years. So, while specific technologies referred to in the text may become outdated, the underlying principles of pedagogical implementation will remain. It is important to note, however, that the uptake of innovation is both slow and rarely revolutionary, and the practices described in some schools that are leading the way highlight the effectiveness of digital technologies and how they can enhance learning. However, technology cannot, in and of itself, produce change, because that requires agency from teachers and learners, and for learners to experience fully the affordances of digital technologies that requires pedagogical framing by the teacher.

There is a growing body of literature on the application of digital and Web-based technologies to teaching and learning. However, much tends to be focused on the post and non-compulsory sectors, whereas this book is firmly focused on schools, providing teachers with coherent and balanced coverage of research on digital and Web-based technologies as they relate to school and classroom practice.

Sarah Younie
Marilyn Leask
April 2012

PART 1

History

1 Integrating technology in classrooms: from the microcomputer to 'the cloud'

Overview

The objective of this chapter is to provide the reader with an historical overview of events, which led to the wide-scale expansion of the use of technology in classrooms in the UK; to review past uses of technologies in schools and to examine how computing technology has been introduced into the classroom over the past three decades.

Gaining an understanding of this history will provide a context from which subsequent developments can be understood. The chapter draws on research into the identifiable phases of technology adoption in schools and from the perspective of practitioners, whose voices on the history were captured in the research conducted by Hammond et al. (2009).

The history of technology in education is charted through an account of how computers first came into schools, the changes in hardware and software which followed and then the introduction of the micro-computer and, more recently, mobile technologies. These changes were experienced by practitioners as phases in developments which, although not necessarily distinct, were nonetheless definable by changes in processing speed, reliability of storage and connectivity, diminishing size and portability coupled with increasing personal ownership of sophisticated mobile technology devices. However, while the use of technology in UK schools has changed dramatically over the last three decades, what has not changed to any significant degree is the nature of schooling and teachers' ideas about learning and teaching.

Introduction and context

From the introduction of mainframe computers in the late 1960s, mainly in higher education, to the introduction of micro-computers into schools in the early 1980s, from storage on cassette tape to more reliable disc drives and cloud computing, from Acorn to PC machines, from standalone to networks and wireless hand-held devices, the changes have been and continue to be challenging to education practitioners. The challenge is on two fronts: the speed of development; and the increasing possibilities for the different forms of technology to support improvements in teaching and learning approaches.

In 1981, in the UK, the British Broadcasting Corporation (BBC) Computer Literacy Project for the first time put micro-computers within the reach of teachers from a wide range of curriculum areas (Millwood 2009). One million units were sold in five years (McMordie, undated) and the government supported the Technical Vocational Education Initiative (1984–1990), which ensured these BBC machines were available in schools. Prior to this time mathematics departments in secondary schools often had links to mainframe computers elsewhere, usually in universities.

What is clear from research is that 'computers found their way into schools without a clear [pedagogic] rationale' (Hammond et al. 2009: 49). Consequently, an examination of the phases of development needs to be understood alongside the political agenda driving technology in education; these developments do not stand in isolation: 'it is very difficult to talk about technology without considering parallel developments in policy and pedagogical thinking' (Hammond et al. 2009: 47).

Theory and research base

The chapter draws on research conducted with leading practitioners involved in technology and education over the past thirty years, which involved in-depth interviews with those who have used technology in their teaching, conducted research and worked with teachers (Hammond et al. 2009). This research, known as the 'Voices Project' and funded by IT in Teacher Education (ITTE), aimed to capture the 'living history' of technology developments in schools from those pioneers who were involved from the very beginning. Alongside this, Millwood's (2009) history that supplements the National Archive of Educational Computing provides a narrative to explain the development of artefacts. Using the archive's materials, Millwood outlines the story of technology in learning from the 1970s in the UK (before the micro-computer), through the 1980s (before the office) and 1990s (before the Internet) to 2000 (before the cloud).

Phases of technology development in schools

Since the first expensive and large mainframe computers in the 1960s, there has been continual development in hardware and software and concomitant challenges arising from the changes in the speed, storage and connectivity of machines. Each development required teachers to acquire technical knowledge (how do I operate this?) and think about practice (how does this interact with my pedagogy?). These dual demands highlight the complex relationship between technology (as machines) and teachers' beliefs about teaching and learning. Hammond et al.'s (2009) research noted that teachers held remarkably consistent beliefs about how to teach throughout their

careers and their experiences with technology, despite shifting contexts and technological changes.

There was also a time lag between advances in technology and their adoption in
schools. It must be stressed that at each stage of progression, the changes were driven
by Research and Development (R and D) in industry (Selwyn 1998) and the military
(Millwood 2009) rather than in response to pedagogical demands from educators.
Teachers were left to adapt these technological advances for school and classroom
purposes: 'this deprived participants and education at large, of a coherent narrative of
what computers in education was all about' (Hammond et al. 2009: 57).

Historically, the first phase from the 1960s up until the end of the 1970s can be
identified with the introduction of mainframe computers, which were chiefly used in
industry or in a higher-education context and led to widespread need for programming skills. Teacher trainers involved in these developments straddled the university and school environments and were fundamental in helping industry produce
teacher-friendly resources; this was achieved through writing specific programmes
for use in the classroom. There was a close working relationship between technology developers and educationalists at this time, and small-scale collaborative projects
were characteristic of this era.

A second phase can be identified with the introduction of the micro-computer
into schools from the early 1980s until the end of that decade. Typically a pupil
would access information in a library and printed encyclopedias, but this changed
in the late 1980s to the use of CD-ROMs. A further phase was detected by Hammond et al. (2009) with the introduction of a graphical user interface (GUI) in 1991,
which practitioners saw as an important shift in the move to personal computers in
schools and commercial software. Then, from the mid to late 1990s, a more advanced
phase can be identified with the introduction of the Internet and the rise of school
networks. For the first time, teachers had access to suites of connected computers
and pupils could access information through search engines with Web 1 technology.
Then, by 2005 Web 2.0 tools and Wikipedia heralded the rise of collaborative, peer-
to-peer knowledge building. More recent developments can be seen in the use of
wireless hand-held devices, which offer greater portability and potential for personalized learning, alongside the move to greater social and professional networking for
information sharing and the use of 'the cloud' for storage of data.

In outlining phases of developments in this way, it must be acknowledged that
this history of technology requires further analysis of a critical political nature,
because the new ways of working made possible by using technology brought concomitant developments in education policy and pedagogical thinking.

Phases of hardware: introducing the micro-computer into schools – 1980s

In 1981 the newly appointed Conservative Minister for Information Technology,
Kenneth Baker, launched the 'Micros in Schools' scheme, which placed an emphasis
on the vocational aspect of technology (Dawes 2001). 'I want to ensure that the kids
of today are trained with the skills that gave their fathers and grandfathers jobs . . .
And that is the reason why we've pushed ahead with computers in schools. I want

youngsters leaving school at sixteen, to actually be able to operate a computer' (Scaife and Wellington 1993: 15).

Research which has captured the experiences of practitioners highlights how the micro-computer marked 'the first decisive moment in the use of computers in school. The new machines offered immediacy and interactivity' (Hammond et al. 2009: 48). All 15 prominent practitioners in the field of educational technology in this research saw the introduction of the micro as a seminal moment in the history of computing in schools.

In the beginning, in the 1980s, funding for the hardware came from the Department of Trade and Industry (DTI), which provided £16 million to subsidize the purchase of British computers in schools. British companies, Research Machines, Acorn and Sinclair (the latter though to a lesser extent) competed with American and Japanese manufacturers (such as IBM, Apple, Atari, Commodore) to equip UK schools with computers (Scaife and Wellington 1993; Millwood 2009).

In addition to purchasing hardware, the Department of Education and Science (DES) provided £23 million to launch the Microelectronics Education Programme (MEP), which was an initiative to explore how computers could be used by teachers in schools. MEP was implemented by the Council for Educational Technology, under the directorship of Richard Fothergill at Newcastle Polytechnic, who led a team of teachers in gathering information, creating materials and disseminating training opportunities. As MEP literature stated, the vision was to 'promote, within the school curriculum, the study of microelectronics and its effects, and to encourage the use of the technology as an aid to teaching and learning'. This ran from 1980 until 1986.

The central team of teachers in MEP worked alongside programmers and publishers to develop software, and 14 Regional Information Centres were created to demonstrate materials to local practitioners. This was a significant part of the MEP vision, as very few education authorities had specialists in the early 1980s and Fothergill understood how multidisciplinary teams working in regional networks were needed to build knowledge, skills and expertise.

Supporting the early use of micros in schools through teachers' centres enabled a powerful mix of facilitating curriculum software development *and* teacher education, which generated conditions for creativity and emerging innovation. This was part of Fothergill's vision:

> Fothergill's real genius lay in knowing how to inspire people without frightening them, and in his staunch belief that we do things better when we do them together. His conviction about what was possible and his healthy disrespect of bureaucracy and pomposity provided valuable lessons. Many were the battles he fought with civil servants of limited vision.
> (Anderson and Page 2004: Obituary)

Many credit Fothergill with the vision of generating the first network of expertise in the UK in the form of specialist teachers, ICT coordinators, advisors and consultants. Indeed, it was Fothergill's untimely death that inspired the 'Voices Project' (Hammond et al. 2009) to capture the experiences of the early pioneers who shaped the beginnings of computer use in schools, particularly, since this history had not been recorded from those involved.

What was deeply understood in this vision was how to create innovation in practice and enable change, through collaborative knowledge building. Leask and Younie (2001a), summarizing the outcomes of research funded by the European Union from 1997–2000 into the pedagogical applications of technologies, identified this way that educators work with technologies as *communal constructivism*. Early educators used communications technology to create and publish knowledge for, and by, one another (Holmes et al. 2001). Previously such knowledge production had been costly and slow.

Through teachers' centres and professional associations small computer programs were developed that teachers could use in the classroom. Teacher professional networks also provided assistance, which was vital as the technology would frequently break down. In a more recent development teachers are using Twitter to provide each other with just-in-time support within personal and professional networks.

Some of the early computers relied on programs which had to be run through tape-recorders. It was not until the introduction of disk drives that a key shift occurred; thereby replacing the unreliability of cassette tapes used previously for the storage of programs. As practitioners recall, the consequences of this lack of reliability were high:

> The cassette recorder turned off a whole generation of very frightened teachers, because it failed so often in the classroom. They put it in even before it was anywhere near reliable. When we got disk drives the world changed, but you'd already lost a whole group of teachers. It was a long, long hard job getting those back in again.'
>
> (Hammond et al. 2009: 49)

Alongside advancements in the reliability of storage came important shifts in software. The development of a graphical user interface (GUI) brought a more user-friendly machine, for teachers and pupils alike, with Apple Macintosh and Acorn Archimedes machines among the first to innovate with GUI (Hammond et al. 2009). This increasing user-friendliness of the interface shifted educational computing out of the 'specialist' domain and into the mainstream of schools.

Early educational computing had focused on programming within the context of specialist 'computer studies' lessons usually located within Maths departments in schools, but the introduction of the micro-computer with pre-prepared software for use in a range of subjects shifted the use of computers to more generalized support across the curriculum.

These developments were further supported in the 1980s by other complementary government initiatives: 1982 was designated 'Information Technology Year' by the Government to increase national awareness of computer technology (Dawes 2001). In 1982 the BBC's Continuing Education Department 'noted the rise of the microcomputer as a pervasive influence on society' and proposed a national campaign (Millwood 2009: 10). Consequently the 'BBC Computer Literacy' project was launched; this involved a book, of which 60,000 copies were sold; a TV programme that reached 300,000 people; a course on the computer programming language

BASIC; and BBC micro-computers, of which 12,000 machines were sold (Hawkridge 1983: 57). This specially commissioned BBC computer was manufactured by Acorn.

This was followed by another major technology initiative launched by the Conservative government in the early 1980s, entitled the Technical and Vocational Initiative (TVEI), which provided further financial aid for schools to purchase computers. However, it transpired that TVEI schools had on average almost *twice* as many computers as non-TVEI schools (Scaife and Wellington 1993: 16). This highlights an emerging disparity of funding between schools for technology procurement: a theme that has continued to re-emerge throughout the succeeding three decades. Also, importantly, TVEI triggered a major political shift in the balance of power in UK education. TVEI was an initiative that radically altered the locus of control in education, being imposed by central government without consultation with the Local Education Authorities or the teaching profession (Leask 1987). However, it did reflect a government commitment to develop technical and vocational education in the 1980s.

As Dawes (2001) reports, this government investment can be seen in 1986, with the Modem Scheme, funded by the Department of Trade and Industry, putting £1 million into enabling schools to buy a modem to link up their micro-computers. In the same year the Microelectronics Support Unit (MESU) was set up with £3 million funding to carry on the work of the Microelectronics Education Programme (MEP), which ended in 1986. Then the White Paper 'Working Together – Education and Training' announced national expenditure of £90 million over ten years to extend the TVEI programme. The Conservative government's commitment to TVEI clearly indicated the importance of technology and in 1987 Kenneth Baker announced Educational Support Grants of £19 million for the expansion of IT in schools.

Phases of software development

In coming to use the same software that has dominated business and industry, schools have adopted commercial applications for word processing, databases and spreadsheets (such as Word, Excel and Access). This has taken away the specialized software designed for education that computers in education first had and has led over the past two decades to a uniformity in schools of software and operating platforms that derive from the business sector.

Prior to this commercial software adoption from business, there were content-free programs, which were especially designed for schools. Hammond et al.'s (2009) research discovered that, among the early programs used in schools, practitioners cited *Branch*, a sorting program, which provided a first step in the idea of artificial intelligence and was often used in primary schools; *Grass* data base; *Cricket Graph*, a data display programme for Apple machines; and the spreadsheet *Grasshopper*. Data logging became popular, particularly in science lessons. There was *Scoopnet*, a newspaper front-page simulation program and the text-revealing program *Developing Tray*, which was popular among adopters.

There was also *Granny's Garden*, which was an early computer game that could be played on the BBC micro. Set in a magical kingdom in the mountains with pupils locating the missing children of the King and Queen, it required the completion of a number of simple problem-solving activities, including logic puzzles, spelling tests and maths quizzes. *Granny's Garden* was later released for use at home on the ZX Spectrum and Amstrad CPC home computer. Another program was the *BBC Domesday Project* with micro-computers, which involved schools collecting data from across the UK (pictures, maps, video, surveys, statistics and personal testimonies), which could be used in conjunction with the BBC Domesday material. The original BBC data was digitally etched into two laser discs and was one of the major interactive projects of the 1980s (Millwood 2009).

Alongside these early programmes came the development of simulations. These modelled real-life contexts, allowing interaction between the user and the software. For example, of those cited by practitioners, there was an archaeological simulation called *Dig*; another programme *Droplet*, which 'simulated the passage of rainfall through the hydrological cycle and, like others, contained a randomising element in it so that the user would get a different output each time the programme was run' (Hammond et al. 2009: 51). As the quality of the graphics has become enhanced, so the sophistication of simulations has increased, with immersive environments gaining in popularity with the development of 3 and 4D (Johnson et al. 2011).

Software development in the 1980s was marked by a significant movement away from educationalists and teachers to commercial providers. Originally, starting with small programs, collaboratively developed between practitioners and programmers, software was created and trialled in educational settings. By the end of the decade general-purpose software could be run on significantly more sophisticated machines and these expensive programmes could only be provided by bigger commercial producers. 'The close link between teachers and developers was being lost and this was marked with regret by all participants' in Hammond et al.'s (2009: 59) research.

Connectivity: the rise of the networked age – 1990s

The introduction of the Internet, in the mid to late 1990s, heralded a new dawn as schools entered the networked age. This signalled the rise of the computer suite. This shift is not to be underestimated as, prior to this development, teachers would only have one or two computers in a classroom. This made whole-class use problematic. Suddenly, with teachers having access to a suite of computers, a whole class could interact with the technology at the same time. Previously the pedagogy of the stand-alone machine meant that teachers tended to 'bolt on' an activity, for pupils to do as part of a rotation exercise with the other lesson activities, or as an extension piece for the more able learners.

While this was the age of networks it was also the time of large-scale introduction of interactive whiteboards (IWBs) in schools. In using interactive whiteboards the focus shifted back to the teacher and their interaction with the whole class. This encouraged more 'leading from the front' with lengthy presentations and 'didactic teacher-centred pedagogy' (Somekh et al. 2007).

However, some practitioners in the Hammond et al. (2009) research felt that, used well, the interactive whiteboard was an 'incredibly powerful, useful resource'. The effect on teaching and learning was largely dependent on the way in which the interactive whiteboard was used. The pedagogy is not inscribed in the technology, but is dependent upon teacher agency and how individual teachers appropriate the technology for their professional practice in the classroom.

Mobile learning and hand-held devices are emerging as the next phases in technology development in schools. As technology develops to provide higher quality computing on ever smaller devices, mobility is going to become a key feature of teaching and learning in schools. This would offer anytime, anywhere learning (AAL) and enhance opportunities for creativity, personalization and support for out of school learning. Table 1.1 below outlines the key developments in technology in schools.

Table 1.1 History of technology in schools

Dates	Technology available in schools	Access	Information storage + retrieval
1970s	library	1 room – multiple books	printed encyclopaedias (Encyclopaedia Britannica)
1980s	micro-computers	1–2 machines per secondary school – in maths department	cassette tapes
1990s	desktop computers + commercial office software	1 machine per classroom – primary & secondary schools	floppy discs / CD ROMs (Microsoft Encarta)
2000s	multiple PCs – in computer labs/hubs	ICT suites – hardwired	Internet + search engines Web 1.0 (read only)
2005	laptops – class sets (mobile trolleys with 15–30 laptops)	wireless connectivity – move to wireless rooms in schools	Web 2.0 (read and write) Wikipedia/wikis collaborative/ peer to peer social/professional networks
2010	mobile devices tablets, smartphones	wireless – across campus	cloud computing semantic Web digital literacy
2015	enhanced mobile devices learner owned – given access to school wireless connectivity	4G learners devices BYOD (Bring Your Own Device)	Web 4.0 advanced digital literacy

Teachers and technology: policy and practice

Throughout these phases of technology developments in schools, from the early 1980s to now, the crucial factor has been teachers – who are after all the key change agents in the implementation of any technology. It is important to document not only the technological advancement in hardware and software, but also to outline how teachers *interact* with these developments and attempt to build a knowledge base about the use of technology in classroom practice for learning and teaching.

Just as Teachers' Centres had provided vital support for knowledge sharing and building in the early days of the micro-computer in the 1980s, so the Internet has led to the emergence of discussion forums in the late 1990s for supporting the building and sharing of new practice. Professional networks have become established for teachers through their subject and professional associations, and special-interest groups, such as Teachers.net and Mirandanet (www.mirandanet.org). More recently, an online teacher network that exploits Web 2.0 tools for knowledge sharing has been created by the *Guardian* to support teachers' professional practice (www.teachers.guardian.co.uk).

The need for teachers to learn from one another about technology for learning and teaching has been a central theme throughout the history of technology developments in schools. Bowles (1999: 31) argued that, since 1984, when TVEI first bought computers into secondary schools, 'teachers have struggled with the new concepts and skills'. The Trotter Report of 1989 identified three specific skills relating to the use of technology that an experienced teacher might be expected to have: practical technology capability; capability to relate technology to the curriculum area and the ability to manage and evaluate technology use. Developing teachers' capability in these three specific skills has been an ongoing challenge (Dawes 2001; Younie 2007).

In fact, there has been rather variable progress in actually developing the technology skills identified by the Trotter report (Bowles 1999). When government evaluators were asked, 'what went wrong in the 80s?' with respect to technology development in schools, the answer was an immediate identification of 'teachers' as a key obstacle. As Scaife and Wellington (1993: 19) found 'this complex chemistry of teacher attitudes has probably been the major barrier to success'. Locating a lack of progress with technology in schools as being the fault of teachers was documented by the National Council for Educational Technology (NCET). In the 1990s NCET published an information sheet, 'Teacher Education and IT', which highlighted how technologies potential to harness education had been largely unrealized – again, due to teachers' lack of capability in employing technology in the classroom.

> The learning potential of IT is far from being realized. There remain large numbers of teachers, in all phases of education, who are not familiar with IT and are therefore not using it in their teaching.
>
> (NCET 1997: 5)

The notion of 'teacher resistance' emerged as a significant concept in the literature of this time and was held accountable for hindering the development of technology in education. However, Dawes (2001) and Younie (2007) believe this is a contestable concept, with little empirical evidence of its existence, and a lot of rhetoric in its explanatory value as to why technology has not transformed learning in the ways visualized by politicians.

Following the development of major technology initiatives across the three terms of Conservative office (1979–1997), the government commissioned a seminal national assessment of the impact of ICT in schools: the ImpacT Report (1993). Conducted by Watson, this was the first major evaluation, which notified government that:

1. the use of technology-based work is primarily dependent on individual teachers' initiatives;
2. in-service provision was a major concern as many teachers felt they needed an ongoing programme of in-service training and,
3. knowledge and awareness of software was not in itself *sufficient* for effective implementation: instead, issues of management, teaching styles and the need for on-going support for professional development were identified as critically important.

In 1997 there came the influential Education Department Superhighways Initiative (EDSI), a synoptic report that first explored the educational opportunities afforded by the Internet, which rightly drew attention to '. . . the considerable managerial and organizational demands placed on those introducing technology of this complexity . . . ' (Scrimshaw 1997: 11).

The EDSI report highlighted the multi-dimensional nature of change and showed that *many conditions* had to be met in order to utilize the educational potential of technology, one of which was: 'the immediate obviousness to teachers of the educational potential' (DfEE 1997: 29). It was clearly evident from this report that teachers would be instrumental in unlocking the educational potential of technology.

Similarly, the School's Curriculum and Assessment Agency (SCAA) report on technology identified the *training of teachers* as the most significant component for 'future work', alongside 'the need for a *long-term strategy*' (SCAA 1997: 12): 'IT training should be a fundamental requirement in initial teacher training and form part of qualified teacher status. There needs to be a strategy for the continuing professional development of all teachers' (SCAA 1997: 14). It is here that the origins of NOF ICT training for serving teachers and the TTA Circular 4/98 that made ICT mandatory to trainee teachers can be found. As Robin Squire, Parliamentary Under-Secretary of State for Education and Employment, asserted in his keynote address at the SCAA conference; '. . . answers can only be produced if teachers themselves become knowledgeable about the technologies and their uses, and confident in their ability to shape them for curricular use' (SCAA 1997: 5).

However, most significantly, the SCAA report also identified that 'there is often a gap between the rhetoric of schools' IT policies and classroom reality' (SCAA 1997: 3).

Common concerns about technology in schools from government reports – 1990s

There are a number of common threads that run throughout the reports considered above. Although the balance of emphasis differs between them, all the reports raise four key issues:

1. *Technology Training* – specifically, the need for thorough training in technology for all trainee teachers and serving teachers that is clearly targeted by phase, curriculum area and previous experience; the reports recommended that this training should cover not just the use of software, but its application to curriculum areas, technology pedagogy and classroom management.

2. *Technology Resourcing* – specifically, the need for more up-to-date hardware, software, more broadband connections to external networks and cheaper connection charges, improved access to computers by pupils and teachers. Also, more human resources in the form of technical staff and teachers with expertise and training in leading technology as a major curriculum area.
3. *School Management* – specifically, the need for senior managers to take responsibility for developing a whole-school policy for technology and the strategy for its implementation; setting realistic budgets for purchasing technology hardware and consumables; training staff and clearly establishing support for technology use at management level, giving technology a high profile.
4. *Curriculum application* – specifically, the need for schools to get a balance between direct teaching of technology skills and their application across subject areas; teachers to evaluate their use of technology and to share good practice; to review how access to networks can help both teachers and learners.

While these four issues were reiterated across all the reports, there were also elements that occurred in some reports, but not in others. For example, raising standards of achievement was referred to explicitly in the documents that originated from government agencies, like Ofsted, but were an implicit sub-text in other reports. All the reports discussed the need for change, to *make more use of technology* and the benefits of making that change. However, one issue that seems to have been either ignored or disregarded is 'the nature of the change that the use of technology will have on a teacher's work in his or her classroom' (Bowles 1999: 24). More technology use by teachers was to become imperative with the election of a new Labour government in May 1997, which made statutory the use of technology across all subjects.

Learning theories and developments with technology in schools – 1980s to now

Research has shown that it is very difficult to consider technology without understanding parallel developments in theories of learning that informed teachers' thinking (Hammond et al. 2009; Woollard et al. 2010). In the 1970s pedagogical thinking was greatly influenced by the work of Piaget (1963) with a focus on discovery and learning as inquiry rather than a traditional instructional pedagogy. This can be seen in the work of Papert who created LOGO at MIT in 1967.

LOGO was an accessible way into programming, which was learner-centred and enabled pupils to control a small turtle-shaped robot. In an open-ended and playful context, LOGO enabled children to learn generic problem solving with a mathematical element and fostered creativity (Millwood 2009). Practitioners in the Hammond et al. (2009: 50) research talked about their enjoyment of seeing pupils 'program' each other around the room as a preliminary to on-screen work with the turtle commands and of giving what they felt was control to pupils over the computer. In turn, the influence of Piaget was superseded by Vygotsky (1978) and a social-cultural view of learning. Today this influence can be seen in the social constructivism of learning with technology in the classroom – for example, the development of dialogic learning with interactive whiteboards (Warwick et al. 2010). Further developments in learning theories such as communities of practice (Wenger 1998) and distributed cognition (Hutchins 1995) can be seen in the collaborative knowledge building of Wikipedia and professional networks of peer support and information sharing.

Applications to practice

Much of the innovation described in this chapter was supported by central govern-ment policies. This was intended to keep the curriculum meeting the emerging needs of society. Research into technology adoption in different countries, which was carried out for the EU and the British Council (Leask and Younie 2001) showed that, without central direction and support, innovation and the adoption of new practices in schools was limited. The UK government elected in May 2010 adopted a hands-off approach to curriculum development with their first act being the abo-lition of the government agency with responsibility for supporting technology innovation in schools (Becta). The evidence suggests that this hands-off approach from government does not advance improvement in education. However, various top-down initiatives undertaken by Becta were also not likely to embed change. A typical approach by Becta was to focus on infrastructure and getting equipment into schools before an analysis of pedagogical applications was available to support adoption by teachers.

In the UK there was a preoccupation with whether introducing computers into schools would lead to measurable outcomes in terms of learning. The most obvious benefit, that in a technologically rich society everyone needs to have the skills to use technology for their own purposes seemed to have been ignored along with other benefits which are difficult to measure. However, all teachers need to manage their professional lives by balancing professional priorities with political initiatives and interventions in education. This is a challenge which teachers can-not avoid and one which calls for continual reflection.

Conclusions

The introduction of technology innovations into an education system provides an opportunity for major change and review through engagement of leading prac-titioners in developing a curriculum fit for society's emerging needs. Critical to the success of any innovation however, is the engagement of practitioners who have to create the new pedagogies for the new contexts that technologies afford. A particular problem with technology integration into schooling has been the lack of knowledge on the part of decision-makers – both policy-makers and school leaders – about the opportunities opened up for new pedagogical approaches with technology.

Further reading

Hammond, M., Younie, S., Woollard, J., Cartwright, V. and Benzie, D. (2009) *What does our past involvement with computers in education tell us? A view from the research community*, Coventry/London: Warwick University Press/ITTE.

Leask, M. and Younie, S. (2001a) Communal Constructivist Theory: information and communications technology pedagogy and internationalisation of the curriculum, *Journal of Information Technology for Teacher Education*, 10(1 and 2): 117–34.

Millwood, R. (2009) *A short history off-line*, Coventry: Becta http://webarchive. nationalarchives.gov.uk/20101102103654/emergingtechnologies.becta.org.uk/index. php?section=etr&rid=14826.

Websites

National Archive of Educational Computing http://www.naec.org.uk/. This website documents the development of learning with technology; through its invention and application over the past half century. In addition, the archive houses technology artefacts, including the original Domesday equipment.

The BBC Computer Literacy Project http://www.mcmordie.co.uk/acornhistory/bbchist. shtml. This website charts the history of the BBC micro-computer and accompanying Computer Literacy Project.

2   Education policy and the rationale for technology development in schools: political drivers

Overview

This chapter provides an overview and rationale regarding government policy initiatives that have driven technology development in schools in the UK, since computers were introduced in the 1980s. While for governments these rationales have tended to be economic and vocational – that is, concerning technology skills for employees in a global economy – for teachers the rationale has been more peda-gogical and curriculum focused, addressing challenges in teaching and learning and the transformative potential of technology. This chapter outlines the major policy directions that governments have pursued since the 1980s and highlights the impact of successive initiatives.

Introduction and context

> 'The introduction of ICT into schools represents one of the largest and most complex curriculum innovations that has ever been attempted.'
>
> (Scrimshaw 2003: 85)

Given the multiplicity of drivers and competing rationales for the introduction of technology in education, this chapter will analyse those with the greatest currency among educational stakeholders. From the number of attempts that have been made to categorize these imperatives, it is clear that from these typologies there is a consensus concerning which rationales have most legitimacy.

While there are political and economic drivers for technology in education emanating from government, alongside a commensurate financial investment, it is important to highlight how, for teachers, this has culminated in a mounting pressure to integrate technology into classroom practice. However, we know from research on policy implementation and innovation in education that systemic change (required at this level in teachers' everyday practices) is either very slow or tends to fail, which again highlights the complexity of the process (Loveless 2001; Younie 2007). At the heart of it is the requirement for teachers to change their pedagogic practice, to make more use of a range of technologies and to exploit the affordances of these technologies for learning.

Theory and research base

This chapter draws on the policy research conducted over the last three decades that has been very important to academics conducting research with teachers on their use of technology in the classroom, which has needed to situate practice within the history and policy of technology development in UK schools (Dawes 2001; Leask 2002; Leask and Younie 2002; Younie 2007). To this end, careful attention has been paid to government policy documents and evaluation reports of government technology initiatives (Younie 2006; Selwyn 2011).

Rationales: policy drivers for developing technology in schools

While there is a 'strong sense of pluralism' with respect to the range of 'perspectives, priorities, expectations and even ideologies' that different stakeholders bring to technology, there is also a shared optimism about the potential technology holds for education (Ham 2010: 30). While it is possible to identify a number of rationales, as Ham (2010) notes these are not 'innumerable'. Ham's analysis shows that globally over the past 20 years, it is possible to discern the key drivers for national investment in technology.

While different stakeholders have different agendas driving technology initiatives, these can be categorized very broadly as: pedagogical for practitioners; economic and vocational for policy-makers; commercial and market orientated for private enterprise, particularly, for the computing industry (Culp, Honey, Mandinach 2003; Loveless 2001; Pelgrum and Plomp 1991; Twining 2005).

For teachers, the rationale for the integration of technology into classroom practice has focused on teaching and learning. Ham and Toubat's (2006) research found that teachers articulated use in terms of increasing 'variety' in their teaching strategies, engaging pupils through opportunities for 'collaboration', acquiring 'content knowledge and information skills' and enhancing 'motivation'. However, probably the most detailed analysis of drivers for educational use can be found in Twining (2005), who cites 19 separate rationales. In an international analysis, Pelgrum and Plomp's (1991) survey of computers in education worldwide identified two leading rationales, which were transformative and pedagogical (with the former changing the nature of schooling and the latter as improving teaching): enhancing learning and raising pupils' achievement. This analysis is supported by Culp et al. (2003), who argue that technology has a transformative element in enabling the shift from didactic instruction to constructivist, inquiry-based learning, and is one that Loveless (2001) terms a 'catalytic' rationale where technology significantly changes teaching and learning.

For policy-makers the arguments concern the economic imperatives that refer predominantly to technology-enhancing global competitiveness. This leads to the concomitant vocational rationale, which asserts that technology skills are essential for employment in 'knowledge based' economies (Brown and Lauder 1997; Culp et al. 2003; Pelgrum and Plomp 1991). The economic and vocational rationales can be traced in government policy documents through both the Conservative and Labour terms of office from 1981 to 2010. As Becta (2010a: 7) asserts, 'the rewards of ICT appropriation are potentially considerable ... [and] will be particularly felt in the area of "knowledge economy" skills'.

Political policy imperatives: economic and vocational rationales

From the beginning, in the 1980s, consecutive Conservative governments were committed to developing technology in their recognition of its economic significance.

> The Government fully recognises the importance of information technology for the future industrial and commercial success of the United Kingdom and the central role that the Government must play in promoting its development and application.
>
> (Prime Minister Margaret Thatcher, Hansard, 2 July 1981)

In addition, in 1981 Kenneth Baker, as the newly-appointed Conservative Minister for Information Technology, added that he wanted to see 'that the kids of today are trained with the skills [for] jobs . . . And that is the reason why we've pushed ahead with computers in schools' (in Scaife and Wellington 1993: 15).

Most significant, however, has been the 'economic ambition' of government ministers for what technology could achieve, which can be found in policy discourse. In 1995 Michael Heseltine launched the Superhighways initiative stating it 'would help with the vital task of keeping Britain competitive in the 21st century' (Somekh 2000: 20). In 1997, at the launch of the National Grid for Learning (NGfL), Blair argued similarly: 'technology has revolutionalised the way we work and is now set to transform education' (NGfL launch, March 1998).

It was the 1997 Labour government's embracing of a post-Fordist economic policy that specified particular requirements for the education system, not least a strong policy drive for generic technology skills (Brown and Lauder 1997; Younie 2002). Technology is pivotal in the global reorganization of capitalism, which entails shifting to post-Fordist production practices, with flexible specialization requiring multi-skilled workers. Foregrounding technology as part of the solution to economic restructuring requires school leavers to be technologically literate (Murray 2006; Piore 1986; Sabel 1982).

> To build an economy that will continue our success in the global market place, we will need an even better educated and more highly skilled workforce. If we are to succeed it will require excellence in our education system and continuous and rapid improvement in our skill levels.
>
> (Estelle Morris, 2001 in Education and Skills: Delivering Results.)

Arguably, it is 'the diminished power of nation states to control economic competition that has forced them to compete in the global knowledge wars' (Brown and

Lauder 1997: 173). As Lyotard critically observes, 'knowledge is and will be produced in order to be sold; it is and will be consumed in order to be valorised in a new production: in both cases, the goal is exchange' (Lyotard 1984: 4). With the resurgence of the British Labour party, Brown and Lauder (1997) identified the 'left modernisers' adopting a post-Fordist perspective that provides an economic and vocational rationale for technology in education. As David Blunkett the Secretary of State for Education and Employment declared in a speech on 16 June 1999: 'Competitive pressures are intensifying. Ours is an increasingly complex and technologically driven world. As a country we need the effort and skill of all our people to compete and succeed' (David Blunkett speech 1999: 1, cited in Younie 2007: 29).

Also, two independent technology reports, McKinsey and Stevenson, both published in 1997, clearly indicated an economic imperative that was critical in influencing Labour government policy on technology for schools. First, McKinsey signified an *international trend* when, in 1993, its American branch reviewed technology in the USA for President Clinton's National Information Infrastructure Commission (NII), which culminated in $2 billion technology investment in schools (Dawes 2001). Brown and Lauder (1997) argued the American rationale for the policy drive on technology in education was also predominantly economic: school leavers needed technological skills to be productive in the emerging new knowledge economy. The international development of technology in education, across leading nations, provides a global context to the developments in the UK in the 1990s.

Proclaiming that 'addressing the issue of ICT' was to be one of new Labour's 'top priorities', the main elements in any new strategy were identified as needing to: 'increase the time given to ICT in both initial and in-service training; make computers available to teachers and develop curriculum-related software' (Stevenson 1997: 7–8). The Stevenson report powerfully concluded that the government would disadvantage the UK in terms of global competitiveness, if steps were not taken to integrate technology into education. The two fundamental conclusions of the Stevenson Report that alerted government to develop a seminal cohesive strategy for technology were: 'The state of ICT in our schools is primitive and not improving [and] it is a national priority to increase the use of ICT in UK schools' (Stevenson 1997: 6).

The recommendations from the Stevenson Report clearly paved the way for Labour's policy drive on technology, which marked the first coordinated national strategy in 1998. In short, over the previous two decades of global policy discourse, it is clear to identify that different stakeholders draw from 'virtually the same list of rationales' (Ham 2010: 32) and that these have stayed stable. The principal policy drivers remain: economic, vocational, commercial and pedagogical, with policy-makers predominantly referring to the first two and practitioners the latter one.

Phases of technology policy development: Conservative to Labour (1980–2010)

The early phase of policy focused on supporting the introduction of computers into schools through developing practitioner networks and encouraging experimentation to explore the potential of computers for teaching. This can be seen in the 'Micros for Schools' scheme from Kenneth Baker in 1981, which introduced computers into schools and the TVEI initiative in 1984. During the 1980s this first policy phase gave way to a more prescriptive phase following the 1988 Education Reform Act. This made mandatory, for the first time in the UK, a national curriculum. While this heralded a move to the inclusion of 'ICT' in the curriculum; it was not until September 2000 that ICT was awarded core subject status (Curriculum 2000). However, following the national curriculum review in 2011 conducted under the coalition government which was elected in 2010, technology has been downgraded to a lower status and now forms only part of the 'basic' curriculum.

Introducing computers into schools: early policy phase 1980s

Technology has been a component of government policy for schools since 1980 (Abbott 2001; Dawes 2001), and Somekh (2000) traces Blair's commitment back to Kenneth Baker and Lord Young in the mid-1980s. In the early phase, however, teachers were encouraged to use computers when their reliability was far from stable and there was an absence of the appropriate software and training. Consequently, in order to guide teachers, policy-makers set up a supporting agency, the 'Microcomputer Electronic Programme' (MEP) in 1980. This was the first nationally financed programme for developing computers in schools. With funding of £2.5 million over four years, MEP had three foci; curriculum development, software development and training of teachers.

Hammond et al.'s (2009) research identified the legacy of MEP, in which practitioners recalled how MEP was pivotal in establishing networks of collaborators, who were catalysts for computer development. MEP was superseded by the 'Micro Electronics Education Support Unit' (MESU), which was set up with a five-year life span. Significantly, the DfES (Department for Education and Skills) at this time also developed the Education Support Grant (ESG), which provided funding for Local Authorities to appoint advisory teachers to support technology use in schools. MESU were given the role of training the newly appointed advisory staff and their role was crucial in guiding teachers' classroom practice in the 1980s.

In the early 1980s, during the first phase of policy, there was a government drive to introduce technology into schools. The government bodies (MEP, then MESU), which were tasked to support teachers, worked with a vision of networking innovators to develop a pedagogical understanding of computers. While this acknowledged the need for support, practitioners reflected that this was 'nothing like on the scale required' (Hammond 2009: 97). Although significant sums were spent on purchasing computers, comparatively little went on teachers' development and training.

Policy development: 1988 Education Reform Act – a national curriculum

The Education Reform Act of 1988 was the most significant act of parliament since the Butler Education Act of 1944 that had heralded free state secondary schools in the UK. The 1988 Act was seminal in launching a national curriculum in which all teachers were compelled to deliver the same content. A positive outcome was the recognition of technology as a subject.

Arguably, the national curriculum was a double-edged sword, which seemed to favour computers by their inclusion, however, it had 'drawbacks as well as benefits: it obliged some to do what they would not have done otherwise [include the subject], but at the same time dampened and constrained others from taking risks', because the curriculum was now prescribed and statutory (Hammond et al. 2009: 99). With the implementation of the national curriculum, some practitioners saw a 'closing down' of teachers' possibilities to experiment with computers, due to the level of prescriptive content from central government. While practitioners had described the early phase of policy as allowing exploration, innovation, flexibility and playfulness, the shift to a standardized, compulsory curriculum diminished these freedoms.

This shift was seen most clearly in the changing status of computer-based learning materials. For example, during the early phase of the 1980s support materials had left teachers 'free on how, and if, to use ICT' (Hammond et al. 2009: 5); now the guidance from government was perceived as obligatory and unavoidable. Some practitioners saw this development as necessary to ensure technology delivery across all schools and to guarantee entitlement to technology.

Overall, this period of prescriptive implementation signalled a major climate change in education concerning the professional autonomy of teachers, which was seen to be radically reduced. While it arguably enhanced the status of technology in the curriculum, it did simultaneously 'narrow' the freedom of the teachers to experiment in curriculum content. As one practitioner pertinently observed:

> We're in such a locked down system . . . we've got loads of kit, but haven't got the freedom to use it in a way that people might find exciting and thoughtful . . . we've got the investment in education, because we've now got a much more accountable education system. The system is imposing, not intentionally, but inadvertently and constrains exploratory practice.
>
> (Hammond et al. 2009: 101)

The government required schools to integrate the use of various technologies into the curriculum via the Statutory Orders in the National Curriculum. Arguably these statutory orders for technology were necessary, as it is not possible to keep experimenting endlessly, but rather to have to address how and where technology is to be implemented in the curriculum. In this sense, top-down policies were essential in addressing inconsistencies in use and ensured a basic entitlement for all for technology. However, it took until 'Curriculum 2000' for the implementation of statutory orders for 'ICT' in *all subjects* and for 'ICT' as a discrete subject to be *awarded core subject status*, as a compulsory foundation subject, along with English, maths and science.

It is against this background struggle for discrete subject recognition, and cross-curricular application in all subjects, that the coalition government's decision to review the status of ICT in 2012 has alarmed so many educationalists. Some fear this may herald a return to the inconsistencies of the past, where technology entitlement and use across all subjects has been replaced by 'luck' – if one's teachers favour the use of ICT (or not).

Evaluating technology policy and progress: 1980–1997

Following the first decade, in the 1980s, of the UK Conservative government's technology initiatives in schools, a seminal national assessment of the impact of technology was conducted in 1993. The ImpacT report highlighted in particular teachers' need for in-service training with technology, as well as a number of other problems, which were reiterated by the McKinsey and Stevenson reports of 1997. Both these independent inquires into the 'issues and opportunities' with technology concluded damningly that the state of technology in UK schools was archaic and it was a public priority to address this. Despite initiatives like TVEI and funding for computers, equipment had become old and development in schools had been piecemeal and slow. At this time, there was also the emergence of the Internet, and access was becoming available for widespread use by schools from the mid-1990s.

There were also a number of other government-commissioned reports published in 1997, which revealed four recurring problems regarding technology development (EDSI, NCET, SCAA). First, there was the problem of technology resourcing, which was judged to be in urgent need of upgrading owing to the aging machines found in schools. Second, teachers required specialist training in order to be proficient with technology. Third, school managers needed to take responsibility for developing a whole-school policy for technology and strategies for its implementation. Fourth, schools needed to address the curriculum application of technology. Arguably the inconsistencies found across schools in the use of technology helped formulate the need for Curriculum 2000. All the reports (EDSI, McKinsey, NCET, SCAA, and Stevenson) indentified the urgent need for *change*; to make *more use of technology*.

This section outlines the development of technology in schools and how government policy has attempted to enhance its use since the 1980s through a variety of technology initiatives. The common concerns found in government reports that highlighted major deficiencies were: technology training, resourcing, whole-school management and curriculum application. During the period of the Labour government from 1997 to 2010, technology was specifically referred to as ICT, and the quotes retain the historical accuracy of this term. This period was an unprecedented time in the history of UK schooling; never before had there been such commitment and expenditure on technology in education. This is to be remembered as austerity measures defined the education landscape post-2010.

UK Labour government policy on technology in schools (1997–2010)

Having identified no coordinated strategy to develop technology in schools, the Stevenson report urged government to develop a cohesive national strategy. Consequently, the new UK Labour government of 1997 focused on prioritizing 'ICT' in schools and developed the most ambitious plans for a national strategy for ICT. The main element of this programme was the National Grid for Learning (NGfL) and New Opportunities Fund (NOF) ICT training for teachers. The NGfL was to provide a network of information, learning materials and funding for school computers (DfEE 1997).

In phase one, the National Grid for Learning, between 1998 and 2002, £657 million was made available to schools in England through a 'Standards Fund' to help develop 'ICT' provision (infrastructure, services and content); and a further £710 million of expenditure was allocated between 2002 and 2004. A supporting national programme of in-service training for teachers and school librarians was financed by the National Lottery's New Opportunities Fund (NOF) (TTA 1998). From April 1999 to December 2003, £230 million from the New Opportunities Fund was made available across the UK (£180 million in England – equivalent to around £450 for each teacher being trained). These programmes were the defining components of the government's national 'ICT' strategy for schools. Their implementation was the responsibility of the Department for Education and Employment (DfEE).

It is worth clarifying at this point what constitutes the difference between a political *initiative* with ICT in education and educational ICT *policy*. It is only 'policy' that contains a mandatory requirement; 'initiatives' do not contain the element of compulsion. With initiatives there is the *desire* to enable change, through teachers responding to the initiatives in the ways the government intended, but this is not a legislative requirement. For example, the NGfL and NOF initiatives provided ICT resourcing and training, with the hope that teachers would, as a result, implement technology use in the classroom, whereas the use of technology across all subjects became a *statutory* obligation for all teachers, with the introduction of national curriculum orders for 'ICT' in 2000.

Launching the National Grid for Learning (NGfL)

In 1997 the Government's White Paper on 'Excellence in Schools', made recommendations for technology based substantially on the work done by McKinsey (1997) and Stevenson (1997). These were converted into clear objectives in the National Grid for Learning documents (DfEE 1997a; DfEE 1998a, 1998b) and indicated the NGfL's intended function: 'the delivery of ICT infrastructure, services, support and training' (DfEE 1998a: 24); 'a framework for a learning community designed to raise standards and improve Britain's competitiveness' (DfEE 1998b: 4). The far-reaching proposals of the NGfL represented perhaps the most ambitious innovation envisaged for UK schools. The emphasis was on ensuring that, at a national level, the ICT infrastructure of every school was upgraded and managed. Specific proposals for teachers focused on training: 'The Grid must be useful. It must lead to the improvement of the skills and confidence of teachers' (DfEE 1997: 14).

In 1998 the task of coordinating content for the NGfL fell to Becta (British Education and Communications Technology Agency), previously NCET (National Council for Educational Technology). Becta were also set the task of evaluating the roll-out of the government's national ICT strategy. This led to a series of important research reports, which in the first phase encompassed the NGfL Pathfinder reports (Becta 2001–2) and ImpaCT2 (Becta 2002), which examined the impact of ICT on pupil learning and attainment. Clearly, 'this was a high-profile initiative the success of which could contribute to perceptions of the efficacy of the Labour government' (Dawes 2001: 13).

Launching the New Opportunity Fund (NOF) ICT training initiative for teachers

Alongside addressing obsolete equipment, policy-makers also identified the need to improve teacher competence (DfEE 1997). As the DfEE (1997: 8) stated, 'the prime importance of developing teacher skills and confidence in the use of ICT is now widely recognized . . .'

David Blunkett announced that the NOF training initiative was to be delivered through Approved Training Providers (ATPs). These were independent training organizations, approved by NOF and quality assured in England by the TTA (Teacher Training Agency). Local authorities were directly involved; over 75 per cent were either accredited training providers in their own right or were receiving direct funding for supporting providers. In England, 96 per cent of eligible teachers signed up for the programme and this far exceeded the target of 80 per cent (Ofsted 2004: 3); in total 394,000 teachers and 99.6 per cent of schools took part (TTA 2002: ii). In total, local authorities received direct funding of £20 million to support the NOF ICT training programme.

Compulsory training for trainee teachers in the application of information and communication technologies across all curriculum subjects was introduced in the UK with effect from September 1998 (DfEE Circular 4/98: Initial Teacher Training National Curriculum for the use of ICT in Subject Teaching), the aim of which was 'to equip every qualified teacher with the knowledge, skills and understanding to make sound decisions about **when, when not, and how to use ICT effectively in teaching particular subjects**' (DfEE 1998b: 17, bold in original). Ofsted (2001) reported favourably on how this policy was impacting on the teaching profession: 'Newly qualified teachers with good levels of ICT skill are beginning to be deployed in schools of all types, and they often provide a good source of stimulus and support for established colleagues' (Ofsted 2001: 10).

However, the situation with serving teachers was more complex: 'the learning curve for many teachers is very steep, but the challenge of changing practice must be faced . . .' (Leask and Pachler 1999: xviii).

One challenge was making sense of this raft of technology initiatives in the late 1990s. Loveless (2001) critically identified how government documents referring to 'ICT capability' failed to prescribe clearly what 'capability' meant for schools attempting to interpret the documents. How to integrate technologies into subjects across the school curriculum was an issue that was fraught with ambiguity. Prior to Curriculum 2000, there was the lack of a clearly articulated strategy for delivering ICT, which had left schools in a variety of positions on how to deliver it. This uncertainty had been identified by McKinsey, who reported 'the lack of clarity over educational objectives for IT itself' (1997: 2).

Similarly, Bowles (1999) argued that a background of continuous change with many aspects of technology in schools had led to much uncertainty, about what ICT to deliver, and on how and where to deliver it.

> The introduction of the National Curriculum in 1991, which included IT, caused much confusion. As in other subjects, different sets of requirements were imposed at least twice; but ICT presented a particular problem. The initial clear link between IT and Technology in the original Orders was broken, being replaced first by nothing and then by standalone orders for IT, but with a very vague Programme of Study at Key Stage 4.
>
> (Bowles 1999: 10)

In particular, there was a 'tension between the delivery of IT - as a discrete subject – against cross-curricular delivery via a number of other core and foundation subjects' (Bowles 1999: 10). This tension was solved, at least at a legislative level, by the implementation of ICT national curriculum orders. Most important, ICT as a discrete subject was awarded core subject status and the integration of ICT into other subject areas was made statutory in September 2000. Consequently, Curriculum 2000 brought clarification to an area where previously there had been much confusion regarding ICT in the curriculum.

In short, the government's NGfL and NOF proposals were ambitious. However, as initiatives these were only intended to provide ICT training and resourcing, with the hope that teachers would, as a result, implement ICT use in the classroom. In order to ensure the latter, the government would have to introduce an ICT policy that had a statutory requirement for teachers to use ICT. Consequently, the difference between government initiatives and policy can be seen in the introduction of Curriculum 2000, which outlined statutory orders for the integration of ICT across all subjects. Implemented in September 2000, Curriculum 2000 contained an integral ICT component for all subject areas, which meant that Ofsted inspections of mandatory orders would ensure ICT's uptake by teachers. These, then, 'were strong indicators that a determined government would allow no choice . . . [and] designed to ensure that teachers would use technology to deliver the curriculum' (Dawes 2001: 8).

An evaluation of the UK's first national technology strategy (1997–2002)

Historically, the Labour government's first term of office from 1997 to 2002 saw an unprecedented wave of policy initiatives designed to embed technology use within the curriculum and organizational management of schools. The UK's first coordinated national technology strategy focused primarily on developing schools' e-infrastructure and training. As the first level of intervention, the NGfL focused predominantly on technology procurement, dovetailing with the NOF initiative for technology in-service training for teachers. Consequently, progress was duly evident: 'As a result of NGfL, improvements can be clearly identified in the levels and quality of ICT resources in schools . . . [and] the increase in teachers' use of computers is a clear benefit emerging from the Government's ICT initiatives' (Ofsted 2001: 4–5).

However, despite these positive outcomes, these were more limited than expected and the overall impact of the initiatives was less penetrating than desired; while best practice with technology in schools could be identified, it continued to remain in 'pockets', rather than the sweeping uptake intended (Pittard 2005). However, it must be noted that, 'The implementation of such a major innovation – one involving procurement and installation of high-cost infrastructure and hardware, and significant changes in management and teaching practices – takes time' (DfES 2001: 4).

Identifying the problems with technology implementation in schools

Given that implementing policy is not a straightforward process, this section examines the roll-out of the national technology strategy. From research on reform in education, it is well known that change is either very slow or tends to fail (Fullan 1991).

Evidence from government reports suggests technology initiatives were not being embedded consistently or fully across schools (DfES 2001–02; Ofsted 2001–02, 2004). However, given the government's aspirations for technology to seriously modernize education, this inconsistency requires an analysis and identification of the specific problems.

First, the government commissioned research to evaluate the national roll-out of the NGfL through Becta; NOF was evaluated via the TTA quality-assurance process (Leask 2002); also the school inspection programme (Ofsted) provided data on the impact of ICT initiatives in schools. From these agencies a number of evaluation reports were produced, which became significant in the appraisal of the implementation of the government's national technology strategy. These were primarily the Becta Pathfinder Series (2001–2, Nos 1–10) and Ofsted Reports (2001–2), which covered Labour's first term in office. Major factors inhibiting the success of the national training programme for teachers included the lack of an infrastructure to deliver high-quality training on a national scale and the lack of access by teachers to reliable technology for use in schools. Emphasis had been placed on providing computers for pupils, but not on computers for teachers (Leask 2002).

Second, through developing an ecological perspective, greater analysis is provided to produce a theoretical framework for understanding the implementation procedures, which exemplifies the interrelated organizational processes involved. Specifically, in the UK between 1997 and 2002 government policy had to be filtered through *macro, meso* and *micro* levels (eco-systems), as policy is mediated through *national* agencies (macro: DfES), *regional* agencies (meso: local authorities) down to individual schools and teachers at the micro level (Younie 2007). National change is a complex multidimensional process with many factors interacting. To understand this, Davis (2008: 142) argues 'it is time to seek a more useful theoretical perspective . . . to inform the diffusion of IT innovation in education'. To this end, it is necessary to understand how a teacher's practice is at the centre (of an eco-system), which is nested within a school (another eco-system), that is nested within a region or nation (eco-zone), which is situated within the global biosphere (the world) (Davis 2008: 142). Consequently the adoption or diffusion of technology in education is complex, because technology impacts 'multiple ecologies' (Davis 2008: 147). These environments (or eco-systems) are impacted on or intersected by other drivers or influences promoting change, such as the IT industry (representing multinational and commercial interests), so it is important to understand the economic and political drivers of technology in education (Selwyn 2002) and the complexity of change across the multiple stakeholders (ecologies). In fact, Crook et al. (2010: 6) in one of the last pieces of research for Becta, argue similarly and claim that 'it may be more helpful to think of an ecology: one in which a complex network of interacting influences is shaping that trajectory in a much more subtle fashion'.

Managing a multi-agency national strategy: leadership

To understand the complexity of the educational landscape and ecologies of change between 1997 and 2002, Younie (2006, 2007) argues it is necessary to identify the role of government agencies. This is because the most discernible factor regarding the Labour government's technology strategy was the number of different agencies involved. As Ofsted (2001: 1) reported, the DfEE (Department for Education and Employment) was given the role of formulating the ICT policy for education and steering the implementation of most aspects of the national strategy. This involved working with the ICT supply industry, local authorities, the Teacher Training Agency (TTA) and Becta. The responsibility for Lottery-funded ICT training for teachers was given to NOF, a non-departmental public body, sponsored by the Department of Culture, Media and Sport (DCMS), via policy directions drawn up in consultation with the DfEE and the TTA. By 2002 the National College for School Leadership (NCSL) had become involved and the DfEE had become the DfES (Department for Education and Skills). This signalled an unprecedented national initiative that demanded long-established agencies and new, emergent agencies to work together for the first time. Added to this (eco-sphere of government agencies) there were also multinational IT companies (supplying hardware and infrastructure), alongside regional local authorities and training providers, and schools. There was a complex interplay between these 'multiple ecologies' at the macro, meso and micro levels.

This was an ambitious multi-agency approach, which was unparalleled in nature and set a precedent in requiring organizational liaison and management across multiple stakeholders, so perhaps it was not surprising that operational relations were found wanting between all the eco-spheres; with no prior histories of dialogues the initiatives were exceptional in scale, necessitating expertise of management personnel that largely wasn't there in the late 1990s, with respect to technology expertise and leadership (Leask 2002). As Ofsted (2001: 13) observed, 'where senior officers failed to give a strong lead, ICT staff often worked in isolation, and this held back both planning and implementation of NGfL-related provision . . .'.

While the extent and newness of the technology initiatives in themselves were challenging, this was complicated further by other educational initiatives that were introduced at the same time. For example: 'the NGfL Programme had links with . . . Excellence in Cities (EICs), Education Action Zones (EAZs), Technology Colleges (TCTs) and the Information Management Strategy (IMS)' (DfES 2001: 3).

Consequently, not only was the government's ICT initiative to be operationalized across multiple-agencies, but there were also other (non-ICT) initiatives that were simultaneously implemented, which, while sometimes linked, were nonetheless often in competition. Although the focus of all the policy initiatives was arguably to 'raise standards', the emergence of competing priorities made for a multifarious and complex landscape of change for schools to manage, with leaders not necessarily in possession of technology expertise, or in a position to know or be able to locate this knowledge elsewhere. It is important not to underestimate the absence of technology leadership in the education system at this time in the late 1990s.

An absence of knowledge: ICT expertise

In the analysis it probably yields no surprise, particularly with hindsight, to find that at the time of the NGfL roll-out there was a discernible lack of technology knowledge in the education profession; schools and local authorities simply did not have the necessary level of technology proficiency among existing senior leaders: a point identified by both Ofsted (2001) and Becta (2001–2) evaluations. Not confined to schools, this was found across the multiple agencies involved: 'The pathfinder local authorities, having had no experience of implementing similar large-scale technology initiatives, did not have personnel in leadership roles at the outset with the prior experience needed to lead the NGfL initiative' (DfES 2001: 5).

Similarly the technology industry had little prior experience of working with schools, and did not always fully understand the needs of the education sector. This led to a fragmented approach, for example:

> . . . using the commercial market to give schools a choice of training provider; and, in allowing schools to use a variety of funding sources to improve ICT facilities. Too much flexibility, coupled with considerable competition . . . has contributed to a fragmentation of effort, with training organizations, local authorities and schools independently seeking solutions to the same problems. This is in stark contrast with the more uniform approach of the NNS [National Numeracy Strategy] and NLS [National Literacy Strategy].
>
> (Ofsted 2001: 4)

The crucial issue regarding the implementation of technology was the need for coordinated leadership. In an already complex field this deficiency could be seen as highly detrimental to schools that lacked technology expertise (internally, among school leaders) and guidance (externally) from local authorities.

> . . . there are few national support networks to share and develop teachers' professional competence in ICT. In consequence, there are too few opportunities to pool expertise to take forward the national initiatives. There is also a danger that the shortage of well informed, commercially neutral and educationally sound advice could be costly at a time of fast-changing technologies.
>
> (Ofsted 2001: 5)

The result was 'too little quality assurance of the implementation of schools' ICT development plans to ensure that initiatives are achieving their purpose' (Ofsted 2001: 5). This was further exacerbated by different levels of funding between schools too. For example, schools that achieved 'Technology College status' had almost twice the amount of funding available for technology as non-specialist schools (Younie 2007).

Disparities of funding for technology

The roll-out of the NGfL Programme has been the largest and most costly single initiative ever to be undertaken by Local Authorities in the UK (DfES 2001: 19).

Despite significant government funding for technology, it was not uniformly allocated and discrepancies 'varied widely among schools [and] this situation was exacerbated by the differing patterns of support in local authorities' (Ofsted 2001: 4). Consequently, different levels of funding led to disparities between schools and 'variation in provision means that teachers and pupils in different schools/local authorities are working under very different conditions' (DfES 2001: 9), which in turn 'raises issues of fairness and social justice' (DfES 2002b: 3).

Examples of funding discrepancies revealed a landscape of inconsistent and fragmented implementation. In addition, there were issues of understanding *technology sustainability*, where maintenance, technical support and upgrading required fiscal expertise: 'problems have arisen due to inadequate prior experience or training for local authority personnel and head teachers in procurement, financial and contractual arrangements' (DfES 2002: 3). Added to which, 'planning for long-term replacement of hardware or the recurring costs of consumables . . . it is not clear whether responsibility for long-term sustainability rests with local authorities, central Government or indeed, individual schools' (DfES 2001: 6).

The disparity of funding clearly impacts on schools' ability to increase the quality and quantity of their technology. Hence, although NGfL funding had raised levels of technology resourcing in all types of school, it was the case that 'in many schools, the quality, age and accessibility of ICT resources pose continuing problems. There also remain significant differences among schools' (Ofsted 2001: 18).

Overall, it is important to recognize that the UK's first coordinated national technology strategy was, up until that time, the most ambitious and expensive changes ever to be implemented in the history of British schooling. Clearly leadership in schools and the local authority were identified as crucial to managing such a complex government initiative. 'Local Authority guidance for school development planning in ICT was, in the best cases, thorough . . . This led to a productive professional dialogue with schools and, where appropriate, to more careful consideration by the schools of how developments in resources, training and curriculum related to each other' (Ofsted 2001: 14).

The harnessing technology strategy (2005–2010)

The Labour government continued to prioritize technology in education in its second and third term of office with the furtherance of new policy initiatives. In 2002 the government's seminal NGfL and NOF initiatives were relaunched as the 'ICT in Schools' programme (ICTiS), with continued earmarked funding for schools to purchase ICT hardware (DfES 2002–5). Other significant projects included: Strategic Leadership in ICT (SLICT 2004, see Comber and Hingley 2004) – a programme of in-service training for senior school staff; Curriculum Online – a learning materials scheme with approved software and funding (e-learning credits, NCSR 2006), and the Test Bed Project, evaluating use in ICT rich schools (Becta 2006).

In 2003 a DfES report openly announced that policy direction had taken a subtle turn; while the period 1997–2002 had concentrated on 'ICT infrastructure, connectivity and professional development', the following period (2003–6), would be concerned with 'ICT pedagogy and whole school improvement' (DfES 2003: 7).

Launched in May 2003, the DfES paper 'Fulfilling the Potential: Transforming Teaching and Learning through ICT in Schools' had the clear aim that; 'every school should be making excellent use of ICT resources and electronic services for teaching and learning and for whole-school improvement' (DfES 2003). In this document, Charles Clarke, the Secretary of State for Education and Skills (2002–2004) admitted that Labour's ICT policy drive had been 'a leap of faith' and, while there had been subsequent 'real evidence of successful practice' since the NGfL (DfES 2003: 4), this highlighted how the initiatives were instigated before the impact of ICT on learning was known. It also hints at the fact that policy had been directed by an economic rationale, concerned with global competitiveness and drive for a technologically skilled workforce, as opposed to a pedagogical rationale, which aligns technology to enhancing learning outcomes. Arguably there were two rationales and agendas that became conflated (Younie 2002).

In short, the Labour government had invested heavily in technology from 1997, prior to the evidence base about effective pedagogic practice being nationally established through research. An estimated £1 billion was spent before ImapCT2 was published in 2002, which, in part, points to an uncovering of other rationales regarding ministers' commitment to technology in education – namely economic and vocational, given that pedagogic rationales and impact on attainment were not fully established beyond a previous small-scale evidence base.

A 'rhetoric gap': between policy and practice

The technology policies of the Labour government were contextually framed by ministers' political aspirations and vision of technology as a panoptic solution to 'raise standards' and prepare school leavers for the new knowledge economy (Brown and Lauder 1997; Younie 2002). Yet, despite heavily funded initiatives (NGfL and NOF) and government policy intervention (Curriculum 2000 statutory ICT orders), there was an identifiable gap between policy and practice. Evidence indicated that the implementation of the national ICT strategy across schools was inconsistent, fragmented and 'patchy' (Becta 2005; DfES 2001–2; Leask 2002; Loveless 2005; Ofsted 2001–2, 2004; Opie and Fukuyo 2000; SCAA 1997; Younie 2007): a 'rhetoric gap' between the political intentions of policies and the actuality of lessons. This highlights the complexity of policy implementation, and how the process is not a direct translation from paper to practice. As the SCAA report found, '. . . there is often a gap between the rhetoric of schools' IT policies and classroom reality' (SCAA 1997: 3). 'While some schools are already pioneering applications of ICT . . . these efforts need to be replicated elsewhere to eliminate the wide variations in the quality and diversity of practice that still exist, both within and between schools' (DfES 2003: 6).

Similar findings were reported in the 2004 'ICT in Schools' survey (Becta 2004), which highlighted disparities of 'e-confidence' between individual schools. Across both primary and secondary schools Becta (2004) found the more e-confident the school, the greater the proportion of the school budget was spent on technology, the more likely they were to have a technology leadership group, and the more likely they were to make technology facilities available outside school hours to pupils (for example, via the school website or learning platform). These factors are crucial in the successful implementation of technology in schools and the complex interplay between them needs to be understood as part of an interconnected, dynamic ecosystem, which in turn is nested in a regional, national and global biosphere (Younie 2007).

In 2005, in order to overcome the disparities between schools, the government launched its new national strategy, 'Harnessing Technology: Transforming Learning and Children's Services' (DfES 2005a). To address the discrepancies, the 2005 e-strategy had four overarching objectives: transform teaching and learning; engage hard-to-reach groups in new ways; build an open accessible system, with more information and services online; and achieve a new level of efficiency and effectiveness in delivery (DfES 2005a). These objectives were echoed in the 2005 Schools White Paper, 'Higher Standards, Better Schools for all' (DfES 2005b), which specified government plans regarding the principal role of technology, which were to be 'designed around the needs of the individual' (Moffatt 2009). As the DfES (2005b) asserted: 'by 2008 all schools will be able to offer access to e-learning resources both in and out of school. We encourage all schools, by this date, to make available a personal online space for every pupil'.

This marks the step change in policy direction to 'personalization' and when the agenda of 'personalized learning' became core themes of the Primary and Secondary National Strategies, 'Every Child Matters' and 'The Children's Plan' that were launched in 2007. In 2008 Jim Knight, Minister of State for Schools and Learners (2007–2008) at the Department for Children School and Families (DCSF), outlined policy plans for the next six years. The revised e-strategy, 'Harnessing Technology: Next Generation Learning 2008–14' (Becta 2009c), specified five key priorities that the government considered essential to deliver 'a technology-confident education system':

1. promoting a technology-related **learner entitlement**;
2. putting in place **universal access** to powerful learning tools;
3. providing **professional tools and support** for better teaching and learning;
4. **mobilizing leadership**, and
5. developing a **fit-for-purpose, system-wide national digital infrastructure** (Becta 2008a: 6, bold emphasis as original).

The 2008 e-strategy highlighted as a goal, the development of 'integrated online personal support for learners', which entailed the provision of an e-portfolio, alongside e-assessment and online reporting to parents. It was envisioned that 'personalized online learning' would be facilitated by these e-strategies, with, for example, online reporting increasing parental engagement (2008b). It specified that all secondary schools should provide online reporting for parents by 2010, and similarly all primary schools by 2012 (Becta 2009b: 12). Moffatt (2009) argues that this strategy was developed in response to research, which shows: 'the single most important factor behind educational achievement is getting parents and carers involved in their children's learning' (Becta 2009c: 3).

To improve the use of technology in schools and to decrease the home–school divide, Becta (2009b) specified that all schools should be making 'effective use of learning platforms by 2010' (Becta 2009b: 14). The role of learning platforms became critical to Becta's drive to embed technology objectives, as identified in the 'Next Generation Learning' campaign (Becta 2009c). This campaign was supported by further government funding via the Harnessing Technology Grant, which had allocated over £600 million to spend on technology in schools between 2008 and 2011. However, with the appointment of a new Coalition government in 2010 and concomitant funding cuts, this funding stream was ended prematurely. Prior to the era of austerity from 2010, it should be noted that the amount of technology in schools as measured by the number of computers to pupils, was achieved. In 2004, the Becta 'ICT in Schools' survey highlighted that the target ratio of 'computer to pupil' from government had been met, which was an average of 1:8 in primary schools and 1:5 in secondary.

With the creation of the Harnessing Technology Strategy, Becta continued to promote technology in schools as a national education policy until 2010. Then, under the Coalition government the agency responsible for technology, Becta, was abolished. The responsibility for technology was subsumed back into the Department for Education (DfE). It took a further two years before the establishment of a new agency responsible for technology in schools was set up. In 2012 the Teaching Schools New Technology Advisory Board (NTAB) was established.

Prior to evaluating the change with technology that was implemented under the Labour government, it is worth recording the principal policy documents that influenced each, successive iteration of technology policy development during the 1990s and 2000s. Table 2.1 outlines the important policy documents and evaluation reports, although given the limits of space this is not exhaustive.

Evaluating change with technology: the nature of complex policy initiatives

From 1997 to 2010 the ICT policies of the Labour government made significant improvements to the provision of technology in UK schools, in terms of infrastructure, connectivity, professional development, pedagogy/curriculum application and whole-school management. Given the magnitude of the task that lay ahead in 1997, it must be noted that the complexities of ICT '. . . are substantial, so the managerial and organizational demands made on all those introducing them will be considerable. Establishing a national development programme will undoubtedly be extremely challenging' (Scrimshaw 1997: 11).

It is important to document the magnitude of this challenge, in order to appreciate the problems of implementing technology as a national strategy and to understand those areas that emerged as problematic:

- insufficient leadership and technology expertise across the multiple agencies,
- disparities of funding, leading to
- differing levels of technology provision, alongside

Table 2.1 UK policy and evaluation reports on technology in schools 1989–2010 (adapted Younie 2007)

Date	Report
1989	**TROTTER REPORT** 'Information Technology In Initial Teacher Training'.
1991	**NATIONAL CURRICULUM** orders for ICT.
1993	**IMPACT REPORT** Watson, Kings College: London.
1995	**NCET REPORT** 'Training Today's Teachers in ICT'.
1997	**DfEE/EDSI REPORT** 'Preparing for the Information Age: Synoptic Report of the Education Departments' Superhighways Initiative'. Department for Education & Employment.
1997	**DfEE** 'Survey of Information Technology in Schools 1996'.
1997	**McKINSEY REPORT** 'The Future of Information Technology in UK Schools'.
1997	**STEVENSON REPORT** 'Information and Communication Technology in UK schools'.
1997	**SCAA REPORT** (School Curriculum and Assessment Authority) 'Information Technology, Communications and the Future Curriculum'.
1997	**OFSTED REPORT** 'Information Technology In English Schools: a commentary on inspection findings 1995–6'.
1997	**DfEE (NGfL)** 'Connecting the Learning Society: National Grid for Learning; The Government's Consultation Paper'.
1998	**DfEE (NGfL)** 'Open for Learning, Open for Business'.
1998	**BECTA (NGfL)** 'Connecting Schools, Networking People: ICT Planning, Purchasing and Good Practice for the National Grid for Learning'.
1998	**DfEE (TTA) 4/98 ITT NC for ICT** 'Teaching: high status, high standards – requirements for courses of initial teacher training'. Circular 4/98. (Teacher Training Agency) (1998) Initial Teacher Training National Curriculum for the use of ICT in Subject Teaching (Annex B).
1998	**BECTA REPORTS** 'ICT in Schools Research and Evaluation Series' First Phase Nos 1–10.
2000	**DfEE/QCA** 'National Curriculum 2000'. ICT as a discrete subject awarded core subject status and the integration of ICT into all subject areas made statutory.
2001	**OFSTED** 'ICT in Schools: The Impact of Government Initiatives; An Interim Report' April 2001. HMI 264.
2001	**DfES/BECTA** 'NGfL Pathfinders: Preliminary Report on the roll-out of the NGfL Programme in ten Pathfinder LEAs'.
2001	**BECTA** 'Computers for Teachers Evaluation of Phase 1: Survey of Recipients'.
2002	**DfES** 'Transforming the Way We Learn: A Vision for the Future of ICT in Schools'. London, HMSO.
2002	**OFSTED** 'ICT in Schools: Effect of Government Initiatives; Progress Report' April 2002. HMI 423.
2002	**TTA** 'The New Opportunities Fund: Training for teachers and school librarians in the use of ICT; Progress review and lessons learned through the central quality assurance process in England'.

(Continued)

Table 2.1 *(Continued)*

Date	Report
2002	**DfES/BECTA ImpaCT2** – The Impact of ICT on Pupil Learning and Attainment (DfES/0696).
	ImpaCT2 – Learning at Home and School: Case Studies (DfES/0741).
	ImpaCT2 – Pupils' and Teachers' Perceptions of ICT in Education (DfES/0742).
2003	**DfES** 'Fulfilling the Potential: Transforming Teaching and Learning through ICT in Schools'.
2004	**PRESTON** 'The Full Evaluation of the English NOF ICT Teacher Training Programme (1999-2003)' (MirandaNet).
2004	**OFSTED** 'ICT in Schools: The Impact of Government Initiatives Five Years On' (HMI 2050).
2005	**OFSTED** 'Embedding ICT in Schools – a dual evaluation exercise. December 2005' (HMI 2391).
2005	**DfES/BECTA E-STRATEGY** 'Harnessing Technology: Transforming Learning and Children's Services'.
2005	**BECTA** 'The Becta Review 2005: Evidence on the Progress of ICT in Education'.
2006	**SOMEKH AND UNDERWOOD** 'Evaluation of the ICT Test Bed Project' Nottingham Trent University.
2008	**DCSF** 'Personalized Learning: A Practical Guide'.
2008	**BECTA** 'Harnessing Technology: Next Generation Learning'.
2009	**BECTA** 'Enabling Next Generation Learning: Enhancing Learning Through Technology'.
2009	**BECTA** 'Harnessing Technology for Next Generation Learning: Children, Schools and Families Implementation Plan 2009 to 2012'.
2009	**BECTA** 'Impact of Technology on Learning and Educational Outcomes'.
2010	**BECTA** 'The Impact of Technology: Value Added Classroom Practice. Final Report'.

- inequable quality of technology training from NOF and
- the limited impact on pedagogy (Younie 2006).

First, the national strategy was ambitious and it was implemented at a time when there were not the necessary multi-agency procedures in place for managing such a nebulous and complex initiative across 'multiple ecologies' at macro, meso and micro levels.

Policy-makers in England working on NOF had not realized that policy-makers in another part of government had dismantled systems at the meso level, which provided the regional subject expert network that NOF relied upon for delivering training (Leask 2002).

In England there are longstanding tensions between the macro and meso levels (Goddard and Leask 1992) with central government having an uneasy relationship with local authorities together with a long history of central government devolving power and responsibility to local authorities only to take them back again within a few years. During the 1990s, following a central government policy to devolve funding to individual schools ('Local Management of Schools'), what had been a well-established regional and local authority network of expert subject advisers was dismantled and replaced by generalist school management advisers, but the NOF programme, which was being developed at the same time, depended on these regional subject experts being available to deliver the training (Leask 2002). Without a high-quality delivery mechanism, success could have been predicted as being difficult to achieve.

Second, there were therefore insufficient levels of technology expertise and leadership within the education profession and commercial companies to orchestrate the strategy. Leaders were struggling to manage the cross-organizational operations inherent in the multi-agency initiative; perhaps a more cohesive or streamlined approach might have been more beneficial. One lesson was that the open market approach to developing an infrastructure from commercial companies and selecting technology training providers required a level of technology expertise and contractual/fiscal experience more characteristic of private enterprise than public sector education or, at least, more experience than most school leaders had in ICT in the late 1990s.

Another outcome was recognizing the disparities of funding, which meant that some schools were significantly better off, which led to differing levels of technology provision between schools (DfES 2001, 2002; Ofsted 2001). The result of that was varying provision affecting access for both pupils and teachers. A digital divide *between* schools technology resourcing emerged that urgently needed addressing (Leask and Younie 2001), and at the time of writing, while minimum levels of computer ratios have been achieved, there still remain major discrepancies between schools.

With training, despite the improvements in teachers' confidence with technology that were the positive consequences of the NOF initiative, there were a number of problems regarding implementation, including: 1) the general lack of technology expertise within school leadership teams, local authorities and ATPs (Approved Training Providers) and the consequent absence of joined-up thinking; and (2) the limited impact on pedagogy and classroom practice. Significantly the quality of training provision varied between providers, and factors at the local level of the school affected the outcomes. For example, the levels of *access* to technology and the extent to which school *leaders supported* the training, had a major impact on the effectiveness of the training for teachers (Leask 2002; Preston 2004).

One serious outcome regarding the lessons learnt concerns the extent to which each of the factors (funding, technology provision, training, leadership), at each level (macro, meso, micro) come together to combine and impact at the local level of the school to affect teachers' use of technology for classroom practice. It meant that the level of knowledge management that was required (across all stakeholders) was substantial and significantly underestimated at the time.

Knowledge management in the education profession

The multi-agency approach inevitably fractured the roll-out of the Labour government's technology strategy. However, this was exacerbated in those cases where technology expertise and leadership within and between agencies was absent or underdeveloped. The strategy required implementing cross-organizational relations, commercial contracts and knowledge management between macro, meso and micro 'eco-systems' – an unprecedentedly complex multi-policy initiative that in reality was deeply fragmented.

As a result, at the time of the national roll-out there was not enough technology expertise in the profession; what knowledge existed was held perhaps by only a few (DfES 2001; Leask 2002; Ofsted 2001). The response to the question, 'how is it possible to get new knowledge into a profession?' is, to network, distribute and extend existing knowledge. The key lesson learnt is the need to build communication networks in order to manage both the cross-organizational aspect of the strategy, and to share and develop technology expertise (Leask 2011). Such encouragement for net working can facilitate knowledge management of technology across multiple agencies and between schools. As critically observed:

> There has been little or no systematic networking of leading teachers and schools to ensure a sound basis for supporting the development of effective subject pedagogy using ICT. As a consequence, teachers with particular interests and expertise too often operate in isolation and lack the stimulus of professional dialogue.
>
> (Ofsted 2001: 21)

Overall, the embedding of technology into schools as organizations, and teachers as individual practitioners, has progressed unevenly, which is due largely to a disjointed and splintered roll-out that, with hindsight, might have been to some degree inevitable, given the magnitude and complexity of such an ambitious, multi-stakeholder national strategy. Perhaps the main lesson learnt is the need to systematically develop communities of practice, between teachers, school leaders and other key stakeholders (commercial companies, trainers, regional and national government agencies), to ensure a sound basis of communication and knowledge building for supporting effective practice using technology (Younie 2007). Leask (2011) proposes a minimum knowledge management system for national education systems which wish to harness innovation and knowledge across the system in order to improve teacher quality and learning outcomes and ensure systemic change.

Arguably in the period after the initial national roll-out, in the second and third term of Labour office (2002–2010), Becta were assigned a more strategic role in facilitating this process of embedding technology in schools.

Given the challenge that such systemic change required and the role Becta has played (for example, providing impartial advice, lists of approved products and managed services, and a research evidence base for technology pedagogic practice), it is with regret that the authors note this agency was shut down as soon as the Coalition government took office in 2010. With a little over ten years since the inception of the far-reaching vision of the national technology strategy, and although inconsistencies inevitably exist between schools, the distance travelled has been considerable – from the 'obsolete, third world' provision that McKinsey and Stevenson found in 1997. With the closure of Becta, the issues of knowledge management pertaining to technology in schools remain more pertinent than ever. In the UK it is now difficult for teachers to find new knowledge and to be engaged in sharing and further developing this with regard to technology for pedagogic practice.

The Conservative–Liberal Democrat coalition government of 2010, and concomitant economic recession, heralds a new era for technology in schools. This contemporary political climate of austerity within the context of a largely global economic downturn requires schools to consider carefully their technology expenditure. This is alongside the removal of foundation subject status, which Curriculum 2000 had awarded to technology and made a statutory requirement of all subjects. The expert panel reviewing the national curriculum recommend changing the status of technology to 'basic', which marks the end of a long fought for battle to see technology prioritized in the eyes of teachers.

> The '**Basic Curriculum**' describes the statutory requirements for curricular provision . . . These are compulsory requirements, but schools are able to determine for themselves the specific nature of this provision. The Secretary of State is therefore not required to produce Programmes of Study and Attainment Targets for subjects and topics in the Basic Curriculum.
>
> (DfE 2011: 18 – bold in original)

This marks a very significant policy shift away from centrally prescribed technology entitlement and consistent curriculum experience, to a technology curriculum that is locally determined. This replaces consistency with diversity and possible disparity. How long will it be before such inconsistencies herald a public outcry, like that of the Stevenson report, which found the state of technology in UK schools was impoverished, owing to a lack of investment and the lowered status of the subject? A cycle of lack of investment and lack of equitable provision for learners could be expected to result from these decisions. But then, in January 2012, the Education Secretary Michael Gove announced that ICT would include more computer science and the DfE announced exactly a year later that the subject will contribute to the English Baccalaureate (EBacc). As the first subject to be added on to the original EBacc (2010), the DfE states that this demonstrates the subjects importance to both education and the economy and that it will count as a science in the EBacc from January 2014. This seems to suggest that the status of technology, when reconfigured with more computer science, could regain its status.

Applications to practice

Technology practice in schools is influenced by the existence of national education policies on technology. Anyone visiting leading UK schools between 1997 and 2010 would have seen the application to practice that resulted from this period of innovation, development and investment in technology (see Chapters 8 and 9, which report on such applications to practice). The research reported in Chapters 8 and 9 (Leask and Preston 2010) brought together the most innovative practitioners from primary, secondary and FE colleges with the purpose of investigating how technology might be used in education both in the future as well as recording effective practice over the past decade. Please refer to these chapters for examples of practice that resulted from the policies discussed in this chapter.

Conclusions

While technology had been developed in schools from the early 1980s, it became very apparent by the mid-1990s that the state of technology in schools was 'primitive and not improving' and it was 'a national priority to increase use' (Stevenson 1997: 6). Problems concerning the major deficiencies were: technology training, resourcing, whole-school management and curriculum application. First, the problem with resourcing was the urgent need to replace obsolete computers. Second, teachers required specialist training to be proficient with technology. Third, school managers needed to develop a whole-school policy for technology, and fourth, there was a need to address the curriculum application of technology across all subjects.

In the late 1990s policy-makers embraced technology and made it a seductively anodyne 'cure all' for education. Arguably, the panacea of technology was cast as the solution to no less than the fundamental problems of education and the economy. As Somekh (2000: 20) argued it was taken 'and offered to the electorate as a talisman'. In turn, this led to the first-ever, nationally coordinated technology strategy and was, historically, the most ambitious and expensive change ever to be implemented in British state schooling. Despite the political idealization of technology and the fact that it may not have had the significant impact on attainment as originally hoped, the Labour government were committed to embedding technology in schools and providing a technology entitlement to all pupils. Arguably the economic rationale was the most politically persuasive regarding the unprecedented financial investment made by the Treasury in technology for schools under Labour 1997–2010 (£5 billion). What remains for the future, in terms of policy development for technology, will be a case of waiting to see.

Further reading

DfES (2002b) *Transforming the Way We Learn: A Vision for the Future of ICT in Schools*, London: DfES.

Somekh, B. (2000) New Technology and Learning: Policy and Practice in the UK 1980–2010, *Education and Information Technologies*, 5(1): 19–37.

Younie, S. (2006) Implementing Government Policy on ICT in Education: Lessons Learnt, *Education and Information Technologies*, 11(3–4): 385–400.

Websites

DfE (Department for Education) http://www.education.gov.uk/

For current policy on technology in schools refer to the government website for education.

National Archives http://www.nationalarchives.gov.uk/

To access Becta research reports, see the national archives, which has records of research into technology and education from 1997 to 2010. Following a change of government, web-based support and provision for education practice was withdrawn by the incoming Conservative and Liberal Democrat government in May 2010. A number of websites with research and evidence-based practice on technology were discontinued: for example, ttrb (teachers training resource bank), multi-verse, Becta.

PART 2

The contemporary context

3 Effective practice in technology-enhanced learning: interactive whiteboards

Overview

This chapter critically assesses the impact of technology on learning and the extent to which there is evidence that technology can enhance learning. It will examine how technology can aid the concentration, motivation and engagement of learners. Attention is given to interactive whiteboards in particular, as Higgins et al. (2007: 221) argue that this technology, perhaps more than any other to-date, has had the widest impact and may be the 'most significant change in the classroom learning environment' in recent years. As interactive whiteboards are a multi-sensory learning tool, so they have the potential to stimulate deep learning. Other technologies such as mobile technologies and learning platforms are referenced in Chapters 8 and 9.

Introduction: using interactive whiteboards

An interactive whiteboard can be described as a 'large, touch-sensitive board which is connected to a digital projector and a computer' (Becta 2003: 1). It is able to run interactive software, connect to the Internet and produce sound. The advantage of an interactive whiteboard over just a computer and a projector is the interactive element. Through tapping on the screen for control, it is possible, using a special pen or finger, to move objects about; highlighting, dragging and dropping and, most important, it provides interactivity for pupils at the screen, unlike a data projector.

In the UK policy-makers' commitment to integrating this technology in schools was matched by financial aid. By 2004 the UK government had invested £50 million in interactive whiteboards (DfES 2004). The UK government investment in technology was reflected globally, amidst a belief that failure to adapt might lead to social and economic disadvantage (OECD 2002). It led to the UK being one of the first countries to adopt interactive whiteboards along with America, Australia and Canada (Koenraad 2008) in the early 2000s, although originally, interactive whiteboards were invented much earlier – in 1991 by SMART Technologies Inc. (Somekh et al. 2007).

Like other technological innovations, it was originally created for business and developed for the boardroom (like PowerPoint) and has since been adapted for educational use.

Theory and research base

This chapter draws both on large-scale empirical studies of the roll-out of interactive whiteboards across the UK, which examine impact, and on more recent, smaller, qualitative work, which examines pedagogical aspects of developing interactivity and dialogic learning with interactive whiteboards. The former draws on the DCSF-funded SWEEP projects (Moss et al. 2007; Somekh et al. 2007) and the latter on the work of Hennessy et al. (2010), Mercer et al. (2010) and Warwick et al. (2010) from the Cambridge University interactive whiteboard research group.

A history of research on interactive whiteboards

Early research on interactive whiteboards focused on descriptions of the functionality of the boards and the software. Methodologically this research tended to be small scale, based on action research by enthusiastic innovators and focused mostly on practices in primary schools (Smith et al. 2005; Koenraad 2008). Research has since developed to include large-scale investigations with more representational samples (Higgins et al. 2007; Moss et al. 2007; Miller and Glover 2006). In England two important studies were conducted in 2007, which were the Schools Whiteboard Expansion Evaluation (SWEEP) projects, in which Somekh et al. assessed the impact of interactive whiteboards in primary schools and Moss et al. evaluated the roll-out in secondary schools from a sample of 30 schools in London (10 per cent representative sample). This research funded by the government found a number of significant advantages to teaching with an interactive whiteboard.

The key question many researchers start by asking is whether the interactive whiteboard only supports teacher-led functions (explain, demonstrate, present, instruct), which in turn supports whole-class, teacher-centred pedagogy and thereby 'sets the pedagogical clock back' (Koenraad 2008: 5). More probing questions are: to what extent can interactive whiteboards support more progressive pedagogies tailored towards greater independent and personalized learning, and more constructivist pedagogies supporting the co-construction of knowledge? To what extent can this technology enhance pupil collaboration and support diversity, and dialogic approaches to learning? These latter questions form part of the current research landscape. For example, more recent studies by Hennessy et al. (2011), Mercer et al. (2010) and Warwick et al. (2010) examine pupil collaborative group work at the interactive whiteboard and are finding innovation is possible if the teacher appropriately frames the activities at the board to extend thinking.

Impact of interactive whiteboards on pupil motivation and learning

'The use of the interactive whiteboard may be the most significant change in the classroom learning environment in the past decade . . .' (Higgins, Beauchamp and Miller 2007: 221).

Somekh et al.'s (2007) evaluation of interactive whiteboards identified a range of potential benefits, which pertain to: enhanced pupil motivation, benefits for teaching and, in some cases, some evidence of increased attainment. This is supported by Koenraad (2008) who found a similar range of benefits. Other researchers identify additional specific benefits: provides *focus* (cinema effect) and more opportunities for *interaction* (Smith et al. 2005), contributes to *concentration* (Kennewell 2004) and motivation (Longman and Hughes 2006), more varied and dynamic use of *resources* (Higgins et al. 2005), increase in *lesson pace* (Cuthell 2006), learners understand more *complex concepts* through visual representations and physically moving objects on the screen (Higgins et al. 2005), provides *multi-modal* and *kinaesthetic* learning opportunities (Miller and Glover 2006), which lead to deeper learning and promotes *metacognition*. In addition, interactive whiteboards can support specific *lesson phases*, from introductions with multimedia stimuli to interim comprehension checks and for the plenary; *debriefing*, reflection and evaluation.

The most cited 'added value' of interactive whiteboards to learning is the impact on pupil motivation. There is a range of evidence to support the claim that this technology does enhance motivation for pupils both primary (4–11 years) and secondary (11–18 years) (Passey et al. 2004; Higgins et al. 2005; Hall and Higgins 2005). Somekh et al. (2005) reported a significant impact in improving pupils' attention, which enabled difficult concepts to be taught more easily and the teachers in their study reported marked improvements in pupil motivation. Higgins et al.'s (2005) research found 99 per cent of teachers perceived that interactive whiteboards did increase pupil motivation. Staff were also positive about the impact of interactive whiteboards on their professional motivation for teaching, with 87 per cent of teachers claiming to feel more confident with technology as a result of the introduction of interactive whiteboards.

Somekh et al. (2007) cites evidence of researchers who found that use of whiteboards affected pupils' attention positively (from Pearson et al. 2004) and pupils stayed on task more, because their attention span persisted and lasted longer with the whiteboard (Glover et al. 2004). In addition, the interactive whiteboard was a visual focus for the pupils, with this increased focus leading to a quicker pace of lessons; use of a greater range of resources, together with multimedia aspects also captured pupils' attention. Pupils also liked seeing their work on the screen (Somekh et al. 2007).

Somekh et al. (2007) found the increase in concentration led to improvement in pupil behaviour. In addition, Somekh et al. (2007) discovered increased participation in lessons and a greater willingness to communicate in class by pupils. Increased contributions were explained by the fact that pupils were less anxious about making mistakes when they used the interactive whiteboard. This in turn enhances creativity, as research on creativity illustrates: when there is a reduction in anxiety and concomitant increase in opportunities to take risks there is more likely to be an environment conducive to enabling creativity (Loveless 2005; Spring-Keller 2010). Freedom from fear of 'getting it wrong' and making errors enables greater risks, play, exploration and discovery, which is conducive to learning (Piaget 1951).

In enabling greater interaction, interactive whiteboards were found to be popular with pupils too. Hall and Higgins (2005) research on pupils' perceptions was unusual in that hitherto, this aspect of interactive whiteboards had rarely been investigated. Pupils were 'very enthusiastic' about the multimedia element of whiteboards (movement, colour, touch, sound) and enjoyed the variety of resources, like games (Hall and Higgins 2005: 102). However, the pupils disliked technical problems and the lack of skills displayed by teachers and supply staff. What pupils did want was the opportunity to touch and use the screen more. 'When asked for their opinions about the interactive whiteboard, pupils are unanimous . . . [they like] correcting errors, moving things about, selecting, changing, and undoing are all regarded as great features' (Longman and Hughes 2006: 14).

> From pupils' perspectives . . . it is important to gather more data about how pupils see this type of technology affecting their classroom life . . . how easily they list . . . examples of how the interactive whiteboard helps them to learn [and] the value that pupils place on the repeatability of demonstrations and illustrations used by the teacher.
>
> (Longman and Hughes 2006: 17)

Although research has found that pupils value and enjoy the pedagogic use of interactive whiteboards in lessons, and the increased concentration and motivation, no evidence was found which showed this impacted in a significantly measurable way on attainment. Consequently, the impact of increased visual and kinaesthetic learning through interactive whiteboards on pupil achievement is less clear than the impact on general motivation and increased attention spans. The patterns on attainment are complex, and where a study may show increase one year, this is not necessarily sustained in the second year (Somekh et al. 2007).

> The key issue emerging from this analysis is that although the interactive whiteboard may alter the way that learning takes place, and that the motivation of teachers and pupils may be increased, yet this may have no significant or measurable impact on achievement.
>
> (Higgins et al. 2007: 221)

The issue is the gap or space between the introduction of digital technologies in schools and the measurement of pupil attainment, which has always been problematic, because of the difficulty of claiming categorically a causal connection, and also the lack of evidence of significant increases in attainment. This is identified as a major 'problem space' (Becta 2010a: 6) and specific 'unease related to the difficulty of finding causal relationships' between technology and learning. The difficulties of finding sustainable answers to this challenge should not be underestimated (Becta 2010a: 6). As argued previously, it may be more helpful to think of this 'problem space' as an 'ecology: one in which a complex network of interacting influences is shaping' the relationship between technology, learning and attainment in much more subtle ways (Becta 2010a: 6).

However, Cox et al. (2004) did find that the 'use of ICT has a more consistent effect on attainment when pupils are challenged to think and question their own understanding' (cited in Somekh et al. 2007: 162). This highlights the need to embed the technology in a sound pedagogy that utilizes constructivist principles to get pupils to evaluate and reflect on their own learning.

To this end, the multi-modal aspects of interactive whiteboards enable teachers to cater pedagogically for a range of *learning styles* – for visual learners, the large screen engenders greater pupil engagement, for audio learners there is the use of sound, and kinaesthetic learners have the opportunity to walk up to the screen, touch and move objects around. Smith et al. (2005: 94) argue that the interactive potential of interactive whiteboards in particular offers opportunities to create educational added value. The added value is the support interactive whiteboards can provide for teachers in scaffolding different learning styles and addressing diversity issues (Cuthell 2003; Glover et al. 2007: 13). As Kennewell (2004:12) argues, 'The degree of engagement and participation was felt to be increased; this was particularly important for the less able children. One way in which this was achieved was by calling pupils up to the board to interact with the material'.

Interactive whiteboards: afford interactivity (technically and dialogically)

One factor that accounts for the motivational effects of interactive whiteboards is the increased interactivity between the pupils and the whiteboard – for example, touching the screen. Kennewell (2006) makes a distinction between interactivity in a technical or physical sense (board functionality such as the production of sound when you touch a picture) and the promotion of cognitive interactivity (question–answer, comprehension check). To this, Koenraad (2008) adds socio-cognitive interactivity, which is the co-construction of knowledge, encouragement of reflection, brainstorming between teacher and pupil and among pupils. Glover and Miller (2002, cited in Somekh et al. 2007) were among the first to argue that interactivity included *a range of interactions*, which include *technical* interactions, between the pupil and whiteboard; *dialogic* interactions, which are between teachers and pupils, pupil and pupil; and *cognitive* interactions, which are between pupils and lesson content.

With respect to developing a pedagogy for the use of whiteboards which utilizes and exploits this typology of interactions, teachers can be placed on a spectrum from traditional and didactic with minimum interactions to progressive and constructivist, which is more interactive. These latter aspects have been explored in more depth recently by the Cambridge research group (Hennessy et al. 2011; Mercer et al. 2010; Warwick et al. 2010) who have investigated how interactive whiteboards can enhance dialogic approaches to learning to support a more constructivist pedagogy. This will be discussed further in the pedagogy section of this chapter.

The benefits of teaching with an interactive whiteboard

In addition to enhancing the types of interactivity outlined above, interactive whiteboards have the potential to benefit teaching by providing greater flexibility, multimedia presentations, support for planning, increased efficiency, and opportunities for modelling technology (Somekh et al. 2007). With respect to flexibility, interactive whiteboards enable teachers to access technical features when required, such as accessing their own online resources, the Internet, and it is also possible to teach the whole class with just one computer. The multimedia aspects allow for a range of materials to be easily accessed in different curriculum subjects and enable teachers to create stimulating 'ways into' subjects. For example, in history interactive whiteboards can link to archive film footage. In maths, rotation, tessellations and transformations, as well as maths games, can be demonstrated, and in modern foreign languages, highlighting phrases and listening to native language speakers via the Internet is made possible (Somekh et al. 2007). Interactive whiteboards also allow for demonstrating difficult concepts through simulations, such as heart function in biology. Handling such resources relatively easily aids the efficiency of a lesson and adds pace (Hennessy et al. 2005).

However, Somekh et al. (2007) found that teaching materials especially designed for interactive whiteboard use, both commercial and open source, were very limited. Most were written for primary schools, and for the secondary curriculum, science had comparably more resources than other subjects (Koenraad 2008). It is considered a challenge finding materials that are completely appropriate: 'a third of teachers (30%) reported that they find it difficult to find suitable interactive whiteboard resources' (Moss 2007: 24). As Koenraad (2008) observes, most of the materials made freely available by hardware suppliers relate to the Canadian and American curriculum. In the UK teachers solve this shortage by producing and exchanging their own resources (Younie 2007). This is corroborated by Jewitt et al. (2007) who found over 70 per cent of teachers made their own materials for the interactive whiteboard. In Younie's (2007) research of 12 secondary schools, departments created materials collaboratively, which not only increased the amount, but also aided the development of a pedagogical understanding of how to embed interactive whiteboard resources into classroom practice, as teachers shared ideas for both resource development and interactive pedagogical instantiation.

Although initially it takes time for teachers to produce learning resources to use in lessons on the interactive whiteboard, the advantage is that these can be saved, stored and shared between colleagues and improvements made year on year. Although this may take time to start with, it is possible to build up a bank of online resources relatively rapidly that can be adapted, updated and progressively developed by teachers as collaborative practice (Glover and Miller 2001; Kennewell 2001, 2004).

There is evidence that interactive whiteboards also increase teacher motivation, and Somekh et al. (2007) cite research from Australia, which showed teachers made significant changes to their classroom practice, such as consolidating learning in a non-repetitive way, and were more creative. Similarly, in the UK Somekh et al. (2005) found teachers enjoyed the creativity of producing their own resources for online use, and consequently increased their technology skills. This shows that the use of interactive whiteboards in class by teachers and pupils provides examples of modelling technology use which can lead to embedding technology skills across the curriculum.

The motivating effects of interactive whiteboards on teachers, who find the easy access to digital resources enriches their lessons, are further enhanced as teachers report that learners are also more engaged, due to the 'cinema effect' (Smith et al. 2005), and because the board is large and the contents clearly visible (Koenraad 2008). This aspect of visualization promotes cognitive understanding through the interactive and multimedia presentation of material, which Smith et al. (2005) found helps pupils to recognize relationships. As Koenraad (2008:10) goes on to argue, '. . . the conditions for engagement can be further optimised by using [interactive white-board] tools to provide even more focus by capturing specific moments of the process for replay or zooming in on particular phenomena'.

By facilitating replays of events and reviewing of processes – for example, with animated demonstrations of models – so Glover et al. (2007) argue that interactive whiteboards provide added educational value to classrooms. The visual representation of complex concepts which pupils can physically manipulate on the screen deepens learning and promotes metacognition, through multimodal and kinaesthetic engagement. The software allows for recap and reinforcement through the flipchart feature, which facilitates the teachers' ability to easily 'flip freely back and forth between screens' (Somekh et al. 2007: 156). Consequently,

> . . . the flow of the lesson was not purely linear; teachers moved backwards and forwards through the content and process of the lesson by scrolling documents, selecting PowerPoint slides, and 'flipping' through pages of the 'flipchart' software provided with the interactive whiteboards.
>
> (Kennewell 2004: 12)

In addition, Glover et al. (2007) found that, when teachers commented on replays of flipcharts that pupils had created, this contributed to pupils' involvement, motivation and self-confidence. The flexibility of using a wide range of Web-based resources that can be applied, adapted, customized and reused (Kennewell 2001) was found to encourage and help teachers to prepare lessons with respect to structuring information and planning comprehension checks (Smith et al. 2005). One consequence of such preparation was the reporting of better behaviour (Moss et al. 2007).

Interactive whiteboards and a consideration of possible disadvantages

However, despite the added value of interactive whiteboards reported above, a number of disadvantages have been found. First, the centrality of the teacher is often reinforced and there can be a reliance on delivering whole-class teaching with a didactic approach in which the interactive features of the technology are not optimized. The relationship between the technology and teachers' preferred style is examined more closely in the pedagogy section of this chapter. Further, irritations reported by pupils due to technical failure or lack of interactive whiteboard skills from teachers and/or learners themselves have been reported by Hall and Higgins (2005). Interestingly, a higher lesson pace, while considered earlier as a benefit, may be also a disadvantage, especially for weaker students (Kennewell 2004) and students with physical disabilities (blind and hearing impaired) (Somekh and Haldane 2006; Somekh et al. 2007). Similarly, Moss et al. (2007) observed that in some cases the increased lesson pace was used for discipline purposes, to keep pupils contained rather than to enhance the learning process.

Interactive whiteboards and teachers' professional development

The introduction of any technology into teaching is multi-faceted as it requires training both technically and pedagogically. There is the technology (functionality), the potential educational benefit (affordances) of that technology and the way technology is integrated into the learning and teaching processes in the classroom (pedagogy). This makes for a complex and multidimensional process that can change the dynamics of the classroom, as briefly considered with respect to the different types of interactivity (technical, dialogic, cognitive) that can be utilized with the interactive whiteboard.

When first introduced into the classroom, teachers have to learn the technical functionality and also consider the various pedagogical instantiations of that technology. For teachers, what is known to help with this process of integrating technologies which are new to them are the following: *familiarity*, if the technology mimics existing classroom practice, such as a board at the front of the class; if pupils act as *co-learners* to help navigate the new functionality and applications; and, if *trial and error* is encouraged within a *collegial environment* of support (Higgins et al. 2005).

With respect to interactive whiteboards, the issue of familiarity is important. The willingness of teachers to engage in deploying interactive whiteboards may be due to the similarity of the technology with a 'normal' whiteboard, which lessens teachers' reticence. Then, the journey 'to travel' is smaller between the technology and teachers' practice, which with interactive whiteboards was shown to be the case. As Higgins et al. (2005) argue, it is precisely because the interactive whiteboard is so suited to supporting whole-class teaching that it has been adopted so rapidly in comparison with other technologies, which leads to the technology 'merely being used to reinforce current teaching approaches, rather than supporting a transforming pedagogy' (Koenraad 2008: 19). However, research by Hall and Higgins (2005) and Pearson et al. (2004) found that the occasions when teachers forgot how to use the interactive whiteboard, while annoying for pupils, did provide a learning opportunity for everyone. Pupils enjoyed the increased partnership with teachers when pupils were able to help solve the technical problems and offer advice. This model of pupils as co learners was also found to be highly effective by Morris (2010).

It is well known that effective forms of professional development involve strategies that foster informal cooperation and a collegial approach (Cuthell 2006; Leask and Younie 2001). As Moss et al.'s (2007: 59) research on interactive whiteboards found, by having an exploratory, trial-and-error approach, where experiences were shared and coordinated by an enthusiastic colleague, training was found to be highly effective. Koenraad's (2008) systematic review of the research also highlighted that implementation is more successful if the possibilities of interactive whiteboards are explored in a spirit of collegial collaboration. Younie (2007) found this to be true, not only of interactive whiteboards, but of all technologies that staff encountered in her longitudinal research of 116 teachers integrating technology into professional practice, from 1998 to 2006 across 12 schools.

With respect to specific interactive whiteboard training, training should be linked to educational theory and practice (Miller and Glover 2007) and it is for this reason that Somekh et al. (2007) regard accredited training programmes for teachers as indispensable. Overall, continuing professional development is successful if it supports teachers' exploration of their current pedagogy, and helps them identify how interactive whiteboard use can support, extend or transform their practice (McCormick and Scrimshaw 2001). However, teachers' 'learning' is not necessarily instantaneous, but rather has been found to evolve through 'stages'.

Stages of teachers' professional development: learning to use technology

With respect to developing pedagogy with an interactive whiteboard, Somekh et al. (2007) cite researchers who traced the stages that teachers work through and ascend when learning to teach with new technologies. For example, they found researchers Glover et al. (2004) and Pearson et al. (2004) both identified three stages in the tech- nology- competence development of teachers. The first stage was defined as 'support- ive didactic' in which the interactive whiteboard is used 'purely as a presentational tool', to support visually teacher-centred knowledge and information transmission (Dewey's 'fact fetish' 1938). The second stage when teachers challenge pupils to think, using illustrations and stimulating pupil responses through the graphical rep- resentations of concepts, is defined as the 'interactive' stage. The third stage is when the technology becomes embedded as an integral part of the lesson and is used to 'stimulate pupils' cognitive development', involving more intensive participation by pupils through exploratory activities and group work. Referred to as the 'enhanced interactive' stage, this is a more process-oriented approach to teaching with an inter- active whiteboard (Somekh et al. 2007: 163). See Table 3.1, which outlines the stages of interactive whiteboard use by teachers.

The identification of stages that teachers go through as they learn how to teach with technology is discussed further in Chapter 5. Suffice to say here that this stage model or 'typological approach' to understanding teacher pedagogical development, for example, from novice to expert, is evidenced by a number of empirical studies in both the UK and America (Hooper and Rieber 1995; Dawes 2001; Tanner et al. 2005;

Table 3.1   Stages of interactive whiteboard use by teachers (adapted from Glover and Miller 2004)

Progression	Competence Development Process	Interactive Whiteboard (IWB) Use	Theory of Learning / Pedagogic Application
First stage	supportive didactic	IWB used as a presentation tool by the teacher; visually support teacher didactic approach	teacher-centred, information transmission model of learning, traditional paradigm
Second stage	interactive	multi-sensory stimuli (verbal, audio and visual) to stimulate learner responses, teachers challenge pupils to think using illustrations and stimulate responses through the graphical representations of concepts	interactive, participatory, teacher – pupil(s) – IWB interactivity, constructivist paradigm
Third stage	enhanced interactive	same as above, with more flexibility, stimulate pupils' cognitive development	more embedded, intensive participation, process-oriented approach, exploratory activities and group work, constructivist paradigm

Younie 2007). Hooper and Rieber's (1995) seminal stage model of teacher progression with technology (from familiarization, utilization, integration, reorientation to evolution) went even further and argued that, if teachers did not progress through these stages, the technology would be most likely to be abandoned.

In addition to Glover and Miller's (2007) scales of 'interactivity' outlined above, other scales construct use in terms of surface use to 'deep integration'. This is similar to West Burnham's (2007) model of learning and stages of progression, from shallow to deep to profound learning. Each are necessary and serve different functions: for example, surface or single-loop learning serves the learning of, for example, mathematical timetables by rote or technical features of computers. Deep or double-loop learners know how to create knowledge and are reflective about what they learn and how they learn. Profound or triple-loop learning is not only about 'the what' and 'the how', but also 'the why'. For example, as a teacher becomes more expert with using the interactive whiteboard, so they progress from using it superficially for 'initiate-response-feedback' stimulus at the start of a lesson (without extension or evaluation), to engaging with more interactive strategies, which demands greater pupil reflection and cognitive challenge.

Higgins et al. (2005) found that as interactive whiteboards became more embedded into classroom practice, so patterns of interaction changed.

> Teachers asked more open questions, repeat questions, probes (where a teacher asks for further information or an explanation of the answer from a pupil), longer answers from pupils, and almost twice the amount of evaluative responses from teachers . . . There was a faster pace, measured by the number of interactions.
>
> (Higgins et al. 2005: 4)

The notion of incremental shifts in the pedagogical use of the interactive whiteboard, like the progression from novice to expert, is akin to Lave and Wenger's (1991) conception of moving from the periphery to the centre in a community of practice, as learning how to use the whiteboard more interactively becomes embedded into practice. However, all this takes time, which leads us to consider those factors that affect the take-up of technology for classroom practice.

Emerging conditions for the effective implementation of interactive whiteboards in classrooms

The key factors identified from research as affecting the implementation of interactive whiteboards were time and costs (Somekh et al. 2007). Although significant government funding enabled the widespread adoption of interactive whiteboards in schools, following the initial expense of installation, came the need to *fund* teachers' training in their use, which also required *time*. Also, it is demanding of teachers' time to produce resources for interactive whiteboard use, as discussed and, although these can be shared and saved for future use, there is still the initial outlay in preparation time. Higgins et al. (2005) found that it typically took one year of using the interactive whiteboard before teachers created their own resources, referred to as 'embedding effects' (cited in Somekh et al. 2007: 164), which appear to be evolutionary and longitudinal – it takes time. In addition to the costs of ongoing training for teachers, there is also the need to train teaching assistants and supply staff. Pupils have cited their frustration with support and supply staff lacking the necessary skills to use the interactive whiteboard (Hall and Higgins 2005).

With respect to time:

> There is a consistent finding across all data that the length of time pupils have been taught with an interactive whiteboard is the major factor that leads to attainment gains. This appears to be the result of the interactive whiteboard becoming embedded in teachers' pedagogy: that is, when teachers have had sustained experience (around two years) of using an interactive whiteboard, they are able to change their teaching practices to make best use of its facilities.
>
> (Somekh et al. 2007: 4)

Interestingly, in some cases Somekh et al. (2007) were able to report improved results, particularly for maths and science, with those teachers who had managed to integrate interactive whiteboards into their classroom practice after approximately two years. This is further supported by Moss et al. (2007:47) who found similar subject variation in take up: 'the relevance of interactive whiteboard technologies was more easily recognised and realised in maths and science' where as in English 'the benefits of the technology seemed less immediately apparent'.

Implementation of whole-class technologies is affected by other school factors, which have been found to greatly influence the impact of any technology. One of the most important is supportive leadership, which is necessary to affect organizational and cultural change in classroom practice (Glover and Miller 2002). Somekh et al. (2007) found that leaders who promoted change, although not necessarily expert themselves in the newly adopted technologies, were effective when they empowered others to learn. This model of 'distributed leadership' is known to be powerful with respect to technology take up in general, not just interactive whiteboards (Lawson and Comber 2004; Younie 2007).

In considering the conditions required for the effective implementation of interactive whiteboards, the conditions that constrain also become apparent. With respect to understanding what constrains teachers' uses of interactive whiteboards (or any technology) the 'old chestnuts' of restrictive curriculum and assessment regimes that prioritize standardized testing come to the fore again. Somekh et al. (2007) in reference to the work of Lewin et al. (2003) cite the need for more flexible curricular and pupil/teacher roles, in order to realize the benefits of technology. Pressures to cover the content of the curriculum 'restrict freedom to make the most of the interactive pedagogies afforded by the interactive whiteboard' (Somekh et al. 2007: 165).

Overall, however, interactive whiteboard use appears to contribute to increasing teachers' technology skills. Interestingly Koenraad (2008: 19) observed: 'one of the more consistent findings is that the adoption process of interactive whiteboards by practitioners is a lot more fluent compared to the integration of the Internet and the use of subject-specific software'. This rapid adoption is supported by Higgins et al. (2005) research, which is explained by teachers' pedagogy, because it reinforces current whole-class teaching strategies. The relatively fluent adoption of interactive whiteboards has, however, led to some changes in pedagogy.

Teachers' pedagogy and interactive whiteboards

The research literature shows clearly that some marked changes in pedagogy have occurred following the introduction of interactive whiteboards into UK classrooms. Somekh et al. (2007: 162) claims that interactive whiteboards have 'changed the ambiance of classrooms significantly' and the clarity of teachers' presentations has 'greatly improved'. However, technology does not necessarily affect pedagogy or teaching style. McCormick and Scrimshaw (2001) argue that technology enables teachers to teach more *efficiently* (as well as having the potential to be transformative), but in essence teachers' pedagogy has hardly changed. Additionally, Kennewell (2004: 61) found that the introduction of technology into schools during the past twenty years or so has 'had relatively little effect on the way teachers teach'.

Somekh et al. (2005) perceptively noted that whole-class technologies such as interactive whiteboards fit well with whole-class teaching approaches, which explains why pedagogy remains relatively unchanged. Consequently, teaching frequently remains didactic as opposed to encouraging greater learner autonomy and teachers continue to control the interactive whiteboard, whereas in fact pupils want more opportunities for themselves to control and use the board (Fraser 2011; Hall and Higgins 2005). Interestingly, Fraser's (2011) research on pupil voice and technology found that when interviewing learners (about what they wanted regarding technology in the classroom, in schools in the Midlands) they frequently requested less teacher talk and more hands-on experience with technology. Similarly, Hall and Higgins (2005) found in their sample of 72 pupils across six local authorities in the north and south of England, the same desire for more access to the technology.

With interactive whiteboards it seems that teachers have not changed their teaching style, in that it still has teachers leading from the front. Instead, new technologies become subsumed seamlessly into traditional classroom practices, so new possibilities become lost amid old routines (Deal 1999). It may be a new pack of cards, but they are shuffled in the same ways, which leads us to question what is required for radical change in practice in terms of pedagogical innovation. As,

> . . . it has been found that interactive whiteboards tend to reinforce established styles of whole-class teaching – sometimes extending the teacher's 'whole-class mode' unproductively rather than promoting new, innovative teaching approaches.
>
> (Higgins 2006, cited in Koenraad 2008: 15)

Interestingly, this finding is corroborated by teachers. In the UK and America teachers have reported that the benefit of the interactive whiteboard is that they can do the same activities (Farrell 2004; Gatlin 2004, cited in Somekh et al. 2007) – for example, using the interactive whiteboard to conduct 'initiate-response-feedback' stimulus at the start of a lesson. Consequently, 'patterns of pupil-teacher discourse were largely unchanged, technical or physical interactivity with the interactive whiteboard was seldom harnessed to produce significant shifts in understanding' (Moss et al. 2007: 44).

Kennewell and Beauchamp (2007) argue that transformation of education in terms of more independent and individualized learning with technology is not widespread in the UK.

> Interactive whiteboards seem to reinforce traditional pedagogies. They do not in themselves afford learner autonomy in the way that laptops, or even desktop PCs do. The long-awaited 'transforming pedagogy' for ICT clearly requires more than regular use of ICT by teachers; it requires a change in pedagogical knowledge and beliefs.
>
> (Kennewell 2004: 17)

It is a similar case in other countries too, data from research on technology use in the Netherlands found that it will take time before interactive whiteboards change teaching practices in innovative ways: 'one reason being that teachers – both in primary and secondary education – appear to apply activities targeted at the transfer of knowledge more frequently than methods to stimulate knowledge construction' (Koenraad 2008: 20). With respect to models of change, it is no surprise that interactive whiteboards have been appropriated without great pedagogical disruption, because they mirror the same practice that occurred prior to their introduction, in this way their assimilation was guaranteed.

What is required for a greater pedagogical realization of interactive whiteboards is the deployment of enhanced dialogic skills to guide pupil group work at the board, alongside specifically designed materials. As Koenraad (2008) asserts: 'The impact of interactive whiteboards is restricted if teachers do not sufficiently realize that for interactivity to take place specifically designed materials (Stranders 2008: 58), dialogical skills (Mercer et al. 2007) and appropriate methodologies are needed' (Koenraad 2008: 20).

Developing a dialogic pedagogy with interactive whiteboards

The interactive whiteboard research group at Cambridge University argue that interactive whiteboards afford the creation of a dialogic space for pupil learning and knowledge building, where the teacher appropriately scaffolds the activity and pupils talk at the board. However, although interactive whiteboards can encourage the creation of a shared dialogic space that allows for the co-construction of knowledge, this only occurs where there is active support and pedagogical framing from the teacher – where the teacher develops active learning and exploits the affordances of the interactive whiteboard, to promote pupil agency. As Warwick et al. (2010: 360) argue: 'the way that the teacher creates a productive collaborative ethos, is central to the success of collaborative work at the interactive whiteboard'.

The functionality of interactive whiteboards requires mediating and pedagogical framing by the teacher. It is important to note that 'technology has no agency – it cannot, in itself, change classroom teaching and learning, but rather requires mediation' (Warwick et al. 2010: 360). The functionality of the interactive whiteboard can be used to support traditional, didactic approaches or support more constructivist, dialogic strategies. As Mercer et al. (2010: 207) argue: '...the effective use of the inter- active whiteboard as an educational tool is not inherent in the hardware, software or even the materials it displays. It is predicated upon the teacher's practical understand- ing of how to engage users and to help them learn.'

To this end, the Cambridge research group, through their publications and web- site, are outlining how teachers can develop dialogic strategies for learning and teach- ing that utilize the functionality of the interactive whiteboard. Because interactive whiteboards can display a wide range of digital resources that use different modalities (film clips, photographs, poems, audio, diagrams, historical documents) these can be pedagogically marshalled in various ways, from acting as a stimulus, to being anno- tated by pupils, then saved, revisited and evaluated. This allows for the temporal devel- opment of learning over a number of lessons, and through pupil interaction with the digital resources and scaffolded discussions with each other, these interactions can be understood as effective dialogic strategies for 'deeper' learning (West-Burnham 2007).

Applications to practice

When considering the interactive whiteboard as a pedagogical tool to enhance learn- ing, the extent of adoption in any school depends on teachers understanding the affordances of the technology. Interactive whiteboards provide a range of features and have the functionality to support a more 'participatory pedagogy' (Kennewell and Beauchamp 2007), but research evidence shows teachers may be more likely to con- tinue with existing pedagogic approaches.

Consider the range of visual, auditory and text-based functions of an interactive whiteboard and how these can be a stimulus for reasoning, encourage the testing of provisional ideas and how individual and collective thinking can be captured, then annotated, reformulated, saved and revisited so meanings are actively created. Devel- oping a set of annotated resources that encourage evaluation and synthesis through group discussion over time arguably supports the temporal development of learn- ing (over a period of time) and generates a learning community, which Mercer et al. (2010) argue are key aspects of dialogic teaching.

As a practitioner you may want to consider how you can enhance your practice through using your interactive whiteboard. For example, you may be interested in developing a more dialogic approach as outlined by the Cambridge research group (Hennessy et al. 2010; Mercer et al. 2010; Warwick et al. 2010). For example, as a practitioner, reflect on:

- How do pupils use the interactive whiteboard when working together on activities?
- Explore and consider, is there a distinctive role for the interactive whiteboard to support productive dialogue and other forms of interaction amongst pupils?

- How can pupils use the interactive whiteboard to share relevant ideas and create new joint understandings?

Rudd (2007: 6) asks, 'how do teachers become critical agents in mediating technology, to provide a more dynamic, interactive and appropriate learning experience?' How would you answer Rudd's question? Importantly, consider how interactive whiteboards can be used pedagogically to support 'exploratory talk'? (Mercer 2000; Dawes 2008). Warwick et al. (2010: 352) state that exploratory talk is talk in which:

- all relevant information is shared
- all members of the group are invited to contribute to the discussion
- opinions and ideas are respected and considered
- everyone is asked to make their reasons clear
- challenges and alternatives are made explicit and negotiated
- the group seeks to reach agreement before taking a decision or acting.

Think about this definition of exploratory talk above and consider the ways in which an interactive whiteboard can support this. Mercer et al. (2010: 201) identified a range of dialogic strategies that the interactive whiteboard could help teachers orchestrate. The aim is that dialogue *'should make reasoning explicit'* and *'support the cumulative co-construction of knowledge and understanding'*. A teacher can use the interactive whiteboard to support any of the following pedagogical intentions:

- scaffold learning
- support the temporal development of learning
- involve pupils in co-constructing knowledge
- encourage evaluation and synthesis
- develop a learning community
- develop pupil-pupil dialogue
- support provisionality of pupils' evolving ideas
- guide lesson flow
- develop pupil questioning (from Mercer et al. 2010: 201).

This approach above concerns the use of dialogue as a way of creating collective meaning. Look for effective ways of exploiting the interactive and multimodal features of interactive whiteboards to support your pedagogic aims. See Mercer et al.'s (2010) paper for more detailed suggestions in further reading and other papers written by the Cambridge researchers, as well as their website listed at the end of the chapter.

Conclusions

Findings from the research to date are largely positive with respect to pupil learning and have found interactive whiteboards enhance whole-class teaching. They have been found to frequently have a significant impact in improving pupils' motivation and attention, and to help teachers in explaining difficult concepts (Higgins et al. 2005; Somekh et al. 2005). 'There is consensus on the contribution of this tool to three aspects of educational practice: the presentation of information and resources, the power of visualisation in the interpretation of concepts and models, the facilitation of interaction and organization of activities with a whole-class focus' (Koenraad 2008: 18).

However, technology cannot, in and of itself, bring about change. That requires agency from teachers and learners. The educational added value is derived from the pedagogical framing of the use of the interactive whiteboards by teachers, situated in classroom practice. Somekh et al. (2007) have illustrated positive results if adequate training is provided and teachers are allowed sufficient time to integrate interactive whiteboards into their pedagogic practice. However, as Koenraad (2008: 18) rightly asserts: 'there is still too little empirical, qualitative, longitudinal and subject-specific research available for firm conclusions'. This affirms the need for further research. As Somekh et al. (2007: 7) argue: 'any distinctive contribution that interactive white-boards can make to pupil learning will be a long-term process dependent on on-going exploration of what the technology can best be used for.'

Further reading

Higgins, S., Beauchamp, G. and Miller, D. (2007) Reviewing the literature on interactive whiteboards, *Learning, Media and Technology*, 32(3): 213–35.

Mercer, N., Hennessy, S. and Warwick, P. (2010) Using interactive whiteboards to orchestrate classroom dialogue, *Technology, Pedagogy and Education (themed issue on interactive whole class technologies)*, 19(2): 195–209.

Somekh, B. et al. (2007) *Evaluation of the Primary Schools Whiteboard Expansion Project*, London: DCSF.

Useful websites

http://dialogueiwb.educ.cam.ac.uk

The University of Cambridge interactive whiteboard group has a number of researchers who publish on using this technology to support classroom dialogue. The website has lesson materials and video footage to support dialogic teaching with the interactive whiteboard. The resources on the website may serve to stimulate discussion, development and trialling of dialogic approaches.

4 Emerging practice with games-based learning

Overview

This chapter critically assesses the research on digital games and the extent to which there is evidence that this technology can enhance learning. The chapter examines theories that help us understand the appeal of gaming, and draws on psychological theories of play, alongside motivational and arousal theories to explain how gaming activities sustain interest for long periods of time. This is set within the context of the research on gaming and current evidence base about games-based learning. The chapter considers applications to practice and barriers to more widespread implementation.

Introduction and context

Digital games-based learning has gained considerable interest since the early 2000s when high-profile proponents (Prensky 2001; Gee 2003) proposed that gaming has an impact on cognitive development. This theory has gained traction in terms of research and interest in the potential effect of games on learning, which has occurred alongside an expansion in the variety of games and gaming platforms.

Computer games are popular with players of all ages and both genders (Johnson et al. 2011). Why is it that games enable players to maintain concentration for such long periods? The principles underpinning the design of successful games are similar to the principles supporting effective learning (De Freitas and Jameson 2006; Douch et al. 2010). In marrying gaming strategies to educational aims and content in order to promote a holistic approach to learning it is possible to get the most out of both gaming and learning together. Working towards a goal, using problem-solving processes and experiencing success are gaming strategies that are replicable and can transfer to games with an educational content.

Educational gaming enthusiasts cite how multiple aspects of interactivity, creativity and problem-solving have the potential to enhance learning; as players are given power and control over the flow of events and learning content, learners' engagement and ownership promotes an enhanced learning experience.

Theory and research base

This chapter draws on recent research into games-based learning and acknowledges the origins of this field in earlier educational research on experiential learning and gaming (non-digital) from the 1960s. However, digital gaming is gaining traction in education and more research is needed on the impact of games on learning (De Freitas and Jameson 2006; Byron 2008; Spring-Keller 2010).

Defining computer games: commercial and educational

There has been an expansion in the diversity of computer games and gaming platforms this past decade of which the most significant has been the evolution of hand-held mobile devices (Douch et al. 2010). Added to this is the increasing interest in digital games for learning (Miller and Robertson 2010). Johnson et al. (2011) point out the wide diversity of games available to educators from simple pencil-and-paper games to complex, massive, multiplayer, online (MMO) role-playing games. Because of this diversity, for the purposes of this chapter, it is necessary to start with a clear definition of what is meant by computer games. Prensky (2001) defines six essential elements to computer games:

1. Rules
2. Goals and objectives
3. Outcomes and feedback
4. Conflict, competition, challenge and opposition
5. Interaction
6. Representation or story.

Additionally, Prensky (2006) argues there are essentially two types of computer games: namely, *'mini'* and *'complex'* games. The latter require more time to master, greater skill set, more problem-solving, difficult decisions, and are consequently more intensely effective in engaging the player. However, complex digital games are not specifically designed for educational purposes. So, there is a distinction to be made between games specifically written for educational purposes and commercial off-the-shelf computer games, known as COTS. There has been a growing interest in the potential of COTS in the classroom (Johnson et al. 2011; Kirriemuir and McFarlane 2004; Miller and Robertson 2009, 2010).

With respect to COTs, it is worth briefly outlining the variety of complex computer games in order to understand how these may be appropriated for educational purposes. There are immersive fantasy games, simulations, massively multiplayer online (MMOs) games, augmented reality games (ARGs), serious games and game 'modding'. Immersive fantasy games, like *Myst* and *Riven*, require players to solve puzzles in virtual environments; augmented reality games also require players to find clues and problem solve, but the boundary between game and real life is more blurred. Simulations, like *Sim City*, are role-playing games, which require the adoption of different identities. There is also game 'modding', where players can actively modify a game, which is possible with open-ended games. Examples of computer games where players create their own game and characters are also referred to as evolutionary games, the best known example of which is *Second Life*. This open-ended game has very few rules and roles as users create and develop everything themselves (Spring-Keller 2010).

More recently there has been the emergence of the Serious Games movement, which is a genre of games that 'layer social issues or problems with game play, helping players gain a new perspective through active engagement' (Johnson et al. 2011). There is also the development of massively multiplayer online (MMO) games designed for learning. The commercial counterparts to these are entertainment focused – for example, *World of Warcraft* – or training based – such as *America's Army*, both of which bring together multiple players to work on exercises that require cooperative, strategic problem-solving. These games are complex and include solo as well as group goals, which are collaborative, but can also be competitive. MMOs are organized around a storyline or theme and are often goal-oriented, but 'the highest levels of interaction and play require outside learning and discovery' (Johnson et al. 2011: 21). What makes MMOs so compelling is the variety of sub-games, or paths of engagement, available to players, with short- and long-term goals to attain and interesting back stories that set the context. The challenge that needs to be addressed is that of embedding educational content into the nature of such immersive and compelling games.

Having outlined commercial games above, it is important to distinguish between recreational games and learning games, where the former are framed by leisure and play and the latter by an education context. Games that a learner chooses to play on their own machine where the main purpose is play are differentiated from digital learning games, where learning is the main purpose; for this, the term 'digital games based learning' (DGBL) applies.

The development of educational content is gaining more interest; there are examples of single-player online games, such as those developed by Persuasive Games, which explore advocacy issues and engage players in serious questions concerning health, policy and social problems; and *Oligarchy*, a game that focuses on international oil drilling (Johnson et al. 2011). The premise behind these educational games is that learners read about a topic, which is then actively explored through online playing. As Johnson et al. (2011) assert, these games lend themselves to curriculum content, requiring learners to discover and construct knowledge in order to solve problems.

The *New Horizon Report* (Johnson et al. 2011) outlines recent examples of developments in augmented reality games (ARGs) and educational content. For example, the *ARG World Without Oil* is a 'collaborative, social imagining of the first 32 weeks of a global oil crisis'; and *Superstruct*, is a game in which players face 'daunting environmental, political and health challenges in a world ten years in the future' (Johnson et al. 2011: 21). Similarly, *The Tower of Babel* is designed for schools, for learners of all ages, for learning languages other than their own. These three examples are designed specifically to outline curriculum content, which help learners gain new perspectives and insights through engaging keep in the topics in more complex and nuanced ways (Johnson et al. 2011: 21).

Just as there has been an increase in the diversity of games, so too has there been a propagation of technology platforms on which to play games.

Types of games and technology platforms

Originally computer games were designed to be played on desktop machines in the 1980s and 1990s; however, more recently (since 2000) there has been a proliferation of gaming platforms, which now include specialist games consoles and hand-held devices. Today games can be played on a variety of platforms, of which there are essentially three types: personal computers, gaming consoles or mobile devices. Personal computers have the functionality to support games, whether they are desktops, laptops, or tablets (netbooks or iPads). Games consoles, however, are specifically designed for game playing, and the two market leaders are Sony X-Box and Nintendo Wii consoles. Hand-held devices range from mobile phones, PDAs, which again support gaming, to specific devices designed solely for game play; of the latter, the two market leaders are Sony PSP (PlayStation Portable) and the Nintendo DS (dual screen).

Just as there are different types of technology platforms to play on, so there are different types of games to play, which require a more nuanced categorization. The most effective is taken to be the Herz system (Herz 1997) which identified eight *types* of games. These are: action, adventure, fighting, puzzle, role-playing, simulation, sports and strategy games. The range and types of games is staggering: for example, there are over 1500 games available for the Nintendo DS device alone. These types of games can also be characterized as *genres*, of which Douch et al. (2010) found six. These were:

- action genre (*Grand Theft Auto*)
- strategy genre (*Tom Clancy's Endwar*)
- puzzle genre (*Crash Bash*)
- simulation genre (*The Sims*)
- shooting genre (*Call of Duty*)
- sports genre (*Wii Fit*).

Young people in Douch et al.'s (2010) research expressed a preference for one particular genre over others, which could be explained by reference to the subject matter that interested them, such as animals, sport or exercise, or contained characters they could relate to.

Douch et al. (2010) argue that the most accessible games for schooling environments are those that have a dual aim of entertaining and educating and can be played via a digital hand-held device. Those with puzzle, problem-solving, literacy and numeracy games are now designed to be much more engaging and offer teachers flexible tools to use in the classroom – for example, 'Dr Kawashima's Brain Training' (Douch et al. 2010). Similarly, such hand-held devices offer additional functionality, from camera mode for photo images, videoing, audio recording, texting options,

Internet access, even global positioning (GPS), which provide teachers with an additional tool box of technology options.

However, when it comes to the history of computer games in education, the earliest types were more basic 'drill and skill' types (Kirriemuir and McFarlane 2004).

History of computer games in education: early uses for learning

When it comes to specific education games, Johnson et al. (2011) argue these can be categorized into three groups:

- games that are not digital
- digital games that are not collaborative
- collaborative digital games.

Historically in schools, the early use of computer games was from the second category. Beginning in the 1980s, the emergent use of games was predominantly with young children to improve literacy or numeracy skills. However, these were simple 'drill and practice' activities (Struppert 2010), which didn't necessarily engage the affective or emotional domain of learners. The problem with educational games has been the lack of 'integrating learner affectiveness' (Ghergulescu and Muntean 2010: 72).

Since 2000, Struppert (2010) argues, game designers, researchers and educators have wanted better integration of educational learning and entertaining game-play, which has led to the emergence of 'serious games'. Simulations such as *Civilization III*, *SimCity* and *The Sims*, have been used to teach History, Social Studies, Urban Planning and English (Struppert 2010). Further to this, there are more recent examples of augmented reality games (ARGs) to teach international diplomacy, language learning and environmental management (Johnson et al. 2011).

Why games? – purported benefits

While the reported benefits pertain to the development of a variety of skills and specific content knowledge, arguably, gaming should be understood more holistically when it comes to psychological and socio-emotional development. However, before outlining the benefits of gaming on the affective domain, it is important to outline the cognitive benefits, which key writers have espoused and made popular (Gee 2003; Prensky 2006).

Cognitive benefits of gaming

In 2003 Gee outlined the impact of gaming on cognitive development, which has been supported by subsequent research (Douch et al. 2010; Miller and Robertson 2010). For example, in 2006 Prensky argued that complex digital games engender a number of cognitive skills, notably through exploration and discovery: players learn to manipulate and manage complex environments, which require strategies to problem solve in order to move onto the next level of challenge in the game. Most significantly, because players are not informed of the rules in advance, but rather learn through playing, this develops deductive reasoning skills.

Douch et al. (2010) argue that complex games require the synthesizing of information from a variety of sources (even beyond the game) and the creation of tactics and/or strategies to overcome obstacles. Games that simulate real-life scenarios involve a broad range of cognitive skills, from organizational competences and decision-making to strategic thinking. It is the design of games that contains effective learning strategies, as players naturally engage in learning when discovering how to play them. Players are not told in advance how to progress in the game, but rather learn through unearthing possibilities about how to proceed. Consequently, players also learn 'not only about the direct consequences of their actions, but also about second order consequences' (Douch et al. 2010: 19).

In addition to developing deductive reasoning, Johnson et al. (2011) argue that MMOs, immersive environments (in 2 and 3-D graphics) engender 'conceptual blending', which is required in navigating the real world and virtual spaces simultaneously in game play. Additionally, they also argue that players gain an understanding of 'procedural logic' or meta-level analytical awareness of game design, which is useful in 'helping students garner a deeper understanding of systems' (Douch et al. 2010: 21).

With respect to cognitive development, games require making mental maps and games that simulate real-life contexts, can develop career-specific skills (Douch et al. 2010). For example, flight simulators require the user to develop 'visual selective attention', to focus on the most important aspect of the situation, while filtering out the rest, and can support learning of specialized cognitive competences, such as aeronautical navigation (*Flight Simulator X*, Microsoft).

Overall, cognitive benefits include aiding the development of motor skills, hand–eye coordination, recognition of strategies and patterns, problem-solving, concentration, capacity to think in three dimensions and decision-making (Struppert 2010: 365). In addition, games can enhance knowledge of specific content: for example, facilitating a deeper understanding of history, health, environmental issues, urban planning, literacy and numeracy (Douch et al. 2010; Johnson et al. 2011; Struppert 2010).

Affective benefits of gaming

Further to this analysis that has identified impact on cognitive development, the benefits of gaming can be understood at more sophisticated psychological and social levels. With reference to Gardner's (1983) multiple intelligences, both intrapersonal and interpersonal competences can be enhanced through gaming. Consequently, the psychological (more holistic) benefits of gaming can be analysed in terms of the cognitive, affective and behavioural domains.

In addition to cognitive development, games also contain an affective element (Ghergulescu and Muntean 2010; Struppert 2010). Arguably it is the ability of games to engage a learner's emotions that explains the high levels of concentration and motivation also required for learning. There are many advantages in engaging the affective domains of a learner, in terms of excitement, enjoyment and fun. Engaging the affective domains results in a positive affect on behaviour, as the learners are focused on the activity rather than off task, and this lessens the probability of disruption in the classroom. With respect to behavioural domains, positive effects have also been found on learners' levels of cooperation and collaboration, which in turn enhances team working and group communication skills (Douch et al. 2010).

The challenge: engaging disengaged learners

Through engaging all three domains of heart, mind and body, digital games-based learning has been shown to captivate disengaged learners. Proponents of digital games-based learning assert that games can engage learners in ways that other tools and approaches cannot. However, we have to understand how and why this is the case, and, arguably, it is through engaging all domains (cognitive, affective and behavioural – staying on task) that digital games have been shown to enthral hitherto disengaged learners effectively.

Ghergulescu and Muntean (2010: 71) believe that 'keeping pupils motivated for the entire learning session still represents a challenging task' and consequently, assessment and measurement of learners' motivation is a key area of research in the field of gaming and e-learning. Reaching disengaged contemporary learners requires obviating a learning process that may be considered to be boring and forced. Games, however, have the potential to provide an instantly interactive environment, which is often experienced as more engaging, motivating and fun (affective) than traditional, didactic classroom teaching.

Games that build on learners' interests and genre preferences provide opportunities for competitive gaming and can be an engaging learning tool. As Douch et al. (2010: 2) argue, digital games encourage a rich and broad range of skill development: problem-solving, reflection, communication, teamwork, learning rules and mental manipulation of images. Digital games mimic effective-learning strategies, such as active participation, scaffolding, gaining feedback and assessing progress. Significantly there is 'motivational impact', because the goals are meaningful and attainable, through feedback that aids responses to reaching the goals (De Freitas and Jameson 2006). Also, because games are designed with different skill levels, players can find their appropriate level and challenge.

The most important feature is the way games are designed to imitate effective learning processes, which include an effective match between ability and challenge, use of feedback, which is immediate, and aids in attaining goals that are meaningful. Here we can see how gaming mimics the pedagogy of experiential learning based on constructivist theories of learning – through *discovery* and *curiosity* players are *motivated* to *explore* and *learn*.

Benefits – what makes digital games effective for learning and teaching?

The increasing awareness about digital games-based learning in schools is doubly timely given the social kudos of gaming among learners and the level of disenchantment by contemporary learners with dry, didactic methods, which can be ameliorated by gaming (Van Eck 2006). The effectiveness of games is due to their underlying architecture, which imitates the key components of learning. In analysing the essential principles of learning, Oblinger (2004, cited in Douch et al. 2010) highlights eight principles that apply to games:

- Active learning
- Assessment
- Feedback
- Individualization
- Motivation
- Scaffolding
- Social and transfer.

Gaming as a classroom activity is likely to be successful, because it has social status (with peer credibility) and psychological interest with individual motivation. See Table 4.1, which outlines the eight principles of learning that are utilised in games design.

Theories of learning and digital games

Miller and Robertson (2010) argue that the explanations that account for the popularity of gaming can be identified in psychological and socio-cultural theories. The most cited psychological theory is that of 'flow' from Csikszentmihalyi (1990) (in Douch et al. 2010; Miller and Robertson 2010; Prensky 2006; Spring-Keller 2010). It is the notion of 'flow' that explains why so many hours are spent immersed in complex computer games by children of all ages and both genders.

'Flow' describes a subjective, positive state that is achieved when someone is completely absorbed in what they are doing. Csikszentmihalyi (1990) indentified the essential characteristics of flow as high levels of concentration, complete engagement in the activity and full attention in reaching targets. Crucial to this is a match between ability and challenge, alongside receiving feedback on progress that enables one to adapt rapidly, modify responses, which contribute towards a greater sense of personal control. It is this level of complete absorption in the game (of 'losing oneself', 'being in the zone', where 'time flies') that characterizes 'flow' with games (Miller and Robertson 2010).

The key is the balance between the learner's skills and the challenges of the game, which results in the learner being so utterly focused and engaged. Essentially, what creates the state of flow with digital gaming is worthwhile goals, decision-making and adaptivity (Douch et al. 2010: 19). Decisions have to be made to achieve goals. The consequence of those decisions is often instantaneous, and this allows the player to advance a level. There is a clear sense of improvement as the player's ability matches the challenge of the game. With respect to learning theories where the feedback is immediate and the challenge achievable – this can be understood through Bruner's (1960) concept of 'scaffolding' and Vygotsky's (1978) theory of the zone of approximate development (ZPD).

Table 4.1 What makes digital games effective for learning and teaching? (based on Oblinger's (2004) eight principles of learning, cited in Douch et al. 2010: 17)

Principle	The learner	How the principle applies to games
Active learning	The learner actively discovers and constructs knowledge	Games require the player to interact in order to progress. Often the rules of a game are built into the game for mastery as the player proceeds, and the skills and knowledge base is developed through participation in the game's tasks.
Assessment	A learner can assess their progress and make comparisons with their peers	Gamers can assess their progress within a game and reflect on what skills they need to develop to achieve certain goals. They are able to compare their achievements with other players' achievements and also with their own past achievements.
Feedback	Instant and relevant feedback is provided to support learning	Feedback provided by games is usually immediate, relevant and clear in terms of conveying the consequences of correct and incorrect choices, enabling players to learn from their successes and mistakes.
Individualization (personalization)	Learning meets the needs of the individual learner	Games are tailored to the individual through content and pre-set levels; in some complex games the game-play can adapt to the individual's skills and knowledge by making tasks easier/more difficult or by providing/withdrawing support.
Motivation	When the task is meaningful and rewarding, the learner becomes motivated	A player becomes involved in a game for long periods of time with an aim to achieve goals that are both meaningful and achievable.
Scaffolding	Learning becomes gradually more challenging as the learner progresses, allowing for development	Games are often designed to include a number of levels through which a player moves as their knowledge and skills improve. When working in collaboration, players will share knowledge and skills to support the development of their peers.
Social	Learning involves others	Games can be played in multiplayer mode, whether individuals are using the same device or involved online. Some online games rely on large communities of players who work together to achieve goals within the game.
Transfer	Skills and knowledge acquired are not restricted to a single context	Gamers use knowledge and skills learnt through playing a game in other games and in real-world contexts. Potential for learners to become more empowered and 'rehearse skills for the real world' (De Freitas and Jameson 2006: 7).

However, behaviourist theories (Skinner 1953) also provide an explanation as players have to work out cause-and-effect relationships. The classic ABC relations of 'antecedent, behaviour and consequence' are clearly in play during a complex game. Just as in the classic behaviourist experiments, the rats had to find their way through the maze to receive a reward of food, so too players explore the environment and work out how to reach the end of the game. Making a choice of which action to take, under the pressure of time constraints, processing several thoughts very quickly and multi-tasking, requires players to respond precisely and swiftly. These processes are highly motivational and engaging and require self-direction, generating ownership and active participation.

Gaming and socio-cultural theories

According to Miller and Robertson (2010), socio-cultural theories that account for the popularity of game playing can be found in the writings of Prensky (2001), Gee (2003) and Sandford et al. (2006). Enthusiastic game players (like any subculture where like-minded individuals identify with one another) have shared norms, values and beliefs, about the value of gaming, and what counts as worthwhile knowledge. This can be understood as acquiring 'social capital' (Bourdieu 1974); this insider knowledge or social epistemology is what Gee (2003) refers to as 'semiotic domains' – that is, sets of practices that 'communicate distinctive types of meaning' about what constitutes good performance in a game and thereby bestows social status in the group, which is an individual's kudos within the subculture of serious games players.

Critical consideration, however, needs to be given to the dominance in the gaming market by multinational companies and issues of cultural globalization. This relates to the wider debate pertaining to notions of 'childhood', commercialization and digital culture (Buckingham 2007).

Gaming as playing: psycho-developmental theories of learning

If we conceptualize gaming as playing, we need to understand why these activities are so compelling. How do psychologists account for children's love of playing as a spontaneous, carefree activity and what theories aid our analysis of the key drivers and motives for playing, such that they can be applied better to learning activities? To answer this we need to examine psychological theories of play.

The importance of play as a process that enables children and young people to learn was discovered by psychologists, in particular Piaget (1963), who argues about the importance of discovery learning, to aid the development of internal mental schemas, and Vygotsky (1978), who highlights the importance of interactivity with others to facilitate meaning making. Both the constructivism of Piaget and social constructivism of Vygotsky can be applied to gaming, as a form of play that aids development in children. As Foreman (2003, cited in Douch 2010: 7) argues: 'learning through performance requires active discovery, analysis, interpretation, problem solving, memory and physical activity which results in the sort of extensive cognitive processing that deeply roots learning in a well-developed neural network.'

Through playful experimentation, psychologists highlight how play can support and encourage learning. Developmental psychologists believe that play (including playing games, digital and non-digital) can be best understood in terms of drives for exploration, curiosity and manipulation. Even from birth, babies show a preference for novel and complex stimuli. Play is engaged in by children for enjoyment, rather than a conscious decision to find out how things work, because play is intrinsically satisfying and fun.

Piaget (1951) argued that play enables a child to practise developing skills and abilities in a relaxed and carefree manner. In this way, Piaget regarded play as an adaptive activity where children could consolidate newly acquired competences and facilitate the development of cognitive and social skills. Piaget (1963) believed games had important implications for children's emerging social and intellectual capabilities – especially boys, according to Hromek and Roffey (2009), and a function of games was to practise working with rules and to develop self-discipline, which underpins society and social order. Mead (1934) argued similarly with respect to learning about morality and that role-playing games enabled the development of empathy in children. Play is understood to aid the socio-emotional, moral and cognitive development of children, predominantly through rules and roles. Shaffer (2006) argues that children generate simulations of environments they want to understand in relation to rules and roles to better appreciate those environments and understand consequences. Spring-Keller (2010) goes on to observe that every kind of play consists of rules, even open-ended games without specific goals. Consequently, for both Shaffer (2006) and Spring-Keller (2010), the definition of a game can be reduced to two singular aspects: rules and roles. This can be applied to computer games, many of which are role-play simulations. For example, SimCity is an urban planning game in which players take on the role of major and contains numerous rules; whereas the *World of Warcraft* is such a complex massive multiplayer online (MMO) game that, even after 50 hours, a player will not fully understand all the rules (Spring-Keller 2010).

Other psychologists examine the playing of games from the perspective of arousal theories (Arkes and Garske 1977) and argue that we have an inherent tendency to seek 'optimum' levels of stimulation or activity. The motivation to explore the unfamiliar is because it increases arousal. However, the notion of 'optimum' level refers to the fact that, if the new experience is too different and unfamiliar, it will lead to too much arousal and over-stimulation, resulting in anxiety and tension. On the other hand, if the experience is too familiar, little arousal will occur and the under-stimulation will lead to boredom (Berlyne 1960). What games trigger is the curiosity to explore new, novel and complex environments, which can be explained by arousal theories.

Motivation – games are fun: understanding positive emotions in learning

Educational psychologists Hromek and Roffey (2009) argue that playing games and having fun are crucial to development and highly motivating for children. Children's games provide opportunities for hypothesis testing, problem-solving and 'formation of thought constructs that reflect the shared cognitive themes related to cultural understanding' (Hromek and Roffey 2009: 630). Moreover, fun and humour stimulate creativity as the 'brain moves from a cognitive, rule-bound state to a more fluid, relaxed state where the whole body is engaged in problem solving' (Hromek and Roffey 2009: 630). This highlights the holistic nature of 'playing' and how the affective domain can be engaged alongside the cognitive and behavioural to affect creativity for learning through game play.

Looking at the role of positive emotions, psychologists Fredrickson and Joiner (2002) argue that these broaden the capacity to learn and enhance optimistic thinking, which leads to more creative problem-solving capacities. Games can engender positive feelings when winning or solving a problem or completing a challenge and result in joyful experiences (affective), which in turn trigger and stimulate creative problem-solving.

Game players display high levels of motivation, which we need to understand as educationalists. Motivation is a key characteristic of gaming, which keeps players playing for long periods of time and, as a psychological attribute, it is also an essential component for successful learning. Given that motivation is a driving force behind both participation and progression in gaming and learning, it is important to understand the psychological theories of motivation, so that they can be applied to pedagogical activities to sustain interest.

Ghergulescu and Muntean (2010: 72) observe that the literature on motivational theory is extensive and, while it is a 'fuzzy' concept, it can be defined effectively as, 'the energy to achieve a goal, to initiate and to sustain participation', which involves emotions, thoughts and beliefs. With respect to the learning context, motivation refers to the energy to attain, to initiate, and to maintain participation in the learning process, to accomplish the goal of acquiring knowledge, skill and understanding. Games motivate, because they contain three essential elements – autonomy, mastery and purpose. Through having worthwhile goals, players have a sense of purpose, which is meaningful to them. Through decision-making (of which actions and paths to take in a game) players experience autonomy and, because games are adaptive, as players increase their skill level, so a sense of mastery is attained, which keeps players motivated.

Gaming as supporting self-efficacy and resilience

Further to this 'motivational' analysis of game playing is understanding how players develop self-efficacy and resilience, which are arguably important psychological attributes in an increasingly complex and demanding world. In referencing Bandura's (1994) self-efficacy theory of motivation, Ghergulescu and Muntean (2010) highlight how a person must believe that they are capable of solving, executing and pursuing a task. Essentially self-efficacy refers to self-perception of one's abilities, which in turn influences effort, commitment and willingness to engage. Most important, with respect to perceived difficulty level, it refers to the recovery of efficacy following failure. 'The higher the self-efficacy is, the stronger the engrossment [and] the higher the speed of recovery of their sense of efficacy after failure is' (Ghergulescu and Muntean 2010: 72). Self-belief of efficacy enables learners to set challenging goals, to initiate action plans and to develop strong perseverance. This demonstrates how resilience can be developed in young people through gaming. Through experiencing the frustration of losing, players learn to tolerate negative emotions and know they can recover and try again.

This links to self-determination theory, which Ghergulescu and Muntean (2010) cite as a more recent approach to human motivation and personality from Ryan and Deci (2000). This refers to 'the energy, the persistence, and the direction that a person is taking in his/her activities' (Ghergulescu and Muntean 2010: 72), because, when motivated, a person performs. However, motivation is not a singular construct, but a combination of more complex constructs, and it is important to distinguish between different types of motivation: amotivation, extrinsic and intrinsic.

'Amotivation' refers to the inability to act, which results from not feeling competent (internal beliefs of self-efficacy), while 'extrinsic motivation' refers to being motivated by factors outside of one's self; rewards, money, grades, which provide satisfaction that is not given by the activity itself. Most important for understanding gaming, playing and deep learning is intrinsic motivation, which originates internally, from inside the individual; the satisfaction, enjoyment and pleasure of doing a particular activity: 'it reflects the human tendency to seek out novelty and challenges, to exercise capabilities, to explore and to learn' (Ghergulescu and Muntean 2010: 73), which takes us back to Piaget's (1951) theories of play and how our drives and curiosity to discover learning and operate at a cognitive, affective and behavioural level and provides a holistic account of learning.

According to Ghergulescu and Muntean (2010), the three key factors that enhance self-motivation (and thereby alleviate amotivation), are the need for competence, relatedness and autonomy, which arguably can be understood as the key elements of games in terms of mastery (competence), purpose (relatedness) and decision-making (autonomy).

The playful interactive element of gaming allows for games to be adapted to players' individual levels of skill. Gaming provides

> a great deal of control, involves active decision making and provides continuous feedback that lets them know how well they are doing. Players can see the consequences of their actions – often immediately – and learn from them without having to fear any serious real-world consequences. The main motivation for players lies in reaching a goal.
>
> (Struppert 2010: 382)

Pedagogies in schools that recognize the importance of play have long been favoured by early-years practitioners. Children in foundation stage settings (before formal schooling and the national curriculum in the UK) predominantly learn through play, yet this methodology and resultant joy of learning is generally lost after the early years (Spring-Keller 2010). The question then is, can the joy of learning through play be extended beyond the pre-school years? Can gaming help re-engage playful learning through educational digital games?

Games and social emotional learning

With respect to the pedagogical use of non-digital games, Hromek and Roffey's (2009) extensive review of the research literature concluded that games are a powerful way of developing social and emotional learning. These skills, which are needed to play successfully with others are also those needed to succeed in work and adult life. Pro-social skills involve regulating negative emotions, turn-taking, sharing and support 'orientations to others that are fair, just and respectful' (Hromek and Roffey 2009: 626). The natural affiliation between children, play, and the desire to have fun with others makes games an ideal vehicle for teaching. While development of these skills is discussed explicitly in relation to 'circle time' games by Hromek and Roffey (2009), arguably where digital games incorporate the same features, it could be asserted that the same outcomes are possible. For example, in massive multi-player online (MMOs) and augmented reality games (ARGs) that require collaborative problem-solving.

There is a rise in awareness of the importance of social and emotional intelligence as a newly recognized form of literacy, which plays a significant part in well-being. The way these ideas have gained prominence in education over the previous decade has been outlined by Hromek and Roffey (2009). They reference Salovey and Mayer (1990) as developers of the concept of emotional intelligence, building on Gardner's (1993) multiple intelligences, particularly intrapersonal intelligence (knowing oneself and how to manage emotions) and interpersonal intelligence (knowing how to get on with others and develop positive relationships). However, the term was popularized by Goleman (1996), who highlighted the connection between the skills of self-management and managing others, which could be as important as IQ in determining success in life. While this is a contentious area for debate regarding the definitions and parameters of social and emotional intelligence, Hromek and Roffey (2009) argue it has ignited a new education focus on 'emotional literacy', which has become more recently incorporated into a broader focus on learner 'well-being'. This they argue can be linked to an emerging international consensus in education about the need to address well-being and build resilience in children for the challenges of contemporary culture, as outlined by UNESCO (1996), which gaming has been shown to support.

The UNESCO report for the International Commission on Education for the Twenty-first Century (1996) cited the 'four pillars of education', which were 'learning to live together', 'learning to know', 'learning to do' and 'learning to be', which can be seen as pertaining to the social, cognitive, behaviour and affective domains respectively and engendering a sense of holistic education. However, learning through games is not just knowing (cognitive) and doing (behavioural), as Shaffer et al. (2004) argue. Games can combine ways of knowing, ways of doing, ways of being and ways of caring, which supports the UNESCO four pillars of education.

Just as researchers and developers have recognized the importance of motivation in gaming, so too has the role of emotion been acknowledged. Arguably, games help young people to manage their emotions, as playing will bring up experiences of frustration, losing, as well as the elation of winning. Players need to learn to develop self-regulation and in multi-player games, develop social skills to play successfully with others.

Given concerns of 'learner disengagement' and the need to engender 'social and emotional learning', there is the need to identify those practices, like gaming, that can effectively engage learners. This is important given the understanding we now have of the links between the cognitive, affective and behavioural domains for learning. Experience-based learning tools, like games, provide a means to develop the skill-sets, attitudes, values that aid social and emotional literacy and engender motivation and engagement. Interestingly, psychologists argue that higher levels of emotional literacy increase the capacity of learners to learn (Zins, Weissberg, Wang and Walberg 2004, cited in Hromek and Roffey 2009).

Role-play games and simulations designed to develop problem-solving strategies and pro-social behaviour (like educational ARGs and MMOs) require players to learn to manage personal goals alongside those of others, which can also involve delaying gratification in order to play cooperatively and collaboratively and, similarly, managing negative emotional reactions to frustration and disappointment. Digital games can provide as much potential for transformative learning through social interaction, cooperation and collaboration, if, as Hromek and Roffey (2009) argue, the power of games lies in the interactive nature of playing together. Learning to manage emotions through gaming can help engender resilience in young people and links to Gardner's (1983) intra- and inter-personal intelligences, as players have to regulate their own emotions (intrapersonal) and navigate and manage those of others (interpersonal).

Games-based learning: developing resilience and pro-social skills

When it comes to creating emotional resilience, the key is the ability to make internal and external adjustments to adversity and change. Hromek and Roffey (2009) argue that engendering resilience involves three key features: belonging to a supportive community based on caring relationships; opportunities to gain competence in a range of skills; opportunities to contribute and participate – all of which could be developed in schools through multi-player games.

While games can be understood to be effective because they engage the cognitive, affective and behavioural domains, the potential of educational games to enhance psycho-social skills has been seriously underdeveloped. The under-utilization of digital games to increase and enhance social competencies stands in need of serious attention in education and further research.

Struppert (2010), in observing this deficit with respect to socio-emotional competencies, has narrowed the gap by examining the use of the simulation – *RealLives 2010*. This simulation was developed to aid the promotion of intercultural competence, which is a 'combination of awareness, knowledge, understanding, attitudes and skills about one's own and other cultures that allows people to interact appropriately, effectively and successfully with culturally-distinct others' (Struppert 2010: 364). The *RealLives* simulation enables players to 'lead the lives of people around the world from birth to death' (Struppert 2010: 364), thereby enabling players to learn more about different countries and cultures. In the research Struppert introduced

RealLives to middle schools in Australia, America and Switzerland (three international schools), in which she examined the simulation's potential to promote cognitive and affective components of intercultural competence.

Struppert (2010) argues that, although there are other role-play simulations, such as America's Army Adaptive Thinking and Leadership (ATL), which the designers declare improves 'intercultural awareness, knowledge, decision-making, metacognition and communicative skills' (Struppert 2010: 365), the empirical data, however, is scarce. This highlights the need for future research to focus on the ways in which these important skills can be enhanced through games.

Gaming and innovative teaching

A number of researchers argue strongly that gaming enables a more innovative way of teaching that engages contemporary learners (Gee 2003; Egenfeldt-Nielsen 2007; Kirriemuir and McFarlane 2004; Prensky 2006; Shaffer 2006). Struppert (2010) identifies how games, by combining different types of media, such as text, images, sound and video, offer new ways of presenting learning materials that can cater for different learning styles. Egenfeldt-Nielsen (2007) argues it is because games provide an interactive learning environment. It is the interactivity which is enjoyable and motivating, resulting in more attention, with longer playing, which results in deeper understanding and better retention and has the potential to captivate less-motivated learners.

Contemporary learners may be experiencing 'highly seductive media environments outside of school' (Williamson and Payton 2009: 33), which are far more enticing compared to classroom technologies that may be considered restrictive and even banal (Veen and Vrakking 2006; Willoughby and Wood 2008). This dichotomous positioning of learners' relationship to technology, as pervasive and engaging outside of school and uninspiring inside, was popularized by Prensky (2001) in the 'digital natives' debate. Prensky (2001) identified the 'games generation' (or digital natives) as those who have grown up in a culture saturated with digital media, such that regular use has led to a 'very different mix of cognitive skills' (Prensky 2001: 46) compared to previous generations – the digital immigrants. However, this is a contested concept and critiqued for being too homogenous and failing to capture the heterogeneity of young people and technology.

Supporters of Prensky argue that the 'games generation' are able to deal with large amounts of information very quickly, even from an early age, such as autonomous learning using trial and error methods. They are active learners and have been defined as the 'twitch-speed generation' by Egenfeldt-Nielsen (2007: 34). More recently Prensky (2009) has argued that the 'games generation' have 'digital wisdom', which means not only using and manipulating technology easily, but also making wiser decisions because of technology.

Despite the popularist proponents' evangelism, it should be noted that the arguments supporting the use of computer games in education rest on a limited research base, to date. As Byron (2008: 188) argues, there is 'little in-depth analysis of the impact of games on learning and lack of proven evidence'. While research finds that games enhance motivation, attitudes, knowledge and skills (Sandford et al. 2006), critics point to serious methodological flaws, as the 'evidence is neither extensive nor robust' (Miller and Robertson 2010: 2). Although the benefits of games have been identified as pertaining to greater engagement and enhancement of certain skills and attitudes, there is much less reporting on the outcomes of gaming on attainment. To date, there are far fewer studies that measure impact on learner performance.

The research in this field has been seriously critiqued and what is clearly missing is a robust connection between playing educational games and a positive impact on achievement and concomitant increase in learning outcomes. Miller and Robertson (2010) argue that research has focused on beliefs and attitudes rather than performance data, with no measures of learning gains being reported; consequently, many studies fail to inform educators about fundamental issues. Similarly, Miller and Robertson (2010) argue that the research base to date is insufficiently robust to support sound conclusions due to methodological weaknesses regarding the absence of control groups and lack of statistical data in the majority of studies. Reporting has been fraught with problems regarding the quality of the studies – in particular, the dangers of generalizing from small samples. To this end, Miller and Robertson (2010) conducted a study with 634 primary school children, in 32 schools across Scotland on the use of a 'Brain Training' game with 10–11-year-olds using a hand-held console. This was in response to their earlier study in 2009 with 71 children, which indicated gains in mathematical computation for speed and accuracy, but was felt not to be generalizable, unless a far greater number of learners participated.

In the replicated study of 2010, Miller and Robertson examined the effects of a commercial off-the-shelf (COTS) game on children's mental computational skills using a hand-held Nintendo DS console. The aim was to investigate changes in children's mental computational performance over nine weeks using *Dr Kawashima's Brain Training* for 20 minutes at the start of each day at school. From the sample, schools were randomly assigned to experimental or control conditions. Significant gains in accuracy and speed of calculations were found in both groups. However, gains in the experimental groups were 50 per cent greater than those of the control group for accuracy, and twice those of the controls for speed. Miller and Robertson (2010: 3) identified the benefits of gaming in terms of 'faster processing of information, enhanced selection of relevant material and high levels of engagement and interest'. They also found a statistically significant improvement in attitude to school. Interestingly, in comparison, Ke (2008) examined the use of computer games in maths and found more positive attitudes towards the subject, but no significant improvement or gain in mathematics performance. This signifies the complexity of the research to date and the need for further work to address the inconclusiveness and contradictory findings of previous studies.

With respect to the need to generate an *evidence base of effective practice*, the Mobile Learning Network (MoLeNET) published an extensive range of case studies for practitioners, which demonstrated how gaming technologies can motivate disengaged learners; support students with learning difficulties and/or disabilities (LLDD);

Table 4.2 Reported benefits of handheld games technologies for teaching and learning (adapted from MoLeNET 2010: 3)

Benefits	Handheld games technologies can
Skill development	Help learners develop transferable skills
	Support learners to develop skills more quickly
	Encourage reflection, as learners view recordings of themselves and peers
	Improve attendance and achievement
Assessment	Be a non-threatening assessment tool, for learners and teachers
	Facilitate self assessment by enabling collection of evidence of skills/progress
	Assist peer assessment
	Provide immediacy of feedback
Flexibility	Enable learning at different times – anytime learning
	Support learners in varying locations – anywhere learning
	Be used as a resource and stimulus for cross-curricular/further learning
Motivation and engagement	Help to engage learners and re-engage the 'disengaged'; make learning fun
	Motivate learners to progress and achieve
	Improve learner focus and attention
	Provide learners with ownership of their own learning; foster participation
	Stimulate interactive learning and multisensory learning experiences
Social and Emotional well being	Engender learner confidence and increase self-esteem
	Facilitate communication and encourage collaboration
	Promote learners' sense of pride in their work; enhanced by seeing progress made
	Improve teamwork and cooperation; develop/advance peer group dynamics
Personalization	Support learners' individual needs
	Encourage autonomy; goal setting, progress and achievement
	Support learners with low levels of literacy and/or numeracy
	Help to overcome language barriers
	Support those with learning difficulties and/or disabilities (LLDD)

help those with numeracy and/or literacy challenges; reduce behaviour management problems and facilitate an engaging learning environment.

MoLeNET (www.molenet.org.uk) works collaboratively with the Learning Skills Council (LSC) to actively promote mobile learning through shared-cost projects. Additional support and evaluation of the programme has been provided by Learning and Skills Network (LSN) (www.lsnlearning.org.uk), which includes technical and pedagogical guidance. Over £16 million has been invested in three phases of MoLeNET, which started in 2007/8. This is important for building up an evidence base of examples regarding the impact of digital games on learning.

In 2010 MoLeNET conducted 35 case studies, looking specifically at hand-held devices to support teaching and learning and found such devices helped literacy, numeracy and mathematics learning; English as a second language (ESOL) and other language learners; 'engaging the disengaged'; improved behaviour; supported vocational, work-based learners and those with LLDD. The report outlines examples of teachers adoption of digital-games-based learning and is a good place to start reading to get an understanding of the practical issues with implementation.

Overall, MoLeNET (2010) found that hand-held mobile devices are generally easy to use, required little training or additional costs and, most important, a number of benefits to teaching and learning could be clearly identified; see Table 4.2.

Pedagogy – history of games-based learning: before computers

The idea of designing games and simulated environments for learning and teaching was a novel idea in the late 1960s when the first articles were written for the journal *Simulation and Games* (1969 Vol. 1, No. 1) (Ruben 1999). This development emerged in response to the traditional teaching paradigm, which was seen as passive information transfer, without recourse to experience and personal meaning making. The quest for a new paradigm came in the form of experiential-based learning, with simulations and games. The classic instructional model was seen to do little to promote active learning or help acquire the critical skills needed to select and evaluate that which is important among a wide array of competing information. Indeed, issues of emotion and the linkages between the cognitive, affective and behavioural domains were undeveloped. As researchers came to acknowledge 'cognitive skills and knowledge acquisition alone are seldom sufficient for personal, social, or professional effectiveness' (Ruben 1999: 499), so active learning through games gained prevalence and pedagogical kudos in the 1960s and 1970s. In the UK this was seen in the Plowden report (1966), which was influential in promoting child-centred education and the importance of play and learning though discovery, which in turn had been influenced by the work of Piaget (1951).

Interestingly, the theoretical foundations for interactive and experience-based learning, including simulations and games can be traced back to the writings of Aristotle and oral practices of Socrates and were popularized in the 1960s, Ruben (1999) argues, by Bruner (1966), Dewey (1966) and Holt (1967). Following this, the 1970s and early 1980s saw a rush to embrace experiential learning as an alternative to the instructional paradigm and addressed the limitations of 'one-way information dispensing methods', which promoted interactivity, collaboration and peer learning. However, despite this alternative paradigm, the dominance (and limitations) of the classic knowledge-transfer model are still evident in schools today and remain largely unresolved (Prensky 2006; Ruben 1999). Consequently, many teaching environments remain 'too predictable, static, unchallenging and boring' (Ruben 1999: 503).

It is in this context that Prensky (2006) and Van Eck (2006) highlight issues with contemporary learner disengagement and how games-based learning can re-engage and motivate those previously disaffected. Problems with disengagement can be understood when referring to arousal theories, where psychologists argue that boredom sets in, resulting from too little stimulation and low levels of arousal, when an optimum level is required for engagement (Berlyne 1960), because children seek that which is novel and complex (Piaget 1951). What has excited proponents of radical pedagogies more recently is how developments in technology have advanced gaming in the twenty-first century. It should be noted that the problem with large-scale disaffection from learning is not new. Indeed, in the 1960s the Humanities Curriculum Project (1967–1972) was established to address this very issue and, in common with a digital-games-based learning ethos, the focus was on learning as inquiry rather than traditional instruction-based pedagogy (Hammond et al. 2009).

Developing a 'transformative' pedagogy with games

The term 'transformative' learning (also referred to as 'critical pedagogy') describes education that provides opportunities for personal and social change, which rejects dry, didactic methods and favours active learning over passivity. Learners are encouraged to become personally involved in the learning process, and through engendering a positive attitude and confidence it becomes easier to implement personal change. As learners experience negative and positive emotions in games, so they learn to manage themselves. Through the exploration of different identities when role playing, learners also develop social skills alongside psychological resilience.

For example, massively multiplayer online games using virtual media-scapes allow self-created digital characters or 'avatars' to interact. Through the social nature of the design, learning through simulation and interactivity, this can encourage collaboration and cooperation. The safety of a virtual identity can lend new-found confidence to learners, allowing shy children a voice. Meadows (2008: 36) in 'I, Avatar' argues that '75 percent of Internet users feel safer speaking their mind when they use an avatar'. Alongside this, however, critical consideration needs to highlight potential risks and how extreme immersion can lead to addiction (Delwiche 2006) although this is very rare (Byron 2008: 11). Similarly, there are tensions between 'social usage' and the possibility of 'reduced socialisation'. For a further discussion of the negative effects of gaming see the Byron Review (2008).

In schools both the positive and negative can be explored through the pedagogical framing of gaming with a teacher. The open-ended, challenge-based games, which occur in MMOs, draw on skills of research, collaboration, problem-solving, leadership and digital literacy (Johnson et al. 2011). In generating more holistic learning, digital-games-based learning engages the cognitive, affective and behavioural domains. Games can be a form of cooperative, experience-based learning, which are highly motivating to young people. Games designers can take any content (maths, money management, climate change) and can create focus (develop engaging learning) through generating a balance between skill, strategy, hope, competition and fun (Hromek and Roffey 2009).

Pedagogical framing of gaming activities

The teacher's role as facilitator of learning from games is a complex and skilled process. While games are very motivational, the learning effect will be minimal if there is no thorough debriefing by teachers. The findings from Struppert (2010) are that learning for example through simulations requires guidance and support from a teacher to ensure accurate and relevant educational outcomes: '. . . the transfer of knowledge and skills from the playing world to the real world does not happen automatically, but requires support from the teacher and follow-up communication, such as debriefings' (Struppert 2010: 366).

The process of facilitating debriefings is important if conceptual thinking is to be progressed to meaningful conclusions. Hence, 'learning review' is a vital stage, which needs to be planned into the design of the lesson and not left to chance; this involves the learner in reflection, challenge and discussion following a game.

Spring-Keller (2010) goes on to argue that commercial games (COTs) cannot be used for self-regulated learning unless they are modified for specific learning needs. The quality and use of games in schools depends on the teachers, their preferred teaching style, ecology of practice (Stronach et al. 2002) and their knowledge of games (Sandford et al. 2006). Just as we can't understand technology by only focusing on the machines and ignoring the role of the teacher and social environment, so it is the same for games. We need to analyse the activities outside the game, since learning happens through interaction not only between the game and the player or players, but through forums, peers and teachers. In this way knowledge is distributed among learners, characters in the game and players outside the game (Shaffer et al. 2005).

If learning is a holistic experience, then we need to appreciate all the aspects of the classroom and pedagogical framing. Spring-Keller (2010) has identified a research gap when stating that hardly anything is known about the impact of the social environment on gaming, specifically the wider gaming community, peers and teachers.

Challenges for implementation: understanding the barriers to embedding DGBL

From the research digital games can be powerful in supporting learning (Miller and Robertson 2010; Rylands 2010). However, there are a number of barriers facing a broader integration of DGBL, which need to be examined. Although there are pockets of innovation (MoLeNET 2010), the widespread adoption of DGBL is hindered by teachers' perceptions of inappropriate content, additional costs, time and technical training required. This is compounded by the fact that, currently, games are not designed to cover UK national curriculum content.

Initially, for the education profession there needs to be a shift in perception of digital games as many are believed to have violent themes based on exposure to commercial advertising. Second, teachers' knowledge of games needs addressing, as highlighted in the Futurelab (2005) survey of teachers and their attitudes to games and learning. In a representative sample of 1000 primary and secondary school teachers in England and Wales, 72 per cent had never played games and 69 per cent reported having never used them in class. When considering using them, the most cited reason (by 53 per cent of teachers) was that to engage learners as games were perceived as motivational, interactive and stimulating. However, only 18 per cent believed them to be relevant to the curriculum. When asked to reflect on the reasons for not using them, the most cited was, because games had little or no educational value (33 per cent). With respect to the benefits of playing entertainment games, teachers thought that the main gains pertained to motor/cognitive skills (91 per cent), followed next by computer skills (77 per cent) and then higher-order thinking skills (63 per cent). Interestingly, with respect to the practical barriers teachers envisaged, the most cited reason was access to equipment (49 per cent) while the next one was inappropriate content at 14 per cent.

Games content

For teachers, a core concern remains curriculum coverage. Unless a game can be seen to specifically address subject content, it is unlikely to be embedded into practice. Aspects of skill development and learner engagement may be helpful, but it would need to relate to a scheme of work directly if we are to see more widespread use of digital games in classrooms (Byron 2008; Douch et al. 2010).

Interestingly, Nintendo have specifically developed games for the education market and have created games to cover curriculum areas. The most popular are puzzle games that require the use of skills such as problem-solving, decision-making, reflection and recall. These include 'Dr *Kawashima's Brain Training*', '*Professor Kageyama's Maths Training*', and '*Professor Layton and the Curious Village*'. MoLeNET (2010) research found these games enable players to be sufficiently challenged through the different levels, thereby providing an engaging and motivating learning experience and one in which players can compete against the game and each other. Also, as these are played on hand-held devices the advantage of flexible and mobile learning is evident too.

Time

A major barrier, particularly to complex games, which require a lot of time, is the structure of the school day and lesson length. For example *Sim City* can take 10–20 hours to play; however, for a deeper understanding up to 100 hours may be required, and it is precisely a lack of time that Spring-Keller (2010) argues is a striking impediment to creativity. The constraints of timetabling have been noted by Becta (2002) and researchers alike (Clarke 2003; De Freitas and Jameson 2006). More creative uses of classroom time organization are required and there are examples of innovative schools with three-hour teaching blocks or half/whole day suspended timetables enabling greater flexibility in the organization of learning. Other solutions are after school clubs that also enable more freedom.

Training

Teachers have reported concerns over the training required to implement gaming devices into their pedagogy in a Becta schools survey (2002). While this may be addressed through having the learners demonstrate games to other learners, this does not negate the learning curve required of teachers if they are to feel comfortable with using games in the classroom. However, in the MoLeNET (2010) research, teachers reported that hand-held devices were easy to use and required minimal training.

Additional funds

Both the software and gaming devices are expensive, and costs need to be effectively managed by such strategies as incorporating learners' own devices into classroom practice and sharing games across institutions. MoLeNET (2010) research found that colleges that had introduced mobile learning on hand-held devices were looking to engender sustainability in this way of distributed, shared resources between institutions.

With respect to developing the sector, educational games will need investment. This is challenging as games are very expensive to create; as Spring-Keller (2010) observes, commercial games like *World of Warcraft* cost upwards of $40 million. The test here is to ask: 'how can technology support more cost effective methods of developing games for learning?' (Spring-Keller 2010: 83).

The above factors are interrelated and combine to create barriers that hinder the integration of digital-games-based learning into classroom practice. A lack of equipment and funding, insufficient technical training, perceptions of an inflexible curriculum (Sandford et al. 2006), require tackling on multiple fronts (financially, technically, pedagogically). However, these are not insurmountable obstacles to teachers who wish to embrace the opportunities that digital-games-based learning can offer.

Guidance on using digital games for learning and teaching

Wider implementation of digital-games-based learning necessitates pragmatic guidance on 'how, when and with whom and under what conditions, games can be integrated to maximize their learning potential' (Douch et al. 2010: 16). The key factors to consider before using digital games for learning and teaching are: time to set up the devices, the aims and objectives of using digital games, training prior to using and any technical considerations (Douch et al. 2010: 16).

Practitioners in the MoLeNET (2010) research reported that with respect to 'setting up' it was important to consider what prior knowledge and training was required; in short, initially expect that it may be time consuming to set up the devices, but this will subside. Learners need to understand the aims of using the device and have clear ground rules set. Technical consideration must be given to storage facilities, memory capacity and charging. For teachers, sharing practice will aid the process, starting with joint planning to encourage the pedagogical use of shared resources; to collaboratively repurpose learning resources for mobile devices; to develop ways of embedding DGBL into schemes of work. Similarly, it is possible to generate learner voice by listening to how learners think a device can be deployed for learning. Teachers should also be aware of how the competitive element of gaming (between the learner and the game and other learners) can be highly motivating. In addition hand-held devices have other functions, either built in or through accessories, which can facilitate learning, such as digital cameras, sound playing (with recording and editing modes, for capturing voice reflections and practising verbal presentations), GPS, Internet access, texting and pictorial communication facilities. The extra functionality of the devices provides opportunities for mobile and flexible learning.

Applications to practice

The following case studies, which report positive outcomes, are by way of providing examples of how digital-games-based learning has been applied to practice, through using either educational games or COTs.

Facer et al. (2004) 'Virtual Savannah Game' was a PDA-based project with Year 7, where learners assumed the role of a lion in order to explore the virtual savannah. The use of GPS in the game facilitated the simulation by allowing learners to use the outdoors environment as though it was an actual savannah, which they had to navigate to return to their den. This games-based experience developed skills of decision-making, reflecting, evaluating, map reading, navigation, alongside specific content knowledge on savannahs and lion behaviour.

Practitioner Tim Rylands (2010) uses the fantasy game 'Myst' to stimulate creative writing. As a primary school teacher, Rylands has made effective use of the game 'Myst' to develop literacy. The PC game 'Myst' creates an imaginary, immersive, multimedia landscape that learners were invited to explore, as a form of stimulus, prior to conducting creative writing. Through encouraging the learners aged 9–11 years to describe the environment, the teacher found the learners were more inspired to write and demonstrated significant improvements in literacy, with a marked impact on attainment (www.timrylands.com).

The Consolarium (Scottish Centre for Games and Learning) established by Learning and Teaching Scotland, examined the impact of games on teaching and learning in Scottish schools. Two key projects were on the Nintendo DS hand-held console and used 'Dr Kawashima's Brain Training' in three Dundee primary schools and 'Nintendogs' in Aberdeenshire primary schools. The first was reported to improve mathematical computation skills, for both accuracy and speed, and also enhance learner confidence, behaviour and attitudes to school (Miller and Robertson 2009). The second was used to support cross-curricular work, using dog care as a stimulus for writing stories, creating art work, developing numeracy skills, role play and drama, with teachers reporting greater confidence, self-esteem and enthusiasm for learning (www.ltscotland.org.uk/icteducation/gamesbasedlearning/index.asp).

Johnson et al. 2011 outline examples of how games-based learning is being used in higher education. '*Global Conflict*', is designed to help teach concepts in citizenship, geography and media. Developed by Serious Games International, it contains detailed lesson plans and assignments for students. '*Mass Extinction*' is currently being developed at MIT's Education Arcade and is about climate change. '*Peacemaker*' is a game designed to teach concepts in diplomacy and foreign relations. Through role play, one assumes the role of either the Israeli Prime Minister or Palestinian President and is required to find peaceful resolutions to conflicts before their term of office expires.

Future directions

More research is needed to address the current gaps in knowledge. Research omissions with respect to DGBL pertain to needing an enhanced evidence base for the effects of gaming on learning, together with more robust research on learner performance and attainment, the social context of learning and the role and impact of the wider interactive environment beyond the game (teachers, peers, online communities) and the nature of distributed knowledge and building psychological resilience.

Even though the most important elements of game design are known (flow, fantasy, curiosity) more research is needed on how these aspects impact on learning. As Spring-Keller (2010) argues, we need to better understand learners. What makes learners curious? What frustrates them? Other questions for future research concern; how can COTS be re-purposed for learning in classroom environments? How can soft skills in effective teamwork be measured, analysed and enforced? If there are identifiable interpersonal problems with team members, what kinds of interventions are possible? What influence does the social context have on virtual group work?

With respect to engendering greater psychological resilience in young people, Spring-Keller (2010) observes that there are few studies concerning the tolerance of frustration in learning settings and, given that games permit feelings of losing and failure, research in these areas could support an exploration of the different ways of dealing with negative emotions. Also, more empirical studies that investigate the impact of games on learning and the requirements of the surrounding classroom structure are needed. As Spring-Keller (2010) cites, the more we know about the design of games and the impact of motivational aspects, the better we can design games for learning for classroom settings.

Conclusions

The most important elements in designing a game are known. These pertain to the motivational aspects of flow, curiosity and discovery, which are understood through theories of play learning and creativity (Piaget 1963; Csikszentmihalyi 1990). The factors that afford a state of flow in digital games are worthwhile goals, which provide purpose; decision-making and an experience of autonomy and adaptivity, which leads to mastery. As Douch et al. (2010) assert, we need to create digital learning games that build on learners' interests and genre preferences and provide opportunities for competitive gaming, which is a beneficial learning tool. It is a huge challenge to design a game for learning purposes, with the same engaging effects as commercial games. However, the benefits in enhancing psychological resilience and pro-social skills are both educationally defensible and desirable.

Further reading

Miller, D. J. and Robertson, D. P. (2009) Using a games-console in the primary classroom: effects of 'Brain Training' programme on computation and self-esteem, *British Journal of Educational Technology*, 41(2): 242–55.
MoLeNET (2010) *Games Technologies for Learning: more than just toys*. London: LSN.

Useful websites

The Consolarium (Scottish Centre for Games and Learning) at Learning and Teaching Scotland ltscotland.org.uk/icteducation/gamesbasedlearning/index.asp).
Tim Rylands, Supporting literacy with 'Myst'. http://www.timrylands.com.

5 Teachers, pedagogy and professional development

Overview

This chapter considers the processes involved in teachers learning to use technology for pedagogic purposes. How teachers come to understand the affordances of a range of technologies for learning and teaching is more than a simple case of 'technology training'. It is a complex process which involves teachers' subject content knowledge, pedagogical reasoning processes and understanding of how technology affords opportunities for learning. Understanding this process of teachers' 'technology knowledge' development, and possible changes to practice to incorporate technology, also requires identification of the barriers teachers face, the factors involved in supporting technology use and the stages teachers go through when learning to use technology for professional purposes. Learning is at the heart of the process of change, and understanding the learning paths of teachers requires nuanced considerations of distributed cognition and situated learning. Social and communal constructivist theories which take account of these have been developed to explain effective models of professional development and knowledge management (Leask and Younie 2001).

Introduction and context

Having investigated the ways in which technology can encourage greater interaction and engagement in the learning process, through a consideration of technologies and learning theories, attention will turn to the role of the teacher. This section is focused on the ways in which teachers can scaffold learning experiences with technology and incorporate these into their pedagogic practice. To understand how teachers learn to do this, a consideration of the theories of distributed cognition, situated learning, and social and communal constructivism will help illuminate the social dimension of teachers learning to change practice.

If teachers are to be expected to be technologically competent, to understand how to develop teaching and learning strategies that integrate technology, guidance about new forms of pedagogic practice and professional development is required. Arguably, while the techno-evangelists dream of a brave new world for learning, pragmatists argue this is stifled by an education sector that fails to engage with its potential, to such an extent that the profession risks becoming the 'Cinderella sector' of the technological world (Daanen and Facer 2007).The perception of teachers as technologically inept is part of a public discourse perpetuated by, for example, the Prensky thesis (2001), which highlights the differences between digital natives and digital immigrants. With teachers defined as the latter, Prensky argues that educators struggle to accustom themselves to working with new technologies. However, Prensky's thesis of the young as digital natives oversimplifies generational difference. It is important to examine issues in technology uptake, in order to understand more critically the ways in which individuals are situated differently to technology, and, in particular, to provide a more critically informed understanding about teachers and technology.

Theory and research base

This chapter draws on a broad range of research about how teachers learn to use technology for professional practice. Research in this area was plentiful in the USA and UK in the 1990s and 2000s, as computers and the Internet became incorporated into schooling and government funding was available for technology implementation and research (Becta 1998–2010). The research from America was predominantly large scale and quantitative, as it was in the UK with ImpacT2, ICT Testbeds and interactive whiteboard research funded by Becta. However, research on teachers' use of technology (as opposed to the impact of technology on pupils, which the former research projects focused on, though not exclusively), focused on identifying the factors that support and hinder teachers' uptake (Jones 2004; Leask and Younie 2001; Scrimshaw 2004). Understanding what militates against use was also important. This research tended to be more small scale and qualitative and concerned understanding teachers' situated practices and ways of negotiating technology (Dawes 2001; Loveless 2001; Younie 2007). To understand the processes involved in teachers learning to use technology for pedagogic practice, it is important to start by understanding the contemporary context in which teachers work. If technology is to be systemically embedded in practice, it is essential to understand the nature of that practice from the outset.

The contemporary context of teachers' work in schools: political pressures and priorities

There is a need to understand the context in which teachers work and the priorities that drive practice at the individual level of the teacher, which is situated within the context of the school, and the priorities of school development plans. These priorities in turn are situated in the wider context of a national agenda driving education from government policy with particular curriculum and examination specifications. There are complex, multiple and competing pressures and tensions, set within a national and even global agenda of driving up standards as measured by external indicators of educational performance (PISA tests).

Metaphors for capturing the complexities of the contemporary educational landscape

Metaphors, like models, enable us to better understand complex situations and processes. To this end, in education an 'ecological' metaphor has been developed. In an ecological perspective of pedagogic adaptation and change, Davis (2008) argues there is a diversity of factors that impact upon a practitioner's use of technology. These are 'envisioned in layers that frame the classroom as nested within the school, local area, region, and the global biosphere of education' (Davis 2008: 2). From understanding the different factors at each of these levels in a multidimensional model, we come to understand teachers' use of technology as addressing a practitioner's concerns at the time. From Hammond et al.'s (2009) research we understand those concerns to involve teacher's beliefs about learning and how technology interacts with the learning process.

It is important that this ecology model should be understood as describing a dynamic and fluid process, which allows conceptual clarity while being not necessarily stable, but rather shifting and changing to accommodate multiple tensions. It is crucial to keep movement in play in relation to the tensions and contradictions that are inevitably inherent within such complex systems so as to move towards resolutions of these tensions or what are competing priorities. For example, at the macro level, a change of government will most likely lead to change in education policy, and at a micro level, a teacher's need to maintain behaviour in a classroom alongside ensuring attainment and learning outcomes, can present as a range of competing priorities. Teachers' evolutionary 'adaptations' are between the external pressures (government policy and curriculum directives), local contextual pressures (school needs) and teachers' preferred practice (classroom context).

Having outlined the political pressures shaping teachers' practice, specifically the demands of an audit culture, which prioritize public performance indicators (external exams), the contemporary background context to teachers work needs to be appropriately understood. The next set of questions is:

- How do teachers develop their professional practice?
- How do teachers come to incorporate technology into their pedagogy, that is, their set of preferred teaching and learning strategies? This is of particular importance if technology is *not* a preferred strategy.

As Fullan (1982: 256) perceptively observes, 'educational change involves learning how to do something new. It is for this reason that if any single factor is crucial to change, it is professional development.'

Teachers' professional development

There are complex obstacles which teachers face in experiencing ownership of educational change, such as using new technologies for learning and teaching. Critically, as Bell and Gilbert (1994: 493) argue, 'teacher development can be viewed as teachers learning, rather than others getting teachers to change. In learning, the teachers were developing their beliefs and ideas, developing their classroom practice . . .'.

Wright (2001) argues that relearning is at the heart of cultural, rather than cosmetic, change. As Stenhouse (1975) accurately observed, 'teachers must want to change: without the willingness of the teacher to participate in the process of restructuring their own knowledge, any legislation will be to varying degrees ineffective or limited' (Stenhouse, cited in Eckhardt 1995: 155).

Professional development can be understood as: '. . . an ideologically, attitudinally, intellectually and epistemologically based stance on the part of the individual, in relation to the practice of the profession to which s/he belongs, and which influences her/his professional practice' (Evans 2002: 130).

However, such a definition looks only at teachers as individuals and not as part of a community of practice (Lave and Wenger 1991); it is more of an individual understanding of professional development, as opposed to a socially constructed understanding of professionalism, as embedded in a community of shared practices. This is important, as McCormick and Scrimshaw (2001) had criticized the technology research community for not keeping up to date with recent theories of knowledge that stress the social dimension of learning. These theories need to be applied to how teachers learn to incorporate technology pedagogically – specifically, distributed cognition and situated learning.

Evans (2002: 128) argues that the 'knowledge base in the field of teacher development is still underdeveloped' and Fullan (1993) noted such an omission regarding an 'inadequately defined knowledge base about teaching' (Fullan 1993: 112), which is a key obstacle in the evolution of teaching as a profession. In addition, there is insufficient attention given to the way teachers learn to construct new knowledge through participation in a 'community of practice' as a joint venture, in education generally and, specifically with technology (Younie 2007). See Chapter 10 for a further discussion on how to develop the knowledge base of the teaching profession through adopting a communal constructivist approach and online community of practice.

Seeing the value of change with technology

If a teacher is convinced that the effort involved in learning new (technology) skills is not worth the perceived gain, or that the skills will only have a short shelf life, teachers are unlikely to make that effort. This argument is supported by Barnett's (1997) concept of rationalization, on the part of the teacher who is over-burdened through competing priorities and must make informed decisions about what they can focus their time and energy on. Barnett argues that in an era of 'super-complexity' it is not possible for teachers to do (or know) everything, therefore a rational decision needs to be made about what can and cannot be done.

Doyle and Ponder (1977) argue similarly when they state that the benefits of introducing something new (technology) are counter-balanced by the additional effort required to organize it, which is conceptualized as the 'practicality ethic'. Tagg (1995) supports this argument by claiming that successful teachers, in particular, will be unwilling to drop approaches that work for the sake of something new unless teachers can see that it is similarly effective. Having examined teachers' professional development in general terms, the next step is to evaluate specific models of professional development for technology.

Models of continuing professional development for teachers about technology

Historically, the preferred model of technology in-service training has consistently been that of *'cascade'*, and this has been hugely unsuccessful (Russell 1995). Typically, this model has three components: a session with a focus on the innovation itself, followed by the teacher being responsible for translating the skills and knowledge gained into the context of the classroom and curriculum, and concluding with a responsibility for dissemination, consisting of the teacher reporting back to colleagues on the skills, knowledge and implementation of technology in the classroom. As Casey (1996) observes:

> We derive little benefit by 'wowing' teachers with demonstrations of new computing technology if we fail to connect its use to the curriculum. Teachers may resist changing to a practice that someone outside the classroom decides is of importance for teachers to do inside the classroom.
>
> (Casey 1996: 16)

During the 1990s and 2000s the 'ICT coordinator' emerged as a key figure in many schools, providing both formal training and informal, day-to-day support and troubleshooting (EDSI 1997; NCET 1995; Pachler 2011). Having warned of the need to change teachers' beliefs before they adopt new methods and the difficulties in effecting even slow changes in teachers' beliefs, Veen (1993) identified four consequences of this for technology CPD. First, it must fit with the existing beliefs of teachers. Second, a differentiated 'bottom-up' approach, appropriate to different subject areas, is needed. Third, change will be slow, since it requires planning and leaders must persist; and fourth, it should be school-based.

What are the underlying theories of learning inherent in these models of in-service training for technology? Rhodes (1989) identified two different approaches to technology CPD for teachers based on contrasting theories of teachers as learners: the deficit model and the skills model. In courses based on the deficit model, the primary barrier to overcome was a teacher's fear of the innovation; the emphasis is on giving the teacher confidence in and with the technology, with educational issues assuming a secondary role. However, Rhodes (1989) argues that this model de-skills teachers, reducing them to novices and makes the new techniques seem distinct from their normal work. Conversely, the skills model 'acknowledges teachers as experts . . . the barrier to innovation is seen as psychological . . . and the emphasis is on encouraging teachers to use the technology in the classroom and then return in order to discuss educational outcomes' (Rhodes 1989: 5).

However, both are 'deficit' in the sense that they regard teachers as being 'barriers' to be addressed rather than as experts willing to engage with new ideas for teaching with technology.

Technology CPD: stage-models and typologies

A number of more detailed models for teachers' continuing professional development with technology have been put forward, which can be characterized as 'stage models'. For example, Novello's (1989) five-stage model, entitled SAPID (self-familiarization, authoring, presentation, integration and design); Dwyer, Ringstaff and Sandholtz's (1991) five-stage evolutionary model; Comber, Lawson and Hargreaves' (1998) 'familiarization-adaptation' model, which was based on Hall's (1979) 'concerns-based adoption' model. Also there has been the emergence of typologies that describe different types of technology users, Dawes (2001) in the UK and Hadley and Sheingold (1993) in the USA.

Dwyer et al.'s (1991) major study into how technology-rich classrooms changed teachers' beliefs and practices over a period of years discovered that the changes were significant, but only occurred after teachers had confronted deeply held beliefs about the nature of learning and the efficacy of their pedagogical activities. Using an American study, the changes were theorized into a five-stage evolutionary model, which teachers pass through in order to become fully competent users of technology in the classroom: entry, adoption, adaptation, appropriation and invention.

1. *Entry* – teachers struggle to cope with technology
2. *Adoption* – successful use of technology at a basic level
3. *Adaptation* – discovery of potential in a variety of applications and can troubleshoot
4. *Appropriation* – mastery over the technology and use it to accomplish various classroom goals
5. *Invention* – active development of new learning techniques using the technology.

Dwyer et al. (1991: 13) observed that, initially, teachers demonstrated 'little penchant for significant change and, in fact, were using their technological resources to replicate traditional learning activities'. Consequently, they argue that teachers have little 'incentive or direction for making changes which might jeopardise . . . performance on existing criteria . . . They did not seek to create new approaches to [pedagogical] excellence' (Dwyer et al. 1991: 13). However, by the fourth stage change did occur. This was evidenced by teachers' personal appropriation of the technology and was seen as particularly significant, since it enabled new pedagogical strategies. Teachers had gained a new perspective on how they could change classroom practice using technology. This stage would be classified as 'transformative' using McCormick and Scrimshaw's (2001) model, which includes how technology can also change the nature of the subject itself – for example, art and the rise of digital technologies.

In the UK Comber, Lawson and Hargreaves (1998) developed a two-part model connecting teacher attitudes to technology with actual use of technology. Comber et al. (1998) refined a three-stage model (familiarization – utilization – adaptation) in light of the work done by Hall (1979), Hall and Hord (1987) on a 'concerns-based adoption' model. The new model identified six 'stages of concern' that represent changing attitudes towards technology innovation, which move from concern about the immediate impact of technology, through to those which relate to introducing technology and concerns about its impact on working with other teachers. The affective and behavioural components of the model are closely connected, so each stage is associated with a level of use. Other models developed to capture 'levels of use' have also come out of the 'concerns based adoption model', such as Loucks et al. (1998), which devised a scale to determine quality of technology use.

With respect to typologies, in the UK Dawes' (2001) research led to the development of a typology of different types of technology user, which her sample of teachers confirmed through member validation questionnaires. Dawes (2001) concludes that change occurs in individual and groups of teachers as they develop professional expertise and the motivation to evolve from being 'potential users' (through the stages of 'participant', 'involved', and 'adept') to 'integral users'. In America Hadley and Sheingold (1993) had constructed a similar typology. These models of CPD and stages of progression help us understand the change process with respect to teachers and how they come to incorporate technology into their professional practice.

Legislative change: the first statuary technology competencies for teachers

The most important legislation regarding 'technology and teacher competence' came in April 1998 from the DfEE with 'Circular 4/1998', which specified that teachers must be able to use technology for teaching. The DfEE stated in detail exactly what was expected in relation to technology for both newly qualified teachers (NQTs) and for serving teachers.

The technology standards for qualified teachers set out in DfEE 4/98 were statements about teachers' technology capability presented in the form of a list of competencies, which applied to all newly qualified teachers from July 1999. The DfEE (1998: 17) stated 'it is concerned with the ways in which technology can be used effectively in teaching' and set out an Initial Teacher Training National Curriculum for the use of technology in subject teaching, which would 'equip every newly qualified teacher with the knowledge, skills and understanding to make sound decisions about when, when not, and how to use technology effectively' (DfEE 1998 Annex B: 17).

This led to the development of the 'technology standards', which had to be met to achieve 'qualified teacher status' (QTS) in the UK. At the time of writing these standards are under review.

Factors affecting teachers' uses of technology

Even if teachers received effective technology CPD, the landscape is more complicated than simply receiving training and then implementing it seamlessly into pedagogic practice. Hence, it is important to understand the issues that affect teachers' uses of technology in the classroom. The first issue concerns research on factors that prevent teachers from using technology. The second on factors that encourage teachers to use technology, and third, the learning experiences of teachers in technology-rich and support-rich contexts.

Factors hindering teachers' uses of technology

It is important to identify the factors known to inhibit teachers' use of technology: these can be classified as *material* or *cultural*. The former refers to artefacts, like computers or finance, the latter refers to the prevailing practice and values surrounding technology. These two types of barrier can be further analysed as *external*, first-order barriers, such as lack of resources, lack of technical support, and *internal*, second-order barriers, such as teachers' approaches, resistance to technology and forming cultural barriers. Additionally, attention must be given to the broader ecology of how these factors interact. Jones (2004) argued it is the complex relationships between these that are in need of further research. To this end, Younie (2007) investigated the multidimensionality of integrating technology into professional practice, specifically the material and socio-cultural factors affecting teachers' pedagogical take-up of technology.

Historically, technology has suffered from masculine, cultural connotations, which Somekh and Davies (1997) thought led to 'cultural alienation' as a problem facing schools trying to promote the use of computers in the 1990s, because it was seen as predominantly male and overtly technical at that time. More recent forms of cultural alienation experienced by teachers pertain to pupils being perceived as digital natives, where they are seen to be more technology savvy than teachers. With respect to the research studies, which examined why teachers do not use technology in their teaching, the following inhibitors were identified (from, Dupagne and Krendle 1992; Winnans and Brown 1992; Hadley and Sheingold 1993; Rosen and Weil 1995; Leask and Younie 2000; Pelgrum 2001):

- Lack of technology availability
- Lack of teaching experience with technology
- Lack of classroom-based support for teachers using technology
- Time investment required to successfully integrate technology into the curriculum
- Lack of in-service training to develop teacher technology skills and confidence
- Inadequate financial support.

Interestingly, Pelgrum (2001) conducted an international comparative survey of the obstacles to technology integration and found the same factors consistently emerged across all 24 countries in the research; namely the lack of computers and the lack of technology knowledge among teachers. While Pelgrum's results were from a 'worldwide assessment', the UK was not a participating country. However, Opie and Fukuyo's (2000) research in the UK did discover that inhibiting the use of technology was also a lack of resources and training as Pelgrum had found. OECD research (Leask 2001), which tested Rogers' theory of diffusion of innovations against the model for adoption of technologies in innovative schools worldwide, found a 'fright and flight' phenomena operating in UK schools, where teachers who were not comfortable with technologies soon left leading schools where technology adoption was expected of the staff. This movement of technologically illiterate staff to other schools can over time be seen to have the effect of making it increasingly difficult for schools left behind in technology adoption to catch up.

Relationships between barriers

Understanding the barriers to the uptake of technology by teachers requires more analysis regarding the relationships between the barriers (Younie 2007) – for example, access. There are different kinds of access problems, ranging from a lack of resources to the poor quality of resources available, to noting that even where 'sufficient quantities of quality resources were available, teachers were still experiencing problems, as a result of the organization of those resources' (Jones 2004: 11). One example would be, if the majority of computers were housed in technology suites that needed advanced timetable booking. Add to this lack of technical support and the frequency of technical problems (due to old, poor-quality hardware), then technical faults lead to lower levels of technology use; recurring faults and the expectation of faults during lessons cause teachers to avoid using technology (Jones 2004: 16), just as the lack of reliability 'lost a whole group of teachers' in the 1980s (Hammond et al. 2009: 49). However, by moving to mobile devices, including pupil's own, which are more robust and reliable with advances in technology, these earlier barriers should disappear.

Similarly, the issue of training is complex and concerns a multiplicity of interrelating factors. Examples are: the lack of time for training, which Snoeyink and Ertmer (2001) identified as a significant barrier; the lack of pedagogical training (Veen 1993); lack of skills training (Preston, Cox and Cox 2000) and lack of leadership support (Preston 2004). Yet, from the wealth of research evidence, we know that effective technology training is crucial if teachers are to implement technology in classroom practice (Kirkwood et al. 2000). This barrier is more complex, however, than the singularly identified element of 'training'. Rather, it is how the training is supported by other crucial factors, such as ongoing technical support, leadership and levels of collegiality, which are both material and cultural (Younie 2007).

Factors supporting teachers' use of technology

Interestingly, apart from the previously mentioned OCED study into the adoption of technologies in schools (Leask 2001), the research that has examined the factors supporting teachers' uses of technology has tended to be large scale, quantitative and American, with little qualitative research (Hennessy et al. 2005). No surprise, too, is the fact that what facilitates technology integration is the corollary of what prevents teachers using it – most notably providing access to technology resources and training. With the advent of affordable computers and access to the Internet in the 1990s, there was an international drive to integrate technology into teachers' practice (Pelgrum 2001; Leask and Younie 2000). In America, the following large-scale, quantitative studies all used survey data to identify the key factors that support teachers' uptake of technology (from Sheingold and Hadley 1990; Kerr 1991; Hadley and Sheingold 1993; Becker 1994; all USA, and 'world-wide'; Pelgrum 2001).

Sheingold and Hadley's (1990) nationwide survey of teachers identified three consistent key factors where teachers were 'accomplished' in their use of technology: first, teacher motivation and commitment to their own development; second, the support teachers experienced in their schools, and third, access to sufficient quantities of technology. Teachers reported that their classroom practices became more learner-centred with the integration of technology in their curriculum. Sheingold and Hadley (1990) saw wider success among teachers if: '. . . ample technology, support, and time for teachers to learn the technology are provided, and if an academic and cultural structure exists to encourage teachers to take an experimental approach to their work' (Sheingold and Hadley 1990: 25).

Becker's (1994) work reveals other positive factors that encourage teachers to use technology, notably: collegiality among teachers using computers in their school; resources for teachers' development; smaller class sizes; and more dedicated technology training.

With respect to research from Europe, in Holland, Veen's seminal research (1993) revealed that school factors played an important role in how teachers made use of technology, in particular the essential technical support offered (20 hours per week) and the positive attitude of the head. The emphasis on the importance of leadership was echoed in the UK by Lawson and Comber's (2004) research.

A review of the research literature identifies a complex interplay of factors that affect the integration of technology into teachers' pedagogic practice. However, these research findings do not provide an understanding of teachers' learning paths or professional practices which teachers engage with to help them integrate technology: in short, how teachers learn and create new knowledge about technology for pedagogical purposes. An analysis of the factors that affect teachers' use of technology does not, in and of itself, reveal insight into teachers' learning processes for implementing technology.

What research has accomplished is the identification of the factors that support teachers using technology and the corollary: of those which, when absent, hinder teachers' uptake of technology. Politically these factors were directly addressed through the UK government's first national technology strategy in 1997, which attempted to rectify the major barriers that had been identified. This included providing the necessary infrastructure to develop technology in schools: namely, technology resources in the form of computers and funding (NGFL) and training (NOF).

Teachers learning to use technology in technology-rich contexts: lessons learnt

This analysis considers the most significant research findings from America and the UK regarding 'support intervention' through technology-rich projects in schools. A widely acclaimed technology research project was the 'Apple Classrooms of Tomorrow' (ACOT), which focused initially on technology-rich classrooms in America (Dwyer et al. 1991; Sandholtz et al. 1997). In supplying the hardware, software and training, this programme of technology-rich intervention aimed to help teachers learn how to integrate technology. This longitudinal research identified an 'instructional evolution' through which teachers progressed. Teachers began with the 'entry phase', where teaching remained largely unchanged as they grappled with technical problems. In the 'adoption phase' teachers began integrating technology into their classroom practice and their own personal attitudes changed, resulting in increased self-confidence with technology. Finally, at the 'invention phase', 'teachers experimented with new instructional patterns' and ways of relating to learners and to other teachers (Sandholtz et al. 1997: 44).

From this research ACOT developed a new model of teacher development. This included week-long 'practicums' during the school year, four-week summer institutes and support from project staff to visit schools during the year. This 'situated teacher development' programme enables teachers to observe ACOT classrooms, work in teams and plan technology-supported projects.

In the UK Somekh's (1991) acclaimed PALM Project (Pupil Autonomy in Learning with Microcomputers) deployed an action research strategy for developing teachers' computer skills. The theory of 'situated cognition' helps to explain teachers' learning in PALM since they acquired most of their computer skills in the classroom when working alongside the pupils. PALM also provided three full-time project officers, who supplied teachers with both educational and technical support in lessons. Given the high level of resourcing involved, in equipping technology-rich classrooms and support staff, such projects raise issues regarding the lack of transferability to all schools.

Clearly these early research studies of technology-rich contexts have relied exclusively on specially funded technology projects, for resources and training support, which by their very nature of being 'one-offs', are not nationally sustainable or transferable. Even though the research demonstrates the advantages of these intervention projects (teachers becoming motivated and integrating technology), Mumtaz (2000) argues that there is a lack of research into the teachers' use of technology after these projects have ceased. Such research fails to explain the way technology becomes embedded (or not) once initial projects have finished and funding and support have gone; the question of how technology use is to be sustained remains.

What the research on technology-rich and support-rich contexts does demonstrate is that it is a combination of factors that is critical to the integration of technology – namely, abundant technology that provides access alongside technical support, together with hands-on training. Also, one key factor appears to be the role of 'situated cognition' in learning about technology alongside other teachers, with opportunities for discussion and reflection. This clearly has parallels with models of CPD that also accentuate the importance of 'situated learning' (Dawes 2001) and 'communities of practice' (Loveless 2001; Younie 2007) that enable dialogue, analysis and evaluation of new skills and knowledge. However, while studies identify specific technological factors pertaining to technical support, access and training, very little research analyses the role of situated learning and the significance of belonging to a community of practice in relation to technology: in short, the socio-cultural dynamics of learning and change with technology.

Although, interestingly, some UK research does exist relating to a major national development, it is not in the public domain. Leask (2011) commissioned research on situated learning in online communities of practice in her role in developing and launching a successful and award-winning national Web 2.0 environment for local government in the UK (see also Chapter 10). She used Rogers' diffusion of innovation theory to develop the user base progressively and found that two types of online community developed quickly. Each was driven by particular user needs in the particular community of practice.

One type of community was driven by national policy officers to meet national policy goals and provided an example of social constructivist learning theories in practice – this means there is a more experienced leader, and others learn from being within a zone of proximal development – that is, being able to learn from a leader with more knowledge. A second major type of community was found to be of an entirely different nature. This community was self-forming. It consisted of groups with similar responsibilities who, in order to show they were using national resources effectively wished to share their ideas and to develop and then benchmark practice against others with similar responsibilities. This way of working provides an example of Leask and Younie's (2001) communal constructivist theory in action with a group of experts coming together to work collectively on shared problems to generate new knowledge. In order to justify ongoing expenditure on the online environment the savings to local authorities of both ways of working were measured to identify financial benefits.

Facilitating change: teacher ownership of technology

One answer to the question of how to embed sustained technology change with teachers is through providing them with their own mobile technology. Research on 'laptops for teachers' proved to be very successful, demonstrating significantly improved teacher competence (Becta 1998; Stager 1995; Selinger 1996). Becta's 'Multimedia Portables for Teachers' project reported by Youngman and Harrison (1998) found the degree of computer literacy of many teachers increased to the extent that even relatively inexperienced teachers were quickly able to use their computer to evaluate software packages and select information to better suit their own curriculum purposes. Teachers' confidence and skills improved and teachers reported their knowledge had grown 'substantially'.

Specifically, the project identified four success factors: training, personal ownership, portability (between work and home) and technical support (combination of formal and informal). The findings of this national research were also strongly supported by the evaluation of local and regional schemes (Loveless and Stevens 2002). Overall, the research projects found that providing laptops for teachers led to a significant enhancement of technology use.

To summarize then: the key factors supporting and hindering teachers' use of technology are multiple and interrelated. The research into teachers' use of technology identified the barriers teachers face, the factors involved in supporting technology use and the stages that teachers ascend when learning to use technology for professional purposes. Barriers included: lack of access to technology, lack of technical support and lack of appropriate technology training. The quantitative survey research (Hadley and Sheingold 1990; Sheingold and Hadley 1993; Becker 1994; Pelgrum 2001) that explored commonalties among 'accomplished' technology-using teachers also identified significant factors such as: support and collegiality in schools; access to sufficient technology; commitment and resources for teachers' professional development and learning; provision for technology training. Further research is needed for us to have a better understanding of the learning paths for teachers using technology in context and to understand how to build up the professional knowledge base for teachers to facilitate more systemic technology use across all ages and subjects. (See Chapter 10 for more details of how this can be achieved.)

Pedagogy and technology

> . . . developments in technology are making the role of the teacher much more complex. In addition, teachers' beliefs about the value of technology for learning are important in their pedagogical reasoning, but there is evidence that teachers beliefs and practices do not change automatically as a result of classroom experience . . . enabling teachers to adapt their pedagogical reasoning and practices in response to learning opportunities provided by technology is likely to be a very difficult and complex process.
>
> (Webb and Cox 2004: 278)

What are the challenges for teachers? When integrating technology into pedagogic practices, what processes do teachers undergo? Is teachers' pedagogy transformed? Or is it that the technologies slot into existing strategies without significantly changing the teaching style and learning processes? Does learning remain predicated on a information-transmission model (Ruben 1999) or social constructivist model of dialogic knowledge creation (Vygotsky 1978) or even a communal constructivist model (Leask and Younie 2001)?

The challenge for teachers is to understand what technologies there are and how they can relate (and possibly change) teachers' beliefs, knowledge and pedagogic strategies. Starting with teachers' knowledge; teachers have a range of specialized knowledge domains that relate to each other. There is subject knowledge (the content of the curriculum area, discipline specific concepts and skills), pedagogic knowledge (what makes for effective teaching and deep learning, alongside classroom management) and then there is technology knowledge, knowing a range of types of technology, hardware and software.

However, it is not enough to know about a range of technologies, in and for themselves. What teachers need to understand is how these technologies interact with and provide opportunities for learning, which lies in the relationship of the technology to the wider learning environment, constituted by other resources, learners and teachers. It is the totality of the environment and ways of organizing interaction with technology in that environment that gives rise to new affordances for learning.

Webb and Cox (2004: 269) argue that teachers need to identify the range of affordances that technologies can provide and evaluate those in relation to their teaching objectives. This requires teachers to develop a much deeper understanding of technology resources if they are to be used effectively.

Types of technology and pedagogic practice

With respect to developing technology knowledge, teachers need to understand the capabilities of a range of technologies. The main innovations in educational technology have been interactive whiteboards, the Internet, portable computers, followed by developments in virtual learning environments, software programmes, hand-held mobile devices and Web 2.0. With standard software packages there is little disputing teachers' growing confidence; what is more contestable is the knowledge of the affordances offered by more recent developments in technologies. Not only does it take time to understand such affordances, the inclusion of these into lesson activities requires investment in planning by teachers. The challenge is to create pedagogic activities to relate the affordances of particular types of technologies to the learning objectives.

A seminal review of the literature on technology and pedagogy was conducted by Cox et al. (2003) for Becta, and further reported by Webb and Cox (2004) in the journal *Technology Pedagogy and Education*, which assessed international research on teachers' practices. A range of technologies were identified, but widespread use of the range was found to be limited. Across subjects and age phases, the types most used were: the Internet, simulations, modelling software, programming, LOGO, data-logging and multimedia editing software.

With respect to the Internet, Webb and Cox (2004) found that teachers needed to identify more effectively the range of affordances this technology provides. More promising were simulations. These enabled learners to 'engage with powerful ideas and conduct explorations that are not usually possible in classrooms' (Webb and Cox 2004: 270) and were found to promote conceptual change in science and geography in secondary schools. Rather than wasting lesson time on the mechanics of setting up experiments, simulations afforded the opportunity to focus on the concepts and processes under investigation. Additionally, animations could permit the representation of processes not visible, such as heart function and blood flow, which aided learner's conceptual development. This finding is supported by later research on interactive whiteboards, which highlights how the multimedia aspects of the technology, which support simulations and animations, aid metacognition through the visual representation of complex processes (Miller and Glover 2006).

Modelling software was also found to enhance learning in science, geography and mathematics in primary and secondary teaching. With respect to programming, LOGO is an often-cited example of technology-enhanced learning, in which LOGO has been shown to aid the development of mathematics skills and higher-order thinking. However, controversy surrounding LOGO concerns how much learning by autonomous discovery should be expected, showing how critical is the role of the teacher and how teachers still need to scaffold the learning experiences with LOGO (Webb and Cox 2004).

Data-logging is used in science to capture experimental data in real time, which is converted into graphs. This eliminates the need for pupils to plot graphs mechanically, which is an activity known to induce boredom and mistakes. Significantly, in the research on data logging it was shown that learners are better at interpreting the findings of their experiments 'when they use real-time data collection with graphing than when they construct their own graphs' (Webb and Cox 2004: 271). Multimedia editing software was also found to be used in a number of innovative practices internationally, but again Webb and Cox (2004) warn of the need to understand the affordances so that teachers can plan activities carefully that relate the affordances to the learning objectives.

Changes in classroom interaction

One of the most important findings of the Webb and Cox (2004) review on pedagogy and technology concerned how increasing uses of technology changed classroom interaction. In particular, there was more learner–learner and learner–teacher interaction, alongside a tendency for less whole-class instruction and increased independent work.

Drawing on the work of Hennessy et al. (2003), there was evidence that teachers were increasing their interactions with individual learners and small groups. As teachers developed and refined their pedagogic strategies (in a sample of 115 teachers), 'using technology was associated with a decrease in teacher direction and exposition, a corresponding increase in student control and self regulation, and more student collaboration' (Webb and Cox 2004: 274). Similarly the research of Mosely et al. (1999) found teachers 'who favoured technology were more likely to value collaborative working, enquiry and decision making' by learners (Mosely et al. 1999).

Increasing interaction and developing pedagogic practices for collaborative learning with technology fits a social constructivist view of learning. With the move from an instructional model of knowledge transmission (traditional paradigm), to a facilitation model of knowledge creation and social constructivism, so the role of the teacher changes. As technology is integrated, so the teacher moves from the role of 'sage on the stage' to 'guide on the side', from expert to facilitator (Sellinger 1996) – to guide learners to useful resources, stimulate debate, support problem-solving, probe thinking and encourage meaning making. Increasing the use of technology was associated with changes in pedagogical practices towards a more pupil-centred model involving collaborative learning. Significantly, like Hammond et al. (2009), Webb and Cox (2004) discovered that decisions about whether to use technology depended on teachers' beliefs. To enhance the uptake of technology, they argue, teachers need to reflect critically on the underlying theories of learning that influence their work, and then to review their beliefs in light of the new evidence regarding the affordances of technology for learning.

Models for characterizing pedagogy with technology

This section is based on the influential work of Mary Webb, who has done much to clarify the thinking in the field of pedagogy and technology. Webb (2010) helpfully outlines models which help to classify pedagogy with technology, and starts from the premise that models help to communicate processes and relationships and aid our

Table 5.1 Model of technology–learner interaction (adapted from Webb 2010: 93)

Instructional paradigm	**Theoretical base** – Skinnerian/behaviourist theory **Learning** – drill and practice
Revelatory paradigm	**Theoretical base** – Bruner/spiral curriculum **Learning** – discovery/experiential: simulation, problem-solving
Conjectural paradigm	**Theoretical base** – Piaget, Papert/constructivist **Learning** – learner has control and computer used as tool (word processing, data handling)
Emancipatory paradigm	**Theoretical base** – efficiency, to reduce workload **Learning** – occurs in tandem with one of the other three

understanding of phenomena. The phenomena in question are complex, because they include teachers' pedagogy – that is, their classroom practice which, in turn, includes teachers' pedagogical reasoning processes (planning, teaching, assessing and evaluation and the knowledge needed for these processes) and the affordances that various types of technology may provide for learning. However, Webb (2010) argues, recent developments in cognition, meta-cognition and the way knowledge is co-constructed in learning communities makes conceptions of pedagogy that more complex, as do advancements in technology, which give rise to new affordances for learning.

Models of 'technology use' concern first, the 'technology-learner' interface, followed by wider interactions including with the teacher and then quantitative measurements of technology use. Among the early models to characterize learning with technology were those that focused on the learning relationship between computer and user. Initial models examined how technology could support the learning process. Influential to this day is Kemmis et al.'s (1977) four paradigms for computer-assisted learning outlined in Table 5.1.

However, while characterizing the role of technology in the learning process, such early models ignored other salient features, most notably wider interactions in the learning environment. By drawing attention to these, Webb (2010) highlights the next set of models that do take account of the interactions between learners, teacher and the technology (or designer, as embodied in the software). In particular, it is Laurillard's (1993) 'conversational framework' that can be used to illuminate the learning process with respect to these wider interactions. Thanks to the influential work of Laurillard in this field, it is worth explaining the key ideas of this model in detail.

The conversational model focuses on the learner–teacher interaction and process of negotiation of the learner's views of the subject matter, which occur in light of the teacher's representation of the subject matter and how the learner modifies their views. The teacher and learner are engaged in a conversation exchanging their representations of the subject matter, which involves the process of reflection (discussing what you are doing) and adaptation (modification of what you are doing in light of the discussion) (Atherton 2011). Atherton argues that the critical feature of the conversational model is the way Laurillard (1993) uses it to evaluate technologically supported learning. When it comes to technology, specifically multimedia software, Laudrillard et al. (1993) identified that learners working on interactive media with no clear narrative structure tended to be unfocused. From this observation Laurillard (1998) argues that multimedia design should provide scaffolding for the learner within the software, where narrative structure focuses the learner. Laurillard et al. (2000) found, with respect to multimedia software, there was a clear need for guidance from the teacher and/or the software to promote meaningful learning' (Webb 2010: 94), as analysis of conversations between learners revealed that without appropriate scaffolding and guidance, pupil talk focused on how to operate the technology (the syntax), rather than discussing the meaning of the content (the semantics). Focusing on the syntax (technical functions) rather than the semantics (the meaning) led to only low levels of reflection (Boys et al. 2001).

Other models that characterize pedagogy have focused on quantitative measurements of technology use. Such models have been developed specifically to calculate the amount of computer activity. For example, the first Impact Study (Cox et al. 1993) had a ten-point scale for appraising teachers' frequency of use. Similarly, Twining's (2000) 'Computer Practice Framework' (CPF) facilitates quantitative analysis of computer use and enables reflection on how the computer is used to support curriculum objectives, which could be through supporting, extending, or transforming those objectives. (This pedagogical analysis is similar to McCormick and Scrimshaw's (2001) model for understanding teachers' curriculum use of computers, whether the technology is deployed to make teaching more efficient or is transformative). However, while quantitative models determine the frequency of use, they do little to analyse the quality of that use.

The most detailed comparison of models for examining pedagogy with technology, including ones not discussed here, can be found in Webb (2010), to which the quantity and range of models is indicative of the complexity and changing nature of pedagogy and technology as advancements are made in both fields. Critically, Webb (2010) argues that, while all these models are useful for characterizing technology use within pedagogical practices, they do little to help us understand teachers' pedagogical decision-making processes and how teachers conceptualize the 'affordances' of technology. It is essential to understand these processes if change is to occur in the profession regarding the take-up of technology.

Understanding affordances of technology

The idea of affordance is one that has been appropriated from ecology and has gained much explanatory power in relation to technology for the unique way in which it encapsulates the relationship between user and tool. For this reason it is worth outlining the lineage of the concept. The term 'affordance', as a noun, was first introduced by Gibson (1979) and evolved from his ecological theory of perception. While the verb 'to afford' was in the dictionary, what Gibson wanted to denote was the relationship between an organism and an object, and the way the former perceived the latter in relation to its needs. Citing the example of a 'tree', Hammond's (2010) synoptic article on affordance outlines how as an object this may offer shelter from the rain or sustenance as food (in which the opportunities the tree affords are different according to need), but the physical properties of the tree remain the same and are invariant. What is fundamental is the perception of the material properties of an object (tree), or tool (computer) as seen by the user.

However, there remains a tension between tool and perception, because perceptions of use are multi-faceted, in that a tool could be used in a variety of different ways. What technology requires is for teachers to allow themselves 'to recognise the flux of possibilities' (Latour 2002: 250, cited in Hammond 2010: 214). With respect to education, the term 'affordance' is used to refer to the opportunities for action, which various technologies provide. What shapes the 'seeing' of a range of possibilities for action with a tool – that is, what influences users' perceptions – are memory and context. Further to this, affordance contains the idea of complementarity (opportunity and constraint), in that technology offers both countless opportunities for actions and countless constraints on actions. In citing the example of interactive whiteboards and how, when fixed to a wall, this provides a physical constraint on use, so does placing an interactive whiteboard flat down on a table provide other opportunities, but other constraints too.

Kennewell's (2001) work with trainee teachers' use of the Internet identifies the different ways teachers perceive the affordance of this technology and how opportunities and constraints are complementary. Crucially, however, Hammond's (2010) critique of Kennewell's research resides in noting the failure of it to offer an account of why teachers should perceive affordances differently regarding the same technology. For a deeper consideration of why teachers perceive affordances in different ways, Hammond (2010) examines further the nature of perception, in particular, the ontological tensions inherent in the concept of affordance and gives an account of how different writers have appropriated this explanatory concept since Gibson's (1979) original inception. Ultimately, though, the significant observation is that 'if a teacher is unable to directly perceive the affordances of technology, relative to well rehearsed goals such as creativity, analysis, authentic learning and so on, then he or she is unlikely to be an enthusiastic adopter of technology' (Hammond 2010: 215). If the affordances of a tool cannot be seen, then it will not be appropriated.

An affordance is then:

> . . . the perception of a possibility of action provided by properties of, in this case, the computer plus software. These possibilities are shaped by past experience and context, [and] can be signposted by peers and teachers. Affordances provide both opportunities and constraints. Affordances are always relative to something and, in the context of technology, relative to desirable goals or strategies for teaching and learning.
>
> (Hammond 2010: 217)

The distinctive insight from Gibson (1979) therefore involves the understanding of the interaction between the user and tool (organism and object) in how the former perceives the latter. This process is more than direct perception of material properties and concerns the meanings that shape how a tool is seen: the lens through which meaning is made and possibilities for action are envisaged. Perceiving the possibilities that technology opens up for learning comes from previous experience, and can be demonstrated and 'signposted' by other teachers. This explains the need to develop an online professional network of teachers to build up a knowledge base about the affordances of a range of technologies.

Additionally, Webb (2005) argues that affordance isn't only about the interaction between the teacher and technology, and its perceived possibilities for learning, but concerns the wider environment and how these interrelate. In a learning environment supported by technology, 'affordances for learning are provided by interactions between the hardware, software, other resources, teachers and other students' (Webb 2010: 96). Affordances are provided not by technology alone, but by the 'totality of the environment', which includes the teacher, other students, other resources and their 'interactions through classroom processes' (Webb 2010: 97). In widening out the interactive processes and how these afford learning (which includes technology), Webb (2010) has developed a framework, which is represented in Figure 5.1 below.

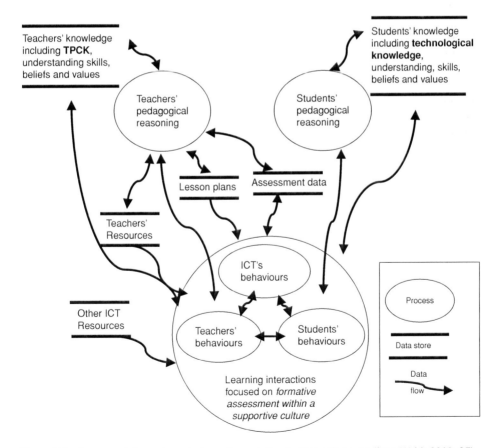

Figure 5.1   Framework for pedagogical practices relating to technology use (from Webb 2010: 97)

Understanding teachers' pedagogical reasoning

Shulman's (1987) model of pedagogical reasoning includes the processes of planning, teaching, assessing and evaluating, to which 'use of technology' was added by Webb in 2002. During pedagogical reasoning, pedagogical content knowledge (PCK) is generated and the crucial process of knowledge transformation occurs during the stages of planning, delivery and evaluation of teaching.

Pedagogical content knowledge refers to a teacher's knowledge about a curriculum area that enables improved teaching of that subject. Further to PCK, the element of 'technology knowledge' was added by Koehler and Mishra in 2005, who introduced the Technological Pedagogical Content Knowledge (TPCK) model. This refers to Content knowledge (C), Pedagogic knowledge (P) and knowledge of Technology (T) and as a model illuminates the dynamic, transactional relationship between knowledge of content, pedagogy and technology. While Koehler and Mishra (2005) argue that teachers can develop TPCK, in particular, greater *technology knowledge* through professional development, Webb (2010: 98) insightfully argues that the 'amount and range of this knowledge makes it unmanageable for individual teachers to achieve a sufficiently comprehensive knowledge set in this domain'.

However, Webb (2010) does provide two solutions to this problem. The first is the development of technical tools to support resource selection, such as digital assistants and search engines. The second concerns reducing the reliance on the knowledge of the individual teacher and enabling pupils to develop their own pedagogical reasoning. Pupils can be encouraged to take responsibility for their own planning and learning through strategies such as AfL 'assessment for learning' (Black and Wiliam 2009). Through feedback from assessment activities learners come to identify what they need to learn (content) and how to learn it (pupil pedagogical reasoning). This Webb (2010) argues is a move to 'distributed pedagogy' where knowledge and pedagogical reasoning in the TPCK model is co-developed and shared between teachers, learners and digital assistants.

Transformation of knowledge in teachers' pedagogical reasoning

Advancements in technology, alongside an increased understanding of pedagogy, following developments in metacognition, have led to a greater appreciation for the processes teachers engage with when conducting pedagogical reasoning (planning, teaching, assessing and evaluation) and the integration of technology into their practice. Crucial in this process is the transformation of knowledge, which occurs with teachers' pedagogical reasoning.

Here the work of Webb (2002, 2004, 2010) has been instrumental in clarifying the complexity of the processes involved and highlights the challenges to teachers when it comes to incorporating technology into practice, since, 'enabling teachers to adapt their pedagogical reasoning and practices in response to learning opportunities provided by technology is likely to be very difficult and complex process' (Webb and Cox 2004: 278). Consequently, the role of professional development is increased.

The knowledge required of the range of technologies and their potential affordances for learning (which are provided by the interactions between the hardware, software, other resources, teachers and other learners) are so vast as to be unwieldy for an individual teacher to maintain a detailed knowledge. Webb (2010) argues this can be supported by a move to 'distributed pedagogies'. For example, pupils are also developing pedagogical reasoning processes as they reflect on their learning and consider how to reach their targets. Similarly, Younie and Leask (2009) argue that the 'technology knowledge' generation required by teachers can be co-constructed through 'distributed professional development' via teachers' online learning communities.

In acknowledging how unmanageable it is for an individual teacher to keep up a working knowledge of technological affordances across an ever-advancing range, we must look to 'distributed' solutions. Teachers working online in distributed networks or teams can share expertise collaboratively and gain appreciation of the affordances of a range of technologies. This will enable teachers to develop appropriate pedagogical strategies, which are only possible when there is an understanding of the various affordances of technologies and how these relate to existing subject knowledge regarding the concepts, processes and skills of specific disciplines.

In understanding the processes that teachers engage with when incorporating technology into professional practice, the research indicates that the technologies most likely to be assimilated are those that match with existing pedagogies (Dwyer et al. 1991; Higgins et al. 2005; Somekh 2007). The most important finding of Veen's (1993) research on factors supporting technology use was that if the software matched the teachers' pedagogy they used it. This is corroborated by Agalianos et al. (2001: 488), who discovered that LOGO was 'more easily assimilated where it fitted with existing practice and caused no substantial changes in content or pedagogy'. Stronach et al. (2001) identified 'ecologies of practice', which referred to teachers' preferred teaching styles. These are put under pressure with changes such as technological innovations and it is the case that technology fits better with some with 'ecologies of practice' rather than others – for example, interactive whiteboards and whole-class teaching.

Hall and Hord (1987) provided a 'Concerns Based Adoption Model' (CBAM) of technology use that emphasized that it is more likely to occur when it is perceived to address the teacher's personal concerns. If we take concerns to be both cognitive and affective, then there is the belief that the technology is aligned to the view of learning. So, how do beliefs about teaching affect the use of technology? Teachers' beliefs about technology play an important role in shaping use and affects whether technology is used as a 'servant' to reinforce existing pedagogy or as a 'partner' to change the way teachers and learners interact with each other and the learning activities (Goos et al. 2003 in Webb and Cox 2004: 258).

Transforming pedagogy with technology

Rather than slipping into existing pedagogies, there is a need to transform and change pedagogy itself. Developments in technology provide new affordances for learning, which give rise to new and emergent pedagogies.

What can technology offer? Technology can offer alternative formats and approaches to teaching and learning that go beyond routine classroom activities. It has the potential to change pedagogy, to transcend the instructional paradigm and move outside a transmission model of learning. Technology can be a catalyst for changing the roles of teachers and learners; it can be used to instigate interaction (talk), collaboration (shared outcomes), higher-order skills (problem-solving) and support creativity.

Technology can support creativity in the sense of learners creating original products with personal meaning. What the technologies allow is the transformation of artefacts, texts, sounds, images, which involve authenticity and control. Similarly, shifts towards higher-order thinking can be supported by technology. For example, computers can carry out routine procedures (datalogging), freeing up learners to focus on higher-order skills of synthesis and analysis. Technology also has the potential to increase interactivity between learner and technology, learner and learner, learner and teacher, where *learner-inquiry* is enhanced – as envisaged in the 'conversational framework' through multimedia software with built-in narrative structures (Laurillard 1993), and dialogic learning with interactive whiteboards (Mercer et al. 2010).

Crucial to such deployment of technology is the way teachers change their roles. Hammond et al.'s (2009) research with innovative practitioners found technology often led teachers to re-think their roles, by freeing teachers up:

> . . . it takes responsibility away from the teacher of having to keep everything going. You no longer have to run round spinning plates. You can give [learners] much more freedom knowing that their interactions with the technology will keep them on task better, so then the job becomes, still inspiring them . . . but having a different kind of context where you really can teach in different ways and you really can change the roles radically of students.
>
> (Hammond et al. 2009: 88)

Table 5.2 Transforming pedagogy with technology

How technology affects:	Potential changes include:
Teacher role – decrease in: teacher direction and exposition, whole-class instruction	Teacher as facilitator – probe thinking, scaffold reflection, guide to useful resources, stimulate debate, reframe
Pupil role – change to learner centred enquiry	Learner control, decision making, self-regulation
Creativity – by supporting authenticity and learner control	Create products, transform artefacts – texts, sounds, images
Interaction – by increasing dialogue, talk, communication	Learner – technology, learner–learner, learner–teacher
Collaboration – cooperation, team work	Working together on a shared product, joint outcome
Higher-order thinking – problem solving	Metacognition, synthesis, analysis, evaluation

Table 5.3 The relationship between technology, application and theory of learning (adapted from Hammond et al. 2009: 89)

TECHNOLOGY Technology offers:	APPLICATION And supports desirable application by involving:	THEORY OF LEARNING – how learning is conceptualized. This is because:
Support for creativity; focus on higher order thinking	A challenge, going beyond the routine, giving element of control to learner	Knowledge is personal, it is about making personal meaning; learner-control and self-regulation
Support for creativity	Doing something the learner would find purposeful	Making meaning requires purposeful activity; learner-led inquiry, decision making
Changing role of teacher, providing alternative means of explaining and clarifying	Going beyond what is taught and how it is taught	Knowledge is unbounded
Focus on higher order thinking; support for talk and collaboration	Communication, interaction, dialogue	Knowledge is not acquired spontaneously, it requires reflection; dialogic learning

These affordances of the technology facilitate learner-centred pedagogical approaches supported by constructivist theories of learning, where learning is conceptualized as a search for meaning in which knowledge is developed through scaffolded reflection and purposeful activity.

In moving beyond routinized practices and changing traditional teacher–pupil roles, technology can transform pedagogy. Table 5.2 provides further information about how pedagogies can be transformed with technology. Also, the following articulation by Hammond et al. (2009) as outlined in Table 5.3 is useful in illustrating the relationship between the applications of technology and theories of learning. Given the potential for technology to transform pedagogy, with its concomitant range of affordances, it is worth reflecting on how this can be achieved in practice.

Applications to practice

Following over 20 years research, Somekh (2007) developed a 'Generic Pedagogic Framework' for teachers to incorporate technology into their classroom activities. The following case study is an example of transforming pedagogy with technology, from the project 'Developing Pedagogies with E-Learning Resources' (PELRS) (Somekh 2007). Working with researchers, teachers and learners in technology-rich schools, Somekh asked the question: 'could we organise teaching and learning in radically different ways now that we have digital technologies?' The project developed strategies to change the traditional role of teachers and learners. By assigning new roles, the project established 'prototype innovatory practices'

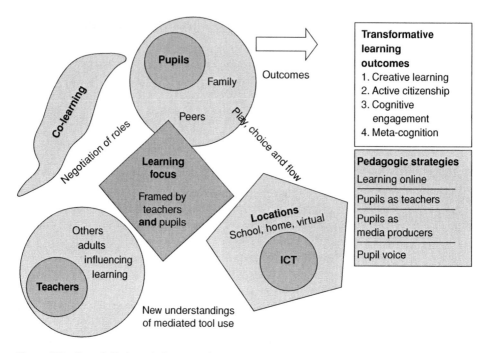

Figure 5.2 Generic Pedagogic Framework

(Somekh 2010: 137), which are represented in the Generic Pedagogic Framework that was developed, as outlined in Figure 5.2.

Teachers reading this may wish to consider Somekh's 'Generic Pedagogic Framework' and reflect how this could be developed in relation to their practice. Table 5.4 provides a framework for teacher's self-analysis of professional practice.

Table 5.4 The role of technology in pedagogic practice: a framework for self-analysis of professional practice

---

Points for teachers to consider when reflecting on practice:

– to what extent can technology support existing teaching/pedagogic strategies already used in the classroom?

– to what extent can technology transform existing pedagogy and enable new things?

– how can teaching and learning be organized in radically different ways?

Research (Webb and Cox 2004) indicates that teachers who favour technology are more likely to value collaborative working, interaction, inquiry and learner-centred approaches.

Teachers may wish to think about these questions:

– how to incorporate more opportunities for interaction in lessons (between learner and learner, learner/s and technology, learner/s and teacher?)

– how to develop more dialogic, collaborative group work and problem-solving activities?

Teacher's beliefs, knowledge about technology and theories of learning

Research shows that teacher's beliefs, knowledge about technology, and theories of learning affect their use of technology. In considering the relevance of technologies to their subject area, teachers may wish to:

- think about how their pupils learn and critically reflect on the underlying theories that influence their work, and
- review their beliefs in light of new evidence regarding opportunities technology affords for learning.

Teacher's technology knowledge

A challenge for teachers is to know how to keep up to date. All teachers need to know how to:

- find out about technology innovations and what other teachers are doing with technology in their subject/age phase
- locate the latest knowledge about the affordances of a range of technologies related to their teaching and subject areas
- contact their professional/subject association for further information on using technology to enhance learning in their curriculum area
- find what other professional development networks they can join to facilitate developing a more detailed knowledge of technology for learning.

Conclusions

With respect to developing technology knowledge, teachers need to understand the capabilities of a range of technologies. It is not enough to know about a range of technologies, in and for themselves. What teachers need to understand is how these technologies interact with, and provide opportunities for, learning. It is the relationship of the technology to the wider learning environment, which consists of other resources, learners and teachers. It is the totality of the environment and ways of organizing interaction with technology in that environment that gives rise to new affordances for learning (Webb 2010). This requires teachers to develop a much deeper understanding of technology capabilities if they are to be used effectively. However, 'enabling teachers to adapt their pedagogical reasoning and practices in response to learning opportunities provided by technology is likely to be very difficult and complex process' (Webb and Cox 2004: 278). Consequently, the role of professional development is increased, making it necessary to look at distributed cognition, situated learning and communities of practice in order to understand how teachers develop new knowledge about technology for pedagogic practice.

Further reading

Mishra, P. and Koehler, M. J. (2006) Technological Pedagogical Content Knowledge: A Framework for Teacher Knowledge, *Teachers College Record Volume,* 108(6): 1017–54.

Webb, M. E. and Cox, M. J. (2004) A review of Pedagogy related to ICT, *Technology, Pedagogy and Education,* 13(3): 235–86.

Useful websites

Naace – http://www.naace.co.uk/

The National Association for the Advancement of Computers in Education (Naace) is the professional subject association for ICT in schools. Naace offers teachers professional development and administers the ICT Mark for schools, supported by The Department for Education.

Vital – http://www.vital.ac.uk/

Vital provides professional development for teachers from The Open University, with funding from the Department for Education. It aims to help practitioners use technology to add value to lessons and find new ways to engage learners.

6   Whole school development, change and leadership

Overview

Research shows time and time again that unless the leadership of an organization is open to the use of technologies to support learning then change will not become embedded in practice (Hargreaves and Hopkins 1991; Lawson and Comber 1999; 2004; Leask 2001).

Research undertaken over 25 years into the adoption of technologies in schools in the UK and across Europe (Leask 2011) shows the key role that national leadership plays in moving practice in schools forward across a country.

When the Internet first became widely available to schools in the mid-1990s, Leask and Younie (2000) found that schools in European countries with strong supportive national leadership were able to move ahead quickly in developing new practices, while in other countries practice in the adoption of new technologies was inhibited by the absence of national leadership and lack of support for the change and of resource allocation. Individual schools may innovate, but they do not have the remit or resources to disseminate new practice to others on a national scale. The findings from the research mentioned above (regarding how to bring about national change) indicate that central governments have a responsibility to support, but not to direct innovation. The passage of time since the early research has shown that innovation can be crushed when centrally driven change takes a conservative turn. England provides an interesting case study in this respect, having moved from the existence of a government agency, Becta, driving leading-edge practice in technologies in education with the full support of the government in power from 1997 to 2010 to, within months of a change of government, Becta being the first government agency to be closed down and the educational resources and evidence banks built up to support practice being removed from government websites. Such websites included Teacher Training Resource Bank, Teachernet, Multi-verse, Behaviour for Learning, the Qualifications and Curriculum Development Agency resources and the General Teaching Council in England's resources. Both the latter agencies were also closed down. The speed of removal of any incentives to innovate through the closure of the leading national agencies supporting innovations, and the removal of case studies and research and evidence from successful innovators on the aforementioned websites

provides a memorable lesson about the fragility of innovations and the need for support from national governments to support continuation. In England educators will
need to develop independent professional bodies which support and publish innovation to avoid such a scenario occurring again.

Introduction and context

Understanding change management is essential for school leaders who wish to innovate. Developing a high degree of political awareness will help school leaders understand the level of innovation that their stakeholders are prepared to tolerate.

For example, in England there was a history of rapid change in expectations
about the use of technologies in schools before the demise of government agencies
as outlined above. With the establishment of the first national ICT strategy in 1997,
education policy on technology in the UK required schools to implement a technical
infrastructure to support virtual learning environments and to integrate technology
across the curriculum. Government investment was around £3.65 billion (Doughty
2006) with a further £639.5 million (Becta 2010a) invested in the years following
2006. The Harnessing Technology strategy (Becta 2008a) published priority guidelines for schools, which included improving learning services, such as learning platforms and email, and the provision of more high-quality digital learning resources
for schools.

Research evidence from this innovative period showed the greatest improvements to learning occurred when technology was used across the curriculum and
not just delivered in discrete subjects (ImpacT2 2002). This demonstrates the need
for technology implementation to occur at the whole-school level, with a holistic
approach from senior leaders. More recent corroborating evidence from Becta (2010a)
can be seen in the connection between e-maturity of a school's processes and school
performance. E-maturity describes 'an organization's readiness to deal with e-learning
and the degree to which this is embedded in the curriculum' (Underwood 2010: 24).
Robust evidence can be cited of a relationship between e-maturity and school performance showing that individual performance was correlated to e-maturity.

Theory and research base

This chapter draws on research conducted over the past 25 years that has examined
the diffusion of innovations, making it possible to understand technology implementation as part of a process of diffusion; the research has also investigated the role
of leadership in embedding technology into schools, as part of a whole-school process; then, research which has analysed the relationship between subject cultures and
technology, since it is known that curriculum subjects have appropriated technology
in different ways and to varying levels.

Engaging staff in change

When it comes to change, it is known that the most effective place to start is with teachers. Advice to leaders about creating a general vision for the direction of a school is that it is best practice to involve all staff (DES 1989; Hargreaves and Hopkins 1991).

However, in the case of embedding digital technologies in the functioning of an organization or department where expertise in new practices may not be held within the whole staff body, an incremental approach appears more effective (Younie 2007; Kington et al. 2001).

This means that effective practice needs first to be demonstrated as working by leading practitioners. Others can then follow and adapt these models to meet their circumstances. OECD ICT for school improvement research (Kington et al. 2001) showed that Roger's Theory of the Diffusion of Innovations (2003) operates effectively in schools which are integrating digital technologies into practice. Roger's theory operates on the basis that, with respect to capacity and willingness to innovate, staff can be divided into five types – innovators, early adopters, early majority, late majority and laggards.

'Innovators' are staff who see the potential of an innovation and will test out ideas without being discouraged by barriers – they develop and demonstrate through their practice the proof of concept of the innovation. They are, however, too far ahead of other staff in their thinking and practice for the majority of staff to be able to follow their lead.

When 'early adopters' who are senior and respected staff adopt the ideas of the innovators into their practice, then the bulk of staff (the early majority) will start to follow this lead. Staff in the 'late majority' category are likely to require some incentives to change practice, and staff performance reviews can play a valuable role in setting requirements for such staff to adopt certain practices. The staff group making up the 'laggards' require special attention and support to change practice. In the UK-based OECD research, the 'laggards' left innovating schools to find schools where such new practices were not demanded. Leask, who was the UK lead for the OECD research, has subsequently applied this theory successfully to a national change-management initiative – the introduction of *Facebook*-type online communities environment for local government (Leask 2011): innovators developed a proof of concept, demonstrating how working online could be more effective than not working online, and managers soon adopted the approach and required all staff in what was a central government agency to adopt this way of working with their national networks. Chapter 9 provides information about the theories concerning the motivating of staff to adopt new practices.

School leadership and technology

Lawson and Comber (1999, 2004) made a strong case for recognizing the relationship between integrating technology and effective leadership.

Schools that had effectively integrated technology were identified as having a common feature, notably leaders who had promoted an ethos that embraced technological change. Whole-school support was signalled by leaders via school technology policy, often: '. . . it was exemplified by a long-term view of investment in technology in a climate of innovation and the recognition of the efforts of those involved in promoting good practice with technology in the school . . .' (Lawson and Comber 2004: 145).

However, the shortage of heads with technology expertise was recognized as a 'stumbling block' in innovation. This recognition led to Becta and NCSL creating The Strategic Leadership of Technology (SLICT) professional development programme, which focused on developing effective strategic leadership skills for technology integration across the school.

Lawson and Comber (1999) identified *leadership* as a key factor in moving towards what they term the 'integrative' school, through 'the knowledgeable and enthusiastic involvement of the head teacher who is capable of promoting a *school ethos* that embraces technological change' (Comber and Hingley 2004: 2). NAACE (2001) acknowledged a supportive head as critical to the integration of technology. However, as Comber and Lawson (2003) and Earley et al. (2002) highlight, such leaders were in relatively short supply, certainly until the advent of SLICT, which was precisely what SLICT sought to address.

Sherry and Gibson (2002) argue that innovative or integrative technology practice will remain an isolated phenomenon, restricted to individual classrooms or departments, if the support of leaders is absent or withheld. Clearly, leaders who support technology engender a school ethos that facilitates the implementation of technology. This highlights the importance of school culture, which was found to be a significant factor that shaped the outcome of previous technological innovations.

While the school improvement literature has recognized the importance of leadership, it is only more recently that leadership has become recognized as a major factor regarding the integration of technology in schools (Lawson and Comber 2004; Preston 2004; Younie 2007).

The school context: the impact of subject cultures on using technology

A further criticism of research to date is that teacher development and use of technology has been mainly conceptualized at the level of the individual teacher. There is nominal awareness in some research of the importance of *school culture* and the issue of *collegiality*, particularly at *departmental* level. This is specifically an issue for secondary schools with the existence of specialized curriculum subjects.

One important factor in how technology is perceived and used by teachers is the 'community of practice' associated with their subject. 'Each subject community could be said to share a set of tools and resources; approaches to teaching and learning; curriculum practices; cultural values, expectations and aims' (Hennessy, Ruthven and Brindley 2002: 3).

Hennessy et al. (2002) argue that there has been little research analysing how and why subject cultures affect teachers' use of technology differently. The cited exceptions are Goodson and Mangan (1995) in Canada and Selwyn (1999a) in the UK. The former found that technology can colonize some curriculum areas, whereby the subject subculture co-opts and utilizes computer technology, whereas for some subjects there may be little colonization.

This argument is followed by Selwyn (1999a), who asserts that the computer is more congruent with some subject histories and more easily integrated into practice than with others. Traditionally computers were the domain of Maths, Science and Technology departments, and this legacy may account for the ways in which different subject areas employ computers. Subject cultures are an important influence in explaining teachers' differential level of technology integration.

In 2002 Hennessy, Ruthven and Brindley noted that many 'teachers' commitment to incorporating technology was tempered by a cautious, critical approach to harnessing its potential' wherein only 'a gradual process of pedagogic evolution appeared to be taking place' (Hennessy et al. 2002: 1).

Selwyn (1999a) argued that the computer is less congruent with some subject cultures and histories, and interestingly 'resistance' is again raised as an explanation, which refers to the culture of the subject and how this shapes teachers' practice.

Consequently, to conclude from the research, the barriers to using technology for *subject teaching* included: a subject culture's resistance to technology; teachers' lack of confidence, experience, motivation, time and training; lack of adequate access to technology and timetabled use of dedicated technology suites; unreliability of equipment; and pressure to conform to curriculum and assessment demands. These contingencies provide an array of explanatory factors to account for differing levels of technology implementation across secondary school subjects (Younie 2007). Further detailed information about barriers to adoption of technology is provided in later chapters.

Criticisms of the subject-specific analysis

The weakness of analysis at the level of curriculum subject departments is that it fails to explain how it is that some subject departments have greatly integrated technology in some schools, while in other schools the very same subjects have not managed to integrate technology. For example, how it is that some science departments have fully embedded technology, while other science departments do not engage with technology for subject teaching? It cannot be the subject alone that accounts for technology use and pedagogic integration. However, analysis can be offered at the level of 'a community of shared practice' – that is, teacher habits and culture at department level – rather than the specific subject taught within those departments (Younie 2007). Motivating staff to change beliefs, attitudes and practices to adopt new practices with technologies is a key challenge of school leaders (see Chapter 9).

Applications to practice

A Futures Education research project funded by Becta and undertaken by Leask and Preston (2010) brought together leading innovative teachers with a view to synthesizing existing knowledge about effective practice in the adoption of and use of innovative technologies in schools. The following applications to practice section draws on this advice from teachers recognized as leading innovators with technology.

Leadership, technology and change: the challenges facing teachers/practitioners

Leaders need to ensure there is a shared vision for the use of technologies to support learning and that barriers to appropriate use are recognized (see Chapter 9). There is considerable literature on planning for school development. Hargreaves and Hopkins (1991) provide an introductory text to those unfamiliar with how to engage whole staff in planning school development. The vision should address the use of technology for

- administration, accountability and monitoring
- communication within and beyond the school
- pedagogy
- the deployment and development of human and material resources.

Choice of appropriate technology tools is a key role of school management. It is easy to spend money on developing and implementing tools for administration, accountability and monitoring. There is potential to collect endless amounts of data – but to what end? Any data collected need to be for a clear purpose and to be used.

Table 6.1 summarizes advice to school leaders about the characteristics of effective technology-based tools and digital resources used to support administration, accountability and monitoring from the research undertaken by Leask and Preston (2010). The information in the table provides a management tool for checking that investments meet the standards defined by leading teachers.

Table 6.1 Characteristics of effective technology-based tools which support curriculum administration, accountability and monitoring

Characteristic	Tools should:

Pedagogical characteristics	• support formative assessment and improving learning rather than focusing on summative outcomes: i.e. the technology should support the processes of learning rather than just recording the outcomes of learning
	 • not just focus on target-led approaches and measurable outcomes. Subject specific assessment tools should not be abstract but should include applications to the real world.
	 • enable more generalized thinking and higher-order skills development
	 • ensure exchange of data with a variety of devices by:
	  – linking with e-portfolios – enabling teachers to easily record and monitor learners' progress: for example, in recording evidence for the areas of achievement enabling learners to upload e-portfolio material
	  – linking with PDAs which are used for recording learner progress data: e.g. observation data
	  – providing hyperlinks between assessment evidence and grades
	  – dealing with digital data: for example, videos

Characteristic	Tools should:

Design characteristics	• support communication between stakeholders, by
	  – being open to scrutiny by learners, teachers, parents and management
	  – supporting blogging to engage and interact with parents and learners
	  – being intuitive to use
	  – being easily updatable by whole school/college workforce
	  – sending alerts
	• be simple and strongly visual e.g. outliers on graphs should be highlighted, using a traffic-light system when learners are falling behind or achieving well to enable target setting and half-termly reporting
	• provide immediate access and updates, by
	  – providing feedback to learners and teachers on demand
	  – identifying irregular attendance patterns and communicating this to teachers and parents
	  – being updatable quickly by the whole school/college workforce in response to events

Technical characteristics	• provide one tool with multiple functions, and for multiple purposes e.g. OFSTED, school/college, formative and summative needs. One teacher reported having to work with four different systems.
	• be comprehensive – provide management of all pupil data: e.g. SEN, medical, child protection
	• be Web-based – access has to be Web-based for parents and whole-school/college workforce access
	• be robust – 'one crash and everyone loses faith'
	• be secure – 'one loss of privacy and everyone loses faith'
	• be flexible – with high standards of interoperability between commonly used packages – e.g. homework information on the learning platforms – should be linked with homework returns by email and alerts about homework missed
	• allow staff appropriate access
	  – there are different levels of access depending on 'need to know'
	  – teachers need easy access to learner data useful for lesson planning.

In choosing e-tools to support administration, accountability and monitoring, care also needs to be taken to ensure:

- Pursuit of data does not replace discussions between teachers and learners about progress: . . . ticking boxes means a lot of qualitative information is now lost . . . formerly teachers would meet at the year's end to discuss the progress of individual learners and rich information would be passed on. Now the focus is on data, which ticks other people's boxes rather than meeting the needs of the teachers and, more important, the learners'. A child must not be reduced to a set of targets (Leask and Preston 2010: 24).

- Software which just gives numerical data to schools/colleges does not help assessment for learning approaches.
- care needs to be taken to limit the volume of data collected to that which can be used.

Using e-tools for communications between people within and outside the school/college

Institutions need a communications strategy to ensure effective and managed use of tools for communication within and beyond the school.

Leask and Preston (2010) report a variety of ways in which technology-based tools were used to facilitate communication both within the organization, and between the organization and the wider community. Undeveloped opportunities for technology tools to support knowledge sharing and building between education colleagues and the wider communities their organizations serve were identified in this research. For example, teachers identified potential for new collaborations between school staff and subject experts and specialists through e-networking as well as schools/colleges and other services or agencies with responsibility for children and young people. But barriers to communicating with technology-based tools were also identified:

- Schools/colleges in competition with others may not want to share resources with other schools/colleges, which may be competing for pupils/students. Local authorities in England have tried setting up cluster-based networks and have found this a problem because of competition between schools for pupils.
- The availability and inter-operability of learning platforms and tools depend on local authorities and broadband consortia.
- There are ethical problems:
  - learning platforms: staff and parents have concerns about pupils' photos appearing online even if their profile is in a password-protected section. Protocols with respect to pupil information, ethical use, access, storage need to be established.
  - there is anxiety about public/private personas – e.g. teachers having social networking accounts, which can be accessed by parents and pupils and the need for positive representation of the individuals, and the organization.
- Parents without Internet or mobile phones are excluded from these forms of communication. There are issues with poverty, culture, religions and skills as well as physical access.
- Professional networking online is not part of the culture for many current teachers.

- Joint projects with other countries depend on the school's technological infrastructure. Even in Europe, schools/colleges technology provision is unreliable and in developing countries it may be more unreliable.
- Access to relevant professional networks: the forums relevant to individual teachers are scattered in too many different places, making it hard for teachers to keep up with or find relevant discussions.

Leask and Preston (2010) report teachers' concern that the digital divide is widening. For some families, poverty is the issue; for others a lack of the level of literacy needed to access the Internet is the barrier, as it is still text-based in the main.

A majority of learners who do have computers at home only use them for information retrieval, so creative tasks, collaborative networking and publication are not in their repertoire.

Teachers' engagement in the digital culture is also variable. Teachers may work in a pedagogical climate driven by a 'tick box' approach to education. This appears to generate a mechanistic approach to technology among teachers which prevents further exploration of creative technology uses. The emphasis on teaching tools – for example, interactive whiteboards rather than learning with and through technology – appears to lead to a distortion in the ways in which the resources are being used. School leaders will wish to check pedagogical strategies for the use of technology in the school to ensure teachers are not just focusing on short-term and low-level uses of technology rather than more challenging applications.

One model of pedagogy uses technology for low-level information dissemination rather than offering creative opportunities for learning beyond the classroom.

Leask and Preston (2010) reported that, while the introduction of learning platforms has led to opportunities for connections between staff, students, parents and other stakeholders, there are barriers to uptake which in many institutions need to be addressed.

These include:

- confusion in senior management teams about who should be in control of the platform: administration, senior management or curriculum specialists?
- inappropriate interactions taking place on social networking sites including incidents of cyber-bullying
- new learners who arrive in the middle of sessions from countries or cultures where they do not have technology resources and the same easy access to the Internet
- a culture of individualism and a reluctance to share resources between staff members
- the creation of materials for supporting teaching that can be disproportionately time consuming
- the danger that, when resources are uploaded to the system, some teachers will become ossified in their use of them
- a minority of teachers not wanting to share their work with others
- an individual using a memory stick to remove data from the system

- learners bringing homework in on memory sticks might introduce viruses and prohibited devices into school/college systems
- senior management being concerned about the risk of losing confidential data to mobile devices
- a lack of skilled facilitators deterring learners in collaborative environments
- learning environments that are not appropriate for collaboration
- poor design of e-resources for CPD
- poor understanding of online pedagogy reflected in the design.

For some teachers searching the internet is a significant barrier to the up-take of digital technologies.

This group:

- resent the time it takes to find relevant materials in Web-based searches
- are disorientated by their lack of knowledge.

School leaders making decisions about a school's policy for the use of technology may find the information in Tables 6.2 and 6.3 helpful in guiding decisions. The tables list the characteristics of effective technology-based tools and how they aid communication within and beyond the institution.

Table 6.2 Characteristics of effective digital tools and resources used for communication

Characteristic	Example
Pedagogical characteristics	effectiveness of any tools depends largely on the people who use the tools
	tools should facilitate collaboration between teachers and learner for joint projects and support for inter-school/college and inter-country projects such as wikis, professional networking
	online courses should expect and stimulate collaboration
Design characteristics	tools need to be flexible and able to be adapted for different uses: e.g. tools should be able to be added to learning platforms
	tools should be easy to use, cheap, free, accessible to all, receptive to different formats such as Skype, mobile phones, wifi hotspots, social networking, videoconferencing
	software needs to be intuitive
Technical characteristics	tools need to be fit for purpose e.g. supporting asynchronous and synchronous communication
	time-saving efficiencies need to be apparent: e.g. group call enables parents to receive messages on their mobiles; a service alerting parents to events provides clear added value
	tools should support wireless networking/cloud computing

Table 6.3 How technology-based tools and digital resources help communication within and beyond the institution

How technology tools help	Example
Communication with peers in other schools/colleges and school/college staff	• use of Outlook calendar instead of bulletins, sharing calendars is helpful for school/college trips • email is the best tool we have (but some staff do not look at email). Twitter helps 'just-in-time learning' • finding schools/colleges for projects: e.g. through e-Pals for curriculum projects • forums and discussion groups, are good but there are too many in different places • email to staff and other schools/colleges can save time if not over used
Teaching and whole-class and group learning – personalizing learning	• PDAs and tablet devices used for individual group work • mobile phones and voting technology • easy to find, accessible, user friendly, immediate, targeted communications, use of video clips (small size is important) scaffolding learning • IWBs and visualizers have changed the ways teachers are teaching. Learners are more likely to share and comment on each other's work and the quality of their evaluations is better • showcasing learners' work through plasma screens and through the website is motivating for learners • live video streaming e.g. showing live artists working • integrating digital photos into reports of visits or school/college guides is motivating learners to write and work together • discussion can be held online and then revisited and reflected upon whereas a class discussion might not be remembered
Administration	• all learners' education plans are on the system and staff update these online this saves time
CPD – formal and informal – saves time	• video clips for demonstrators, mini-clips • able to share resources via the learning platform by placing handouts and documents about the use of technology on the VLE • access to courses and 'how to' resources

Communication with parents

Leask and Preston (2010) reported that there are few communication channels which do not rely on technology and that, while some primary schools/colleges had a preference for face-to-face communication with parents, others had well-developed e-communication systems. Sensitivity of the information and parity of access to technology mean that schools/colleges cannot replace all non-technology channels of communication with technological ones.

Communication with learners

For some learners technology is a barrier, and paper-based methods work better. This problem needs to be recognized and dealt with.

Teacher-to-teacher communication outside the school/college

Because of the isolated nature of specialists in schools and colleges, opportunities to meet and network with colleagues with similar responsibilities are valued and are invaluable for the sharing of practice. The costs of face-to-face meetings can be high, particularly in rural areas. Opportunities for online CPD are under-developed. Online discussions and blogs, while they can never fully replace face-to-face contact, do have a role to play, and some professional associations are providing online services to support this.

Teachers contributing to the Leask and Preston (2010) research cautioned senior leaders against relying too much on e-communications. Effective ways of working without technology which they wanted retained include:

- pastoral care and CPD from outside the school/college including support from expert practitioners
- coaching triads
- CPD that involves other schools/colleges
- briefings (which are better face to face than in email)
- pigeon holes: these should be used for some form of communication rather than email. One teacher reported that in the time taken to reply with one email, a teacher can deal with 10 pieces of information on paper
- 'coffee machine conversations': these are difficult to replicate online (although focus group members using Twitter say this fulfils this purpose)
- 'off the record' chats: these are important, since more emotive issues are best dealt with face to face; anonymous suggestions can be collected – for example, in a box
- 'issues groups': these can create ideas and recommendations
- open-door policies: these are good for open discussion of issues.

Learning styles and preferences must be taken into account in choosing communication strategies using technology.

Processes for making decisions to adopt digital tools and resources

Largely because of networking capacity and licensing issues, and depending on the tools, it is now usual for the local authority, headteacher, senior management team or the network manager to make decisions about the adoption of digital tools and resources. Previously, with standalone computers, individual teachers were able to choose resources. Best practice is that teachers are engaged in these decisions.

In adopting major new tools and resources the impact on learning outcomes has to be a first priority. So, an open-minded leadership team is essential if technology use is to develop. The Leask and Preston (2010) research reported that teachers found heads who are not well informed were sometimes easier to work with than those who were better informed, because they hand over more responsibility to the teacher for delivery. Other staff also need to be convinced about the benefits of technology for teaching and learning and brought into the technology selection process. Sometimes it was also appropriate to include governors and local authorities.

Effective in-school/college processes which support decision-making include engaging staff in opportunities to trial and evaluate products, providing opportunities for demonstrations and knowledge transfer from expert users, as well as time to experiment and test out the software.

Embedding new tools and resources into practice

Once decisions are taken, implementation and embedding the tools in practice becomes the next challenge. The length of time taken for new systems to be embedded depends on 'need to do basis' and on the type of tool and its immediacy: that is, the complexity and relevance. So, adoption time could be one week or could be several years.

Factors that were identified in the Leask and Preston (2010) research as helping embedding are listed in Table 6.4.

New e-tools have to be interoperable, and standardized. Training has to allow teachers time to play. The best way to embed new tools into professional practice in the school/college is teachers seeing the tools in operation improving teaching and learning. Chapters 5 and 9 provide further information about staff development.

Table 6.4 Factors that help embed digital tools and resources in practice

Familiarity	pedagogical support	training including on the job training and informal peer training
Sharing of good practice and open minds	school/college ethos	ways in which teachers can share what they are doing with others
Technical support	security sorted	pre-release issues sorted such as data protection
Funding	compulsion	strong management
Teachers seeing immediate benefits in supporting their everyday work	IWBs	pragmatism and reduction of work load – the new technology helps people do essential jobs better

Technical support is also an important element in embedding tools alongside teachers' competence and confidence. Teachers should not be expected to manage and maintain equipment.

Learning platforms are useful in extending the teachers' range of pedagogic approaches seamlessly as long as the design is flexible and adaptable.

There are, however, a number of factors hindering implementation – the key one being the assessment system. If the ability to demonstrate technology-tool use as appropriate across subject areas was a required part of the assessment system, then adoption and implementation would be accelerated.

Those choosing technologies to support learning are advised to consider the key factors hindering the embedding of digital tools in practice as set out in Table 6.5.

Less important factors that teachers identified as hindering embedding tools in practice are listed in Table 6.6 in no particular order.

Effective use of staff time

A critical factor supporting the successful adoption of technologies in schools is the impact on staff time. Who should enter the data from pupil assessments? If teachers are entering data, this leaves less time to be spent on learners' issues.

Improving the transferability of pupil data between schools was raised as an issue by teachers contributing to the Leask and Preston Education Futures research (2010). These concerns were around:

- data that do not provide the next school with enough information about the learners themselves, where they are up to and what they need to do next
- the variability of data between different feeder schools
- the variable data needs of different secondary schools/colleges
- the inordinate volume of data collected, making it increasingly difficult to gain a meaningful overview as well as a useful picture of the individual learner.

Leask and Preston (2010) found factors that inhibited teachers from mastering adequately the knowledge and practice required from complex administration, accountability and monitoring tools included the following:

- coping with 24/7 access
- finding time to learn new processes and programs
- incompatibility with home systems
- appropriate levels of access
- the complexities of converting data.

Other concerns were the need to:

- back up data, offsite storage of data – security issues/data protection
- operate safely and remain within the law

Table 6.5 Major factors that hinder embedding digital tools and resources in practice (Leask and Younie 2001; Leask and Preston 2010)

Factor	Impact
National assessment systems	There is a dilemma which teachers face in high accountability systems where it is directly measurable results which count. Learners may benefit considerably from extra-curricular activities but if these are not counted in a culture where that which is measurable is that which counts, then pupils are losers. Too much emphasis on measurement of individual parts of learning rather than the whole learning experience is a feature of such systems; and attainment is valued over achievement. Teachers contributing to the Leask and Preston (2010) research asked: 'Surely technology-based resources could be developed which allow more credit to be given to a range of outcomes which encourage learners to explore, accumulate, reflect and demonstrate in a range of forms?'
Transferable skills aid adoption of new systems	The capacity to change tools depends on similarity to previous systems so schools/colleges can hit the ground running and so that pedagogical applications are known.
Filtering systems	Filtering systems often prevent access to educationally beneficial applications – teachers suggest the philosophy should be: 'educate for responsibility rather than ban and block (Leask and Preston 2010). Filtering policies vary between local authorities and are reported as a major constraint in innovation. It seems that filtering systems are perceived as excessively rigorous and are causing teachers and learners to work outside the system just to use applications which are now considered part of the toolkit of Web users. A transparent code of practice providing a base line for good practice together with a rationale for this is needed. Some Local Authorities (LAs) restrict the use of equipment for personal use – e.g. a laptop cannot be used at home for Facebook, Hotmail or booking trips – even if these uses are school/college related. Some LAs block website access so that online resources such as games which might have an educational application cannot be accessed.
Lack of demonstrable pedagogical benefit	One of the primary education groups for the Leask and Preston (2010), research expressed concern about the value of learning platforms in the primary school and considered it will be a long time before they are accepted. There are concerns about maintenance and technical aspects of keeping them running – plus the skills needed for creating the tools. It was considered the money might be better spent elsewhere and the question: 'where are the pedagogical claims backed by evidence?' was asked. 'Just because a technology exists does not mean it is going to be useful for schools/colleges of all types'. The value of learning platforms for secondary schools/colleges was acknowledged by participants in this research.

Table 6.6 Other factors that hinder embedding digital tools and resources in practice

Factor	How it is demonstrated
Staff issues	• staff attitudes: age of staff, people's preparedness to change • availability of the skills needed to maximize the impact of the tools • lack of time for teachers to become pedagogically confident • lack of CPD: lack of support post implementation • teacher pedagogic style: sometimes teachers resist the locus of power transferring from teachers to learners. Some teachers find it difficult to understand that learners can discover knowledge for themselves as well as 'infecting' other learners with enthusiasm
Technical issues including reliability	• security e.g. the more mobile, the more likely it is to be stolen • interoperability • reliability – increased workload and duplication of effort because the technology cannot be trusted to work 100% of the time • ability to download is not always available for free products – because of filters • potential for subversion of the system e.g. learners swapping swipe cards around • lack of teaching experience of those who write software • compatibility of resources between schools/colleges, home and universities
School/college management issues	• ethics, for example, issues over biometric data and security, the terms under which it is stored, civil liberties issues, future use of data issues: e.g. fingerprint identification • the lack of culture of use of technologies for internal communications • accountability – loss of evidence trail and concerns over security and privacy: ensuring all parents have given permission for pupils to be photographed and videoed. If there is one child in the classroom whose parents have not given permission then this restricts what technology can be used and how. • health and safety • software management • teachers need to have appropriate hardware and software and be used to using it for example, electronic reporting requires this • lack of joined-up thinking in schools/colleges in different communities • absence of professional culture of sharing • cyber bullying • cost • being risk averse

- generate teacher awareness of issues of confidentiality, and privacy including issues concerning taking data offsite
- discipline those members of staff who tended to 'do their own thing'
- warn teachers who may leave portals open while away from their desk or while at home potentially allowing anyone to access confidential data (the same risk of misuse of data comes from the use of a pen drive to store confidential files).

The *solutions* mooted were:

- the development of protocols/complex caveats around data security and having these agreed by the staff
- a Web-based method of keeping up to date with current legislation and acceptable practice
- advice on managing expectations
- the development of more inter-operable programs
- more access via portals to remove the need for staff to carry data.

Younie (2007) and leask and Preston's (2010) research found that effective CPD is led by subject specialists who are able to demonstrate through their approach good models for practice.

Features of this CPD should be:

- time, appropriate training and support
- peer-to-peer support and professional networking
- departmental organization of CPD
- appropriate materials and online content
- networking and sharing of resources
- ongoing training to acknowledge, encourage and reward progress
- CPD, giving time to experiment with new technology tools and share ideas about applications with other teachers.

Further information about appropriate forms of CPD is provided in Chapter 9.

Uptake of technologies in smaller schools is inhibited by the lack of expertise and staff. Teachers who are technology coordinators in primary schools and who are on call all day, every day, are not best placed to implement learning platforms and other major technologies. They usually have to deal with technical problems, replenishing stock, managing resources, keeping up to date and developing new practice, often while teaching their own class. Solutions to this dilemma include sharing technical staff with other primary schools, secondary schools, private or public organizations nearby and developing parent helpers.

Conclusions

In the course of undertaking research into the effective use of technologies in educational settings over 25 years and in many countries, the authors of this text have time and time again seen huge variations in practice between schools in the same country even where the schools have similar amounts of funding.

The school's leaders play a major role in creating the ethos of the school, and the ethos of a school determines the dominant pedagogical approaches, and the dominant pedagogical approaches influence the allocation of resources.

So, unless senior leaders have a vision for pedagogy within their institution which is underpinned by technology or are prepared to support innovative teachers in the use of technologies to support learning, practice within the school will not incorporate technology.

Individual teachers who wish to work in schools which are innovative in the use of technologies to support learning are advised to ascertain the position of the school leaders with respect to technologies before taking up a post.

Where school leaders want to drive change, they will need to consider the factors inhibiting the adoption of technologies such as those outlined in this chapter, together with theories concerning the management of change and the adoption of innovations. The following chapters will provide more details.

Further reading

Becta [2003] What the Research Says about Whole School Improvement http://portaldo-professor.mec.gov.br/storage/materiais/0000012855.pdf

Kington, A., Harris, S., Lee, B. and Leask, M. (2001) Information and communications technology and whole school improvement: case studies of organizational change, *Education-Line*, September 2001, pp. 1–16. http://www.leeds.ac.uk/educol/documents/00001905.htm

Selwyn, N. (1999a) Differences in Educational Computer Use: The Influence of Subject Cultures, *Curriculum Journal,* 10(1): 29–48.

Useful websites

Becta Self Review Framework – a self-assessment tool for schools to use in assessing and improving their technology use. Although the organization, Becta, no longer exists, the Department for Education has taken over this work.) https://selfreview.becta.org.uk/

Naace – http://www.naace.co.uk. Naace is the subject association that support technology integration in schools. Naace offers the ICT mark for schools, which is a self-assessment tool to help schools assess and improve their technology use.

National College for school leadership (England) – Personalizing learning definition http://www.nationalcollege.org.uk/index/leadershiplibrary/leadingschools/personalizedlearning/about-personalized-learning/what-is-personalized-learning.htm

7 Key classroom principles: across and within subjects and key stages

Overview

This chapter considers the expectations placed on all teachers in state-maintained schools in England to use technology to support their teaching and to maximize pupils' learning. It provides examples and ideas for the use of digital technologies used in different subjects and at different key stages. Through this analysis an expectation of the skills, competences and knowledge of both pupils and teachers in different subject areas is explored and an analytical framework is provided as a self- and institutional analysis tool. This chapter includes a summary table showing different forms of technologies for different curriculum areas.

Introduction and context

Effective practice: using technology for professional purposes

In leading schools, teachers of all phases are expected to be able to use a variety of technologies to support their professional practice (Leask and Pachler 2005). Expectations of their practice include the following:

- For *teaching* and the presentation of ideas and subject content. For example, using the interactive whiteboard and the preparation of learning resources uploaded onto the learning platform.
- For *learning*. Pupil assessment (self, peer and teacher assessment) is normally undertaken regularly and recorded with progress monitored over time and targets set using a range of features of the school's learning platform. In addition to teachers completing records and using data to identify problems with progress, the pupils can access learning-support materials through their networked area on the system and take ownership of their learning.
- For *supporting* a teacher's wider professional roles in school in relation to administration; record keeping and reporting.
- For teachers' *professional development,* which can be supported online through professional networks and specialist subject associations.

Teachers are expected to use technology appropriately to support the teaching and learning process and to use a wide range of particular types of technology – for example, digital cameras, interactive whiteboards, computers – alongside the use of *specialist software* relevant to the subject area – for example, data logging in science. Professional standards for teaching require practitioners to use a combination of hardware and software as deemed fit for purpose to support the teaching of the learning outcomes of the lesson.

Theory and research base

Research continues to show that the effective use of technology in schools to support subject learning and teaching is patchy (Becta 2008a; Harrison et al. 2002; Ofsted 2004). This inconsistency means that, while some teachers use technology effectively to stimulate and expand pupils' learning experiences, others fail to incorporate technology into their pedagogy, thereby losing opportunities to engage and enhance pupils' learning. There is a growing research base of evidence which indicates that, when technology is effectively deployed, pupil motivation and achievement are raised (DfES 2002, 2003; OECD 2007). In such schools teachers can expect to be provided with personal laptops or iPads and to have home and school access to the school's online learning platform and associated devices.

Any planning undertaken by teachers should start from an understanding of how learning takes place – everything that teachers undertake with learners should have this as a foundation (Gardner 2006; Savin-Baden 2007; Wragg 2004). The same applies to the use of technologies in education – the first question the teacher must be able to answer when using technologies is how is this going to help learning. Table 7.1 below repeats the table in the introduction as a reminder to the reader how a deep understanding of learning theories is essential for classroom practitioners. The table summarizes the main learning theories educators need to be aware of today in planning learning with technologies. Further details are available in the texts mentioned in this chapter and in the Learning to Teach in the Secondary School series (Routledge), which covers all main curriculum subjects with a chapter on the use of technologies in each.

Technology and pupil learning

For pupil learning, technology should be used where its use is justified as a method of achieving the stated learning outcomes of any lesson (Bennett and Leask 2005). Becta (2003); Kington et al. (2001); Beetham and Sharpe (2007) and Leask (2001) provide access to a number of reports on the benefits of effective use of technologies. Becta's (2001) list of benefits to pupils of effective use of technology remains comprehensive:

- greater motivation
- increased self-esteem and confidence
- enhanced questioning skills
- promoting initiative and independent learning
- improving presentation

Table 7.1 Theories and approaches to learning

Relevant learning theories	Key ideas	Learning is conceptualized as:
1.1 Constructivism Piaget (1963)	Constructive – individual focus Concerned with how knowledge and skills are internalized Cognitivist Developmental	Learning is conceptualized as individuals actively exploring the world and receiving feedback. Constructivity – is the integration of new concepts and skills into the learner's existing conceptual/competency structures. Pedagogical applications: knowledge building requires interactive environments. Need activities to encourage experimentation and discovery of principles. Need support for reflection and evaluation.
1.2 Social Constructivism Vygotsky (1978)	Constructive – social focus Zone of proximal development Understand learner and scaffolders roles in collaborative activities	Individual learning is scaffolded by the social environment. Teachers/more knowledgeable peers have a key role in dialogue and interaction with the learner; how learners can progress beyond their immediate capability by supportive others scaffolding the learning experience. Pedagogical applications: knowledge building requires interactive environments. Need activities to encourage collaboration and shared expression of ideas/dialogic approach. Need support for reflection, peer-review and evaluation.
1.3 Communal Constructivism (Leask and Younie 2001) Holmes et al. (2001)	Social constructivism – dialogic learning **with** technology Situated learning and distributed cognition, using digital technologies for social/professional online networking for knowledge management	Social theories of learning (peer-to-peer knowledge construction) and the affordances of digital technologies (to create, share and build new knowledge online together; **with** and **for** each other) Learning is conceptualized as collaboratively co-creating knowledge, through cooperative, peer-to-peer, informal learning and interaction, using digital technology.
1.4 Situated Learning Lave and Wenger (1991)	Communities of practice Situative CPD Work-based learning Situated learning	Learning is conceptualized as participating in communities of practice. Developing from novice to expert, focus on situativity attends to the social context of learning. Authenticity of the environment and support for peer-to-peer learning are highlighted.

(Continued)

Table 7.1   *(Continued)*

Relevant learning theories	*Key ideas*	*Learning is conceptualized as:*
1.5 Multiple Intelligences Gardner (1983)	Individuals have multiple cognitive abilities Identifying multiple intelligences in the breakdown of intellectual capacities	Individuals have different and multiple ways of learning and processing information. To date, 8 intelligences have been identified, these are relatively distinct and separate: linguistic, logic-mathematical, spatial, musical, bodily/kinaesthetic, inter-personal, intra-personal, naturalistic; and a possible ninth intelligence, spiritual/existential. Influenced by Piaget and Bruner.
1.6 Emotional Intelligence Salovey and Mayer (1990) Goleman (1996)	Individuals have different emotional abilities/intelligence levels	Learning is conceptualized as the ability to perceive emotions; to integrate emotions to facilitate thought; to navigate social environments and process information of an emotional nature. Whether this is strictly 'intelligence' is contested. However, educationalists acknowledge the link between cognition and emotion, which both affect learning.
1.7 Experiential Learning Dewey (1938) Lewin (1951) Kolb (1984) Beard and Wilson (2006)	Experience is the foundation of learning Learning is holistic, socially and culturally constructed Learning is shaped and influenced by the socio-economic context in which it occurs	Learning is conceptualized as – learning from experience. Experiential learning is the process of making meaning from direct experience, upon which, reflection is encouraged to increase knowledge, skills, values and beliefs. Emphasis on learning by doing. Pedagogical applications: action learning; problem-based learning; emphasis on critical thinking and problem solving. Experimentation/experiential learning are constructivist; focus on how learning opportunities allow progressive discovery of concepts and skills.
1.8 Behaviourism Watson (1924) Pavlov (1927) Skinner (1953)	Classical and operant conditioning Antecedents, behaviour, consequences Stimulus-response Reward and reinforcement Trial and error learning	Learning is conceptualized as association between stimulus-response. Focus is on measureable behavioural outcomes of learning, rather than knowledge, understanding, values, attitudes and beliefs. Associative concern with external behaviours (not with how concepts/skills are represented internally) Pedagogical applications: instrumental teaching, drill and practice, rote learning.

- developing problem-solving capabilities
- promoting better information-handling skills
- increasing time 'on task'
- improving social and communication skills.

More specifically, technology can enable children to:

- combine words and images to produce a 'professional' looking piece of work
- draft and redraft their work with less effort
- test out ideas and present them in different ways for different audiences
- explore musical sequences and compose their own music
- investigate and make changes in computer models
- store and handle large amounts of information in different ways
- do quickly and easily things which might otherwise be tedious or time-consuming
- use simulations to experience things that might be too difficult or dangerous for them to attempt in real life
- control devices by turning motors, buzzers and lights on or off or by programming them to react to changes in things like light or temperature sensors
- communicate with others over a distance.

Becta (2001) also developed and defined pupil 'ICT capability', which could be broadened out to a wider definition of capability for all users, to include teachers and support staff. Technology capability is characterized by an ability to use effectively tools and information sources to analyse, process and present information, and to model, measure and control external events. More specifically, developed technology capability enables individuals to:

- use technology confidently
- select and use technology appropriate to the task in hand
- use information sources and technology tools to solve problems
- identify situations where the technology use would be relevant
- use technology to support learning in a number of contexts
- be able to reflect and comment on the use of the technology they have undertaken
- understand the implications of technology for working life and society.

The UK 2011 national guidance for all teachers was that pupils should be given opportunities to develop and apply their technology capability in the context of all curriculum subjects. The English National Curriculum documentation (2011) sets out the entitlement of pupils:

> Pupils should be given opportunities to apply and develop their ICT capability through the use of ICT tools to support their learning in all subjects [...] Teachers should use their own judgement to decide where it is appropriate across these subjects.

Pupils should be given opportunities to support their work by being taught to:

- find things out from a variety of sources, selecting and synthesizing the information to meet their needs and developing an ability to question its accuracy, bias and plausibility
- develop their ideas using ICT tools to amend and refine their work and enhance its quality and accuracy
- exchange and share information, both directly and through electronic media
- review, modify and evaluate their work, reflecting critically on its quality, as it progresses.

(DfE 2011)

With respect to practical guidance on the use of technology to support learning and teaching, there are a number of detailed texts which act as manuals specifically to do this. Of those to be recommended, the following are regularly updated and provide a plethora of practical guidance: Leask and Pachler (2005) *Learning to Teach using ICT in the Secondary School*, and Leask and Meadows (2000) *Teaching and Learning using ICT in the Primary School*. There are specialist books about teaching ICT as a subject too (see Kennewell et al. 2007). These texts, which are aimed at all practitioners across primary and secondary schools, provide a source of activities, based on tried and tested strategies and supply a wealth of 'hands-on' ways to incorporate technology and address 'how to' issues.

The skills, knowledge and understanding teachers need to incorporate technology into pedagogy are acquired over time. There are many different ways to incorporate technologies into lessons. Technology use, in and for itself, provides no guarantee that learning will take place, which reiterates the point that, unless the technologies used help achieve the stated learning outcomes of a lesson, their use cannot be justified.

Applications to practice

Preparing to use technology in the classroom

From the texts referenced above, a number of common mistakes in planning and preparing to use technology in lessons are identified.

For example, Kennewell et al. (2007: 7) outline a list of the issues and provide advice about how to avoid common mistakes: starting with a plan for longer-term aims and then planning lessons knowing where they fit the scheme of work and medium then term plan.

When using technology in lessons, teachers should:

- always check beforehand that the equipment works, particularly the compatibility of the software on the school computers, as it may be different from that used at home to prepare lessons
- be well prepared by ensuring a thorough understanding of the technology resources to be used in advance, to 'avoid being exposed'

- know how to fix simple hardware problems, like a printer jam or getting the whiteboard display working
- neither overestimate or underestimate the pupils' abilities with the technology
- be flexible and be able to adapt lesson plans to accommodate for the unexpected and have a 'plan B' should the first need to be abandoned
- plan transitions: for example, when pupils move and need to save and log off
- consider health and safety issues. Include other adults in the classroom, like support staff, and brief them clearly about what they need to do when the technology will be used. (Kennewell et al. 2007: 7)

Further practical and useful skills for teachers to develop are understanding the basic network configurations and components found in the schools and how the school technicians and network managers enable teachers to use the network effectively in teaching and learning. Teachers all need mastery of the hardware and software currently used for teaching in the school. This will involve developing a detailed knowledge of the various packages used in the school too (Kennewell et al. 2007: 101).

With respect to incorporating technology into subject-specific teaching, the 'Learning to Teach' series (Routledge) provides a handbook for each major subject which considers the use of technology in that subject.

Kennewell et al. (2007) provide an example of some simple self- and peer-assessment tools for teachers to use in assessing pupils skills with the different technologies. These are very straightforward and provide a scaffold and an example of what can be done and worked up from these (see Table 7.2).

Technology: knowledge and skills required of teachers

Technology is constantly being developed and changed, which makes it very challenging for teaching professionals to keep up to date. The evolution of faster (and smaller) devices and machines is proving more affordable for school departments and families.

Teachers need to audit their own technology skills, knowledge and understanding regularly in order to identify their own strengths and to highlight areas for development. The ECDL (European Computer Driving Licence) provides a structured way of gaining skills through materials freely available from the British Computing Society. The ECDL has international recognition and accreditation (see www.ecdl.org). Examples of audits can be found online and in books, for example, Capel, Leask and Turner (2009: 49–50).

All teachers should have some knowledge of technology, but this will have developed through different experiences and, because technology is always continually developing, a teacher cannot be expected to know everything. Kennewell et al. (2007) suggest that teachers 'be open to advice, not to hide [their] ignorance and be willing to learn new skills and develop a detailed knowledge of the various packages used in the school (Kennewell et al. 2007: 101).

Part of being an effective practitioner is being reflective (Schon 1983, 1987; Stenhouse 1975) and adopting a learning cycle approach to one's own development with technology.

Table 7.2 Examples of simple peer- and self-assessment tools for use with and by pupils (adapted from Kennewell et al. 2007: 129)

Year 8 Group presentations: peer-assessment – Feedback sheet

Criteria	Group 1	Group 2	Group 3	Group 4
Readable font	Yes			
Impactful and appropriate use of images	Yes			
Effective use of animation to aid meaning	No			
Good quality and use of sound	Yes			
Effective use of colour including consideration of colour blindness	Yes			
Overall comment	Like the colour, but sound did not match the images			

Self-assessment

Group	Yes/no		Explain	
Are my fonts clear and readable?	Yes		They are in Arial size 20	
Are the images suitable for the audience?	Yes		My audience is Year 7, so I have used cartoons	
Have I used animation effectively to convey meaning?	No			
Have I used sound effectively to convey meaning?	Yes			
Are the colour combinations suitable	Yes			

Using technology to support practice and pupil's learning in the classroom

Classroom practitioners (from experienced teachers to newly qualified; from SEN support-staff to higher-learning teaching assistants) are all expected to know how to use technology to advance pupils' learning, and to be able to use generic technology tools for the benefit of pupils. Given the advancements and pace of change with technology, this is a demanding expectation. It includes, for example, at the more basic end, office software, such as word processing, databases, spreadsheets and presentation tools; hardware, such as interactive whiteboards, printers, scanners, digital cameras and DVDs; also email, the Internet and the school's learning platform. To add to this, there are more recent technologies such as iPads, smart phones, Web 2.0, wikis, blogs, immersive environments, Twitter and Facebook. There is also an expectation that professionally teachers will use technology to be connected to relevant subject associations, education networks and professional online support. In practice, the range and types of technology used with pupils of different ages and in different subjects varies. However, there is an expectation that whichever is appropriate for the pupils' age and subject, classroom practitioners will have a technical working knowledge of the technology and how it can support deep learning.

When examining the key principles of classroom practice, it is also worth revisiting the key processes involved in teaching information/technology as a subject. Table 7.3

Table 7.3   Key processes pupils should master (from the English National Curriculum for ICT at KS3, 2011)

Finding information

Pupils should be able to:
a. consider systematically the information needed to solve a problem, complete a task or answer a question, and explore how it will be used
b. use and refine search methods to obtain information that is well matched to purpose, by selecting appropriate sources
c. collect and enter quantitative and qualitative information, checking its accuracy
d. analyse and evaluate information, judging its value, accuracy, plausibility and bias.

Developing ideas

Pupils should be able to:
a. select and use ICT tools and techniques appropriately, safely and efficiently
b. solve problems by developing, exploring and structuring information, and deriving new information for a particular purpose
c. test predictions and discover patterns and relationships, exploring, evaluating and developing models by changing their rules and values
d. design information systems and suggest improvements to existing systems
e. use ICT to make things happen by planning, testing and modifying a sequence of instructions, recognising where a group of instructions needs repeating, and automating frequently used processes by constructing efficient procedures that are fit for purpose
f. bring together, draft and refine information, including through the combination of text, sound and image.

Communicating information

Pupils should be able to:
a. use a range of ICT tools to present information in forms that are fit for purpose, meet audience needs and suit the content
b. communicate and exchange information (including digital communication) effectively, safely and responsibly
c. use technical terms appropriately and correctly.

Evaluating

Pupils should be able to:
a. review, modify and evaluate work as it progresses, reflecting critically and using feedback
b. reflect on their own and others' uses of ICT to help them develop and improve their ideas and the quality of their work
c. reflect on what they have learnt and use these insights to improve future work.

---

sets out the 'key processes' identified in the English National Curriculum for ICT at KS3 in 2011. Although, at the time of going to press, the curriculum was under review and may well be different to this, although arguably these processes are essential to learning in a digital age.

For effective practice, teachers need to understand the range of ways technology can be deployed to support professional practice, from specialist subject teaching to general administration. If teachers are to know which specific technology applications are relevant to the subject area and to find out more about learning and teaching with technology, they will need to know where to find this information – from subject associations, CPD courses, practitioner publications, books and online professional networks, which facilitate teachers taking an active role in their own professional development.

Technology resources can be used in a range of ways by teachers to achieve the goals set out in Table 7.3. Practitioners need to be familiar with these and ensure time is set aside to learn the use of any resources which are new.

Teachers need to know how to:

- use common software packages; for example, word processing, PowerPoint presentations and Excel spreadsheets
- input data, interpret data (for example, trends in pupil attainment) and print data from the school's intranet/learning platform
- evaluate Internet resources for their reliability as learning resources
- create digital resources – for example, online worksheets – which are appropriately differentiated – for example, through using more or less complex language and through including tasks of different levels of complexity
- manage international collaborative projects linking schools and pupils around the world (such as e-twinning, see www.etwinning.net and webquest, see www.webquest.org)
- use pupil assessment data to identify where interventions are needed and to set individual and group goals to raise attainment
- use ICT for administration purposes. (Adapted from Younie and Leask 2009: 126)

There are generic skills that all pupils and teachers can be expected to have: for example, knowledge of generic office software packages and Web 2.0 environments for collaboration; management of online collaboration on educational projects; and production of multimedia. Given that technology can be used in so many different ways across subjects and age ranges, it is worth summarizing below specific examples of how technology could be used in each subject. Thus, Table 7.4 shows how technologies can be applied in different subjects. While changes will be inevitable, the essential nature of using technology for learning remains the same (finding things out; developing ideas and making things happen; exchanging and sharing information; reviewing, modifying and evaluating work as it progresses).

From children's earliest time in school they should be encouraged to use technology to support their learning, as familiarity provides a foundation for competence, confidence and innovation and development of new ideas.

Table 7.4 Elements of technology use across various subject areas

Art and design		Maths	
Finding things out	Surveys (e.g. consumer preferences), Web galleries, online artist/ movement profiles	Finding things out	Databases, surveys, statistics, graphing, calculators, graphical calculators, dynamic geometry, data logging/measurement (e.g. timing), Web-based information (e.g. statistics/history of maths)
Developing ideas	Spreadsheets to model design specs	Developing ideas	Number patterns, modelling algebraic problems/probability
Making things happen	Embroidery CAD/CAM	Making things happen	Programming – e.g. LOGO turtle graphics
Exchanging and sharing information	Digital imagery CAD Multimedia for students' design portfolios	Exchanging and sharing information	Formulae/symbols, presenting investigation findings, multimedia
Reviewing, modifying and evaluating	Real world applications – e.g. commercial art	Reviewing, modifying and evaluating	Comparing solutions to those online, online modelling and information sources
Business & commercial studies		Technology	
Finding things out	Pay packages, databases, online profiling	Finding things out	Product surveys, consumer preferences, environmental data
Developing ideas	Business/financial modelling	Developing ideas	CAD, spreadsheet modelling
Making things happen	Business simulation	Making things happen	CAM, simulations (e.g. environmental modelling), textiles, embroidery, control.
Exchanging and sharing information	Business letters, Web authoring, multimedia CVs, email	Exchanging and sharing information	Advertising, product design and realization, multimedia/Web presentation
Reviewing, modifying and evaluating	Commercial packages, dot.com, admin systems	Reviewing, modifying and evaluating	Industrial production, engineering/ electronics
Performing arts		Physical education	
Finding things out	Online information sources, surveys (e.g. PHSE issues)	Finding things out	Recording/analysing performance, Internet sources (e.g. records)
Developing ideas	Planning performance/ choreographing sequences	Developing ideas	Planning sequences/tactics

(Continued)

Table 7.4 *(Continued)*

Performing arts		*Physical education*	
Making things happen	Lighting sequences, computer animation, MIDI, multimedia presentations	Making things happen	Modelling sequences/tactics, sporting simulations
Exchanging and sharing information	Video, audio, digital video, Web authoring, multimedia, animation, DTP posters/flyers/ programmes email	Exchanging and sharing information	Reporting events, posters, flyers, Web/multimedia authoring, video, digital video
Reviewing, modifying and evaluating	Ticket booking, lighting control, recording/TV studios, theatre/film industry	Reviewing, modifying and evaluating	Website evaluation, presentation of performance statistics, event diaries, performance portfolios
English		*Modern foreign languages*	
Finding things out	Surveys, efficient searching/keywords, information texts, online author profiles, readability analysis	Finding things out	Class surveys, topic databases, Web searching/browsing
Developing ideas	Authorship, desktop publishing (balancing text and images)	Developing ideas	Concordancing software, interactive video packages, DTP and word processing
Making things happen	Interactive texts/ multimedia/Web authoring	Making things happen	Online translation tools, interactive multimedia
Exchanging and sharing information	Exploring genres (e.g. writing frames), authoring tools, text./ images, scripting, presenting, interviewing (audio/video)	Exchanging and sharing information	Word processing, DTP, Web/ multimedia authoring, email projects, video/audio recording, digital video editing
Reviewing, modifying and evaluating	Website evaluation, online publishing, email projects	Reviewing, modifying and evaluating	Internet communication, website/ CD ROM language teaching evaluation, translation software
Humanities		*Science*	
Finding things out	Surveys, databases, Internet searching, monitoring environment (e.g. weather), census data etc.	Finding things out	Data recording and analysis, spreadsheets and graphing packages, Internet searching (e.g. genetics info)

Humanities		Science	
Developing ideas	Multimedia, DTP, modelling (spreadsheets/ simulations)	Developing ideas	Modelling experiments/ simulations
Making things happen	Simulations, interactive multimedia/web authoring	Making things happen	Datalogging, modelling experiments, simulations (what if . . . .?)
Exchanging and sharing information	Web authoring, email projects	Exchanging and sharing information	Communicating investigation findings (DTP, web/multimedia authoring, DVD)
Reviewing, modifying and evaluating	Weather stations, satellite information, website/CD ROM evaluation, archive information	Reviewing, modifying and evaluating	Accessing information (evaluating for bias on issues (e.g. nuclear power)

From: Leask and Pachler (2005) (with thanks to Dave Maguire)

Teachers and support staff are expected to be able to use the technology that pupils use in lessons. It is a professional requirement of classroom practitioners that they have the skills needed to support pupils' learning, which means being competent in the range of technology skills relevant to their teaching. The task below is designed to enable a professional audit of an individual's technology skills, which will enable an identification of the areas of competence and those that require further development. For those used to working with the technology the audit will seem too easy, but there are still many people not confident in basic skills – they may have been in jobs not requiring computers or have come from a school or country where access to computers and the Internet is limited.

Auditing staff and pupil technology skills

It is suggested that practitioners begin by auditing their own skills (see Table 7.5) and identify the aspects of technology that are most relevant to the age range and/ or subject they teach (perhaps using Tables 7.2, 7.3 and 7.4 as a guide). Then, having identified the areas for development, consider the ways in which this technological competence can be developed; locate relevant technology training and commit to improving their skills. For technical skills it may be worth considering the previously mentioned European Computer Driving Licence (ECDL), or for more pedagogically focused technology development look at the UK government-funded project Vital from the Open University, which delivers online continuing professional development for school practitioners, and the Naace website.

Efficient use of learning platforms is an area in which many schools can expect to be working over the coming years as practice develops and teachers share knowledge and expertise. Younie and Leask (forthcoming 2013) reported that learning platforms in those schools most advanced in the embedding of technologies across

Table 7.5   Basic technology skills audit

Put a tick beside each skill indicating your level of competence/confidence
(0 = no confidence, 3 = very confident).

General skills	*0*	*1*	*2*	*3*
Choosing appropriate software to help solve a problem				
Dragging and dropping				
Having more than one application open at a time				
Highlighting				
Making selections by clicking				
Moving information between software (e.g. Using the clipboard)				
Navigating around the desktop environment				
Opening items by double clicking with the mouse				
Printing				
Using menus				
How to change the name of files				

Word-processing skills	*0*	*1*	*2*	*3*
Altering fonts – font, size, style (**bold**, *italic*, <u>underline</u>)				
Text justification – left, right and centre				
Using a spellchecker				
Moving text within a document with 'cut', 'copy' and paste				
Adding or inserting pictures to a document				
Counting the number of words in a document				
Adding a page break to a document				
Altering page orientation – (landscape, portrait)				
Using Characters/Symbols				
Using find and replace to edit a document				
Using styles to organize a document				
Using styles to alter the presentation of a document efficiently				
Adding page numbers to the footer of a document				
Adding the date to the header of a document				
Changing the margins of a document				

Email skills	*0*	*1*	*2*	*3*
Recognizing an email address				
Sending an email to an individual				
Sending an email to more than one person				
Replying to an email				

Email skills	0	1	2	3
Copying an email to another person				
Forwarding an incoming email to another person				
Adding an address to an electronic address book				
Filing incoming and outgoing emails				
Adding an attachment to an email				
Receiving and saving an attachment in an email				

Database skills	0	1	2	3
Searching a database for specific information				
Using Boolean operators (and/or/not) to narrow down searches				
Sorting database records in ascending or descending order				
Adding a record to a database				
Adding fields to a database				
Querying information in a database (e.g. locating all values greater than 10)				
Filtering information in a database (e.g. sorting on all values greater than 10)				
Categorizing data into different types (numbers, text, and yes/no (Boolean) types)				

Web browser skills	0	1	2	3
Recognizing a Web address (e.g. www or co.uk, etc.)				
Using hyperlinks on websites to connect to other website				
Using the back button				
Using the forward button				
Using the history				
Understanding how to search websites				
Using Boolean operators (and/or/not) to narrow down searches				
Creating bookmarks				
Organizing bookmarks into folders				
Downloading files from a website				

Spreadsheet skills	0	1	2	3
Identifying grid squares in a spreadsheet (e.g. B5)				
Inserting columns into a spreadsheet				
Inserting rows into a spreadsheet				
Sorting spreadsheet or database columns in ascending or descending order				

(Continued)

Table 7.5 *(Continued)*

Spreadsheet skills	0	1	2	3
Converting a spreadsheet into a chart				
Labelling a chart				
Adding simple formulae/functions to cells				
Applying formatting to different types of data including numbers and dates				

Presentation skills	0	1	2	3
Inserting text and images on a slide				
Inserting a slide in a presentation				
Adding a transition between slides				
Adding buttons to a presentation				

Source: Bennett and Leask (2009) An editable version of table 7.5 is available here: www.routledge.com/textbooks/9780415478724

the curriculum were using learning platforms to support structured and unstructured independent study and collaborative learning for pupils, but most schools were still developing this level of use. Younie & Leask (2013) found the role of the learning platform as an information repository was well established in schools, as was its support for administration and communication between staff, pupils, and parents. However, assessment practice and learning support using the learning platform was developing more slowly, with schools being at quite different stages. It was the exception to find schools which were making more advanced uses of the interactive and collaborative features of learning platforms.

Learning platforms or virtual learning environments

Becta (2006) defines a learning platform as an online environment, bringing together hardware, software and supporting services to enable more effective ways of working within and outside the classroom and between school and home. Learning platforms provide a range of technology-based functions supporting content management for lesson materials and coursework which can be accessed at home or at school; curriculum mapping and planning; learner engagement; administration and communication tools including email, instant messaging, discussion forums, wikis and blogs. Younie and Leask's research on learning platforms (2009) reports that universities were many years ahead of schools in the use of online learning platforms to support teaching and learning and remote access. Teachers who have been university students recently should be able to transfer their knowledge from their university experience into the school context. Examples of the use of learning platforms in schools are given in Table 7.6 and further detailed advice about choosing learning platforms is given in Chapter 9.

Table 7.6 Types of learning platform uses as reported by schools with examples of activities (Younie and Leask 2009)

Types of learning platform use	School examples of activities and functionality
Administration	Usage/access statistics
	Pupil records (tracking, monitoring, reporting pupil progress and attainment) Whole-school data management
	Timetabling
	Some problems with interoperability of SIMS (school information management systems) and MIS (management information systems)– these do not always pick up pupil assessment data **from** the learning platform or publish **to** the learning platform
Communication and information giving	Enhancing school identity and links to the wider community Connections between family of schools (inter-school communication) Whole-school online notice board; department areas; forums (intra-school communication) Home–school links (parental communication)
	Announcements/news and updates Public display boards with links to information and documents such as uniform lists, order forms, clubs and parental news
	Blogging
	Calendar: publishing to parents and pupils key dates of trips, school plays, parents evenings, sporting fixtures
	Podcasting: linked with pupil assessment tasks. Audio files used with less able readers; MFL learning activities in native language. Music and songs (revision rapping of core knowledge) posted on YouTube
Information repository	**Storage** of curriculum materials/online learning resources; links to websites for departments/subject areas
Collaborative working	**Teachers:** communal construction of knowledge. For example: designing resources for sharing; through evaluation of resources; facilitating discursive activity; sharing of lesson plans **Pupils:** Video conferencing; use of online collaborative games
	Wikis: for collaborative group work
	Virtual classroom: extending home/school links
	Forums: discussion/chat rooms
Learning and assessment	**ePortfolios:** uploading and showcasing of pupils' work Pupils' folders and teachers' folders are available to access externally from home
	Self-assessment/peer assessment: formative self-assessment: using quizzes, multiple choice tests, revision exercises
	Formative assessment and feedback: pupils upload files, which are peer-reviewed using a forum for example: reviews of a book or website; group presentations; electronic teacher feedback on assessments

(Continued)

Table 7.6   *(Continued)*

Types of learning platform use	School examples of activities and functionality
	Testing subject knowledge of pupils: online testing and tracking of own results by pupils
	Homework and class work uploaded into the teacher's folder by pupils for marking
Independent working	Pupils can complete homework online and upload and save onto their area or e-portfolio. Supports 'anytime, anywhere learning' (AAL); independent and peer collaboration. For example; in MFL, pupils listening to recordings and, record and compare their own work.

Developing pupils' technology skills

The integration of technology into lessons requires confidence and competence on the part of teachers managing the resources for pupils' learning. For example, the Internet provides a wealth of educational resources; locating and adapting suitable resources, however, takes time. What the Internet does provide are: access to information; the use of interactive tools and resources; participation in and/or creation of online projects; communication with expert others; and publishing and sharing information and ideas. For more systematic use of the Internet for educational purposes some teachers favour the use of webquest-type projects (www.webquest.org), e-twinning projects (www.etwinning.net), and whole-school, cross-curricular projects (see Leask and Williams 2005).

Teachers do need to train pupils in effective use of the Internet, in the evaluating of sources and evidence and in e-safety. Young people have been found not to understand the risks of sharing personal information online, so e-safety training should be part of their school curriculum.

Ensuring e-safety: a key classroom principle

The Internet provides a wealth of information sources; nevertheless, pupils may not have learned how to search for information efficiently or selectively in terms of accuracy, reliability, plausibility and currency of the information. In addition to needing to develop a discriminatory or critical digital literacy, pupils also need to adopt e-safety strategies, in order to avoid unsuitable materials, cyber bullying and manipulation by others.

Promoting e-safety: the UK's first national child Internet safety strategy

The UK was the first country to demonstrate its commitment to child digital safety by setting up the multi-stakeholder UK Council for Child Internet Safety (UKCCIS), which has established the UK as a world leader in child digital safety and, as Byron argues, 'sets a global precedent' (Byron 2010: 5).

UKCCIS published the first UK child Internet safety strategy in December 2009 (UKCCIS 2009). In order to increase awareness of how to keep safe online, UKCCIS advocated following the 'Click Clever, Click Safe Code', with three simple things to remember to help keep learners safe when online – Zip It, Block It, Flag It. This marked the UK's seminal launch of a national digital code to promote e-safety. It followed the 2008 Byron Review, which made a series of recommendations to improve the way learners interact digitally and called for teachers and other practitioners to strengthen the knowledge base about how children and young people use digital technologies.

Following the first Byron Review of 2008, it was recommended that 100 per cent of schools should have 'Acceptable Use Policies', which are regularly reviewed, monitored and agreed with parents and pupils, and that all schools and local children's services use an accredited filtering service (Byron 2008: 9). Ofsted's National Adviser for ICT, David Brown, in an interview to mark 'Safer Internet Day' on 7 February 2012, stressed that the 'most effective schools made e-safety a priority in the curriculum, in staff training, in support for pupils and in raising awareness with parents' (Ofsted 2012: 1).

The process of developing e-safety policies began in 2007 when the UK Labour Government commissioned a review by Byron of the risks posed by the Internet. Following the publication of the review in 2008, Ofsted was then tasked to evaluate the extent to which schools teach pupils to adopt safe and responsible practices in using technologies (Ofsted 2010). The need for e-safety arises because, while the Internet offers multiple opportunities, the emergence of Web 2.0 technologies, such as social networking, online gaming, instant messaging and photo sharing, leads to 'new and serious risks' as observed by EPICT (European Pedagogical ICT Licence). The risks identified vary from browsing inappropriate websites, anti-social behaviour and bullying to releasing private and personal information to unsecured sources.

The Byron Review (2008: 56) highlights 'risk taking' by pupils. Byron reports that 'in Europe, 51% of teenagers use the Internet without supervision from their parents and in the UK, 23% of parents with children under 11 allow their children to access the Internet without supervision at home' (Byron 2010: 10). Children reveal their identity to others far more easily than their parents realize (Livingstone and Bober 2005; Valcke et al. 2006). The Child Exploitation and Online Protection Centre (CEOP 2007), set up to coordinate the central collection of cases for Internet-related abuse in the UK, reported that, while 49 per cent of young people surveyed have given out personal information, such as their full name, age, email address, phone number, hobbies or name of their school, to someone that they met on the Internet, by contrast only 5 per cent of parents thought their child has given out such information (Livingstone and Bober 2005: 22).

Particular issues addressed by e-safety policies include the apparent ease by which some children will give out personal information, the facility for pupils to communicate without censorship and in private, alongside cyber-bullying of some children towards others and the actions of predatory adults, which can lead to pupils being at risk.

Consequently, ensuring e-safety is seen to be an important element of the use of technology across the curriculum and also the discrete teaching of technology in secondary education (Woollard 2007: 16–17). The 2008 Byron Review concluded that 'explicit teaching' of e-safety was necessary at all ages. To this end, Byron provided

Table 7.7   The 3 'C's of e-safety (adapted from Byron 2008)

	Commercial	Aggressive	Sexual	Values
Content (child as recipient)	Adverts Spam Sponsorship Personal info	Violent/hateful content	Pornographic or unwelcome sexual content	Bias Racist Misleading info or advice
Contact (child as participant)	Tracking Harvesting Personal info	Being bullied, harassed or stalked	Meeting strangers Being groomed	Self-harm Unwelcome persuasions
Conduct (child as actor)	Illegal downloading Hacking Gambling Financial scams Terrorism	Bullying or harassing another	Creating and uploading inappropriate material	Providing misleading info/advice Misuse of online info: e.g plagiarism

a strong conceptual framework for e-safety on which the teaching practices and the subject knowledge for e-safety could be hung. The three 'C's of content, contact and conduct (Table 7.7) help focus teaching activities and identify the purposes of the teaching resources used.

The Byron Review (2008) in the UK makes explicit the steps that need to be taken to protect Internet users. The focus on the school is to build 'children's resilience to the material to which they may be exposed so that they have the confidence and skills to navigate . . . more safely' (Byron 2008: 5). Byron argues that what is required is making explicit teaching and learning about e-safety, and the review also concludes that new teachers entering the profession need to be equipped with e-safety knowledge and skills.

E-safety resources for teaching digital citizenship

The idea of 'digital citizenship' is an effective way of introducing the topic of e-safety and encouraging appropriate online behaviour. In addition to pupils' awareness, teachers also need information and guidance on e-safety, which, to date, has mainly been aimed at the professional development of practising and experienced teachers and school leaders (Barrow and Heywood-Everett 2005; Becta 2009, 2010; Teachers TV 2010). With respect to pre-service teachers, concerns expressed in the Byron Review (2008) led to an explicit directive that 'in order to maximise the number of new teachers that enter the profession with the appropriate e-safety training, I recommend that guidance on how to assess trainees . . . should take account of e-safety competency' (Byron 2008: 130).

There is a range of e-safety resources from CEOP, Microsoft, ThinkUKnow, KidSmart, Digizen and Childnet International. Childnet provide materials on their website (www.childnet-int.org). 'Young People Safe Online' (Microsoft 2007) is a set of online resources created by Microsoft aimed at teachers, pupils and parents. The resources are appealing, accessible and well written, and focus on four important stakeholder groups: the pupils, their parents, volunteers working with young people and the teaching profession. 'Staying Safe with Dongle' is from the CBBC Stay Safe website (BBC 2010) and invites children to learn about Internet Safety with Dongle the rabbit and the Stay Safe Quiz.

'The Smart Crew' is from KnowITAll by Childnet International. *The Adventures of Captain Kara and Winston's SMART Adventure* is a series of 3D animations covering the 5 SMART rules aimed at helping younger children understand the importance of keeping safe online. The cartoon clips are relatively short and convey the key message efficiently. There is a range of follow-up activities and full lesson plans provided.

For younger children, specifically primary phase, there is also 'Welcome to Hector's World'™ (KS1), 'Lee and Kim's Adventure' (KS1/2) and 'Cyber Café' (KS2), which are from ThinkUKnow (CEOP). These are all easy to access and are supported by teaching resources. However, some resources on CEOP are only accessible by registered users and some are only accessible by those who have completed the CEOP training. There is a growing number of e-safety training courses available. For example, there is EPICT's e-Safety Awareness Module, which is part of an internationally recognized e-Safety CPD course (there is however a small charge for this teacher accreditation). Alternatively, there are CPD opportunities available from Vital at the Open University. In addition for trainee teachers (pre-service teachers), there are resources from the national subject association IT in Teacher Education (ITTE). To support e-safety awareness raising it is paramount that initial teacher education (ITE) providers create a pathway for trainee teachers, as specified by Byron (2008).

However, there is no 'one-stop' fix for e-safety guidance, but rather a minimal solution for teachers wanting support and teaching aids. Table 7.8 provides a list of useful websites with relevant resources for raising awareness about e-safety (Woollard, Pickford and Younie 2010).

Byron (2010) asserts the importance of embedding the issue of child digital safety within a broader context of building resilience (for example, skills of critical evaluation, risk management and self-monitoring) with a 'clear understanding of the importance of risk experiences and their management for child learning and development' (Byron 2010: 2). The challenge is to empower learners to manage risks and make the digital world safer:

> . . . to be empowered to keep themselves safe – this isn't just about a top-down approach. Children will be children – pushing boundaries and taking risks. At a public swimming pool we have gates, put up signs, have lifeguards and shallow ends, but we also teach children how to swim.
>
> (Byron 2008: 2)

Teachers need to be aware of the threats and challenges to staying safe online, and to support the learners' understanding and adoption of safe and responsible

Table 7.8 Links to e-safety resources

360° Safe – School e-Safety Self-Review Tool	http://www.360safe.org.uk
Association for IT in Teacher Education (ITTE)	http://www.itte.org.uk
Child Exploitation and Online Protection Centre (CEOP)	http://www.ceop.police.uk
Childnet International	http://www.childnet-int.org
Digizen	http://www.digizen.org
EPICT (The European Pedagogical ICT Licence)	http://www.epict.org/
Kidsmart	http://www.kidsmart.org.uk
KnowITAll	http://www.childnet-int.org/kia
Staying safe with Dongle (KS1)	http://www.bbc.co.uk/cbbc/help/web/staysafe
The Smart Crew (KS2)	http://www.childnet-int.org/kia/primary/smartadventure
ThinkUKnow	http://www.thinkuknow.co.uk
Vital (Open University)	http://www.vital.ac.uk/
Young People Safe Online website (Microsoft)	http://www.youngpeoplesafeonline.com)

practices when using technologies. This highlights the trend towards developing learners 'digital wisdom', which encompasses responsible and informed use, an awareness of risks and respect for relevant ethical and legal positions.

Conclusions

Does any parent want their child to leave school not competent and confident in the range of technologies commonly used in today's society? For some communities, the answer will be yes. Usually for religious reasons, some communities turn their back on modern practices but, for most communities, equipping young people with the skills and knowledge needed to work effectively in society is a high priority and is expected to be a prime goal for education. This places responsibility for keeping up to date with technology on the shoulders of school leadership teams and individual teachers.

This chapter provides a number of audit tools for teachers to use in checking their own and their pupils' knowledge of how to use technologies to support learning. Such knowledge should now be part of every teacher's pedagogic content knowledge and subject content knowledge. Keeping up to date is a responsibility of all professionals, and parents have a right to expect the teachers to whom they entrust their child to be using the most up-to-date pedagogical approaches involving technology.

Further reading

Wragg, E.C. (ed.) (2004) *The RoutledgeFalmer Reader in Teaching and Learning*, London: RoutledgeFalmer.

OECD (2009) *Creating Effective Teaching and Learning Environments: First results from Teaching and Learning International Survey*, (TALIS) www.oecd.org.

The Routledge *Learning to Teach* series: all the texts contain chapters about the use of technology in each specific subject area. You may find further ideas for the application of technology in your subject areas in these texts. The Routledge text *Learning to Teach Using ICT in the Secondary School* (Leask and Pachler 2005) provides detailed guidance also.

Useful websites

Regional broadband consortia – all regions in England are covered by the RBCs who provide a range of services including technology access, advice on technology resources to schools and who negotiate with providers of resources on behalf of participating local authorities and their schools. http://www.ja.net/communities/schools/netwokring/regional-broadband-consortia.html

Child Exploitation and Online Protection Centre (CEOP) website Think U Know: http://www. thinkuknow.co.uk .This website reinforces the message about safe Internet use, which is the responsibility of all teachers, and contains useful information for teachers, children and parents.

PART 3

Futures

8 Curriculum and personalizing learning

Overview

The model of schooling most people are familiar with is for the most part a transmission model with an teacher standing and delivering to a passive audience. This approach to teaching, which relies on the learner being totally attentive, is doomed to have minimal impact. The spoken work is too ephemeral – through a few days' absence from school or a few moments' inattention the learner may have missed an explanation of a threshold concept with subsequent long-term impact on their capability in a subject. Such an archaic pedagogical approach seems to be persisting more in schools than in universities where it is the norm in many institutions for lecture materials, including webcasts of lectures, to be available online for learners to go over at their leisure to ensure they have grasped the concept being taught, and for all learners to have a personal tutor. What will it take for schooling to get to this stage? What do new teachers need to know and to be able to do?

This chapter looks to the future and provides a vision from innovative UK teachers.

Introduction and context

This chapter will explore the impact of a pervading access to technological tools in creating 'communities of knowledge' with learner involvement and responsibility coupled with personal learning pathways and mentoring becoming core pedagogical strategies.

Will the future be one where each learner and teacher will have one digital tool that provides freedom from current constraints of only operating in classrooms and learning cubicles? How close is the iPad to such a tool?

Theory and research base

There is a growing body of evidence about how technologies support learning. This chapter draws on the Education Futures research of Leask and Preston (2010) funded by Becta, that recorded innovative teachers' views of future schooling. A sample of innovative practitioners (45 from nine government regions) with expertise as senior leaders and as classroom teachers in primary, secondary, special educational needs and vocational and further education was selected to contribute to the Education Futures research. The knowledge base of those involved in this research was extensive. Many of the practitioners in the sample had more than 20 years experience in innovation in the use of technologies in education, with their experiences and knowledge being drawn from a wide range of countries and educational contexts.

The future – which technology tools would help?

The teachers worked in phase-specific focus groups to create a vision of technology tools for future teachers through discussing the questions: which technology tools would teachers have to have to help them do their job well? What would be the characteristics of these new tools and how and when would they be used? The discussions were focused around the following four dimensions of the operation of schools and colleges:

- Curriculum - subject teaching
- Curriculum – administration, accountability and monitoring
- Communications between people within and outside the school/college
- Use of time and space.

The ideas about technology tools for 'future teachers' from the primary, secondary and FE focus groups were very similar. The knowledge base on which contributors to the Education Futures research drew was both theoretical and practical: theoretical with respect to theories of learning and pedagogy and practical with respect to contributors' experience of what works in practice. (Table 0.1 in the Introduction lists the main learning theories readers may find helpful for this chapter.)

Choosing technology tools for supporting curriculum work in subject areas

A pervading viewpoint amongst developers seems to be that teachers only use technology tools for whole-class teaching or one-to-one interaction. Deep learning as opposed to surface learning is more likely when the learning is relevant to the learner and where the learner has to explain to others what they have learned (West Burnham 2007). Group and project work are pedagogical tools to help achieve this. Educators choosing software and software designers need to consider the changing role of the teacher to 'facilitator rather than dictator' and choose and design tools which support collaborative enquiry and working. An increased take-up of digital tools and resources in subject areas can be predicted as members of the profession not born into a digital age retire.

Well-designed resources have the potential to reinforce the learner centred pedagogical models of the future. Teachers who use technologies effectively to support learning use a pedagogical model where technology tools are used to:

- develop problem-solving skills
- encourage independent thinking
- promote imagination and inquisitiveness
- support multimodal and multimedia assessment of independent projects
- encourage collaborative links with experts.

The teaching profession in England is showing a significant shift away from a focus on content and move towards the process of learning, with particular emphasis on teachers' roles as facilitating the learner. Teachers contributing to the Education Futures research identified three key areas for development for curriculum subject software that related to the process of learning rather than content:

- More *web-based suites* of programs are needed for group teaching, but they need to be developed with teacher experts – for example, 'packages' covering subject areas and curriculum-specific content.
- More software applications are needed that would develop *personalized learning* without losing face-to-face elements of teaching where pupils engage in dialogue with teacher experts who have important, interesting and stimulating things to say about their subject.
- A concentration on sophisticated *search tools*.

Web-based curriculum suites

Teachers specifically made the point that leading institutions are moving away from the purchase of software packages towards subscription-based, Web-stored curriculum resources and cross-curricula programmes purchased by subscription, where subjects are integrated into an overall curriculum vision and design paradigm (see Leask and Williams (2005) for a vision of cross-curricula working at secondary school level using supporting technologies). Teachers contributing to the Education Futures research wanted more cross-discipline learning activities for all phases, drawing on constructive learning experiences in the Foundation Stage (early years, aged 4–5 in the UK) and continuity and progression in Web-based suites of subject-specific software throughout the National Curriculum key stages.

Personalized learning

Technologies support a move towards personalized learning, and innovative teachers are increasingly using different input devices, varied locations and Web spaces for individual learner use. The growth of inclusive technology design – that is, designs which incorporate SEN (special educational needs) – also supports personalization (for example, software that provides opportunities such as vision-enhancing techniques for those with poor eyesight), inclusion of neighbour detection, graphical display, location-sensitive devices and wireless communication. In the most sophisticated environments all these features act in concert to form a single interface that enriches access to information and communication. The use of devices that register who is in the room should be used with caution, as inappropriate surveillance will disturb the trust between teachers and learners. The integration of a wide range of technology tools into software including virtual trips to museums, field trips and attending re-enactments of historical events were considered to be likely to greatly increase the power of the learner to direct their own learning. Greater ownership of the learning is also likely to increase learner engagement.

Sophisticated search tools

Current access to high-quality resources on the Web is not satisfactory, as the evidence base underpinning much material and advice is rarely cited. The teachers in the research, therefore, requested a dedicated *search engine* for educational resources that can be tailored by teachers or technology coordinators to alert them to new tools and resources. Resources for education like folksonomies and website tagging tools, which include user recommendations, would enable teachers to find out what really works. Chapter 10 outlines the requirements for a national e-infrastucture for countries wishing to use technologies to support high-quality knowledge building and sharing in education.

Characteristics of effective technology tools for the future

Digital tool and resource designs need to support *flexibility* in curriculum and assessment: e-tools should provide the opportunity to repurpose tools. Tools should support discovery learning with autonomy devolved to the learner; allow meta-tagging by users; provide taxonomy support with elements that can be disaggregated; and supply repositories of reusable objects and ubiquitous access.

The Education in Futures research (Leask and Preston 2010) report *specific characteristics* of technology tools for the future:

- learning platforms anywhere accessible anytime for anyone (*cloud computing*) with mega bandwidth available both at home and in school/college as well as mobile network coverage
- *interoperability* with software which accepts a range of different formats – for example, images and videos; PC interoperability to be similar to the Apple Mac so that, for example, music written in one computer package could be dropped into another computer presentation package without having to be reformatted; school data and administration software to be interoperable with learning platforms, for example, via Moodle widgets
- Tools built to an accepted set of *cross-platform standards* to ensure software tools and icons are similar no matter which piece of educational software is being used. This reduces the learning curve for teachers. Without this level of technological transferability, the skills (and hence confidence) acquired in one area of technology cannot then be applied to another

- While acknowledging *copyright issues*, the teachers contributing to the Leask and Preston (2010) research pointed out that the more *readily available and accessible* software is, the more likely it will be used – for example, being able to download the Interactive Whiteboard (IWB) software at home without having to enter complex serial numbers would help develop teacher use.

Recognizing the demands on teachers, *solutions* were offered by the teachers contributing to the Education Futures (2010) research to ameliorate the demands on the profession, as expectations of their use of, and knowledge about, technology tools rise:

- A new role of *learning technologist* is needed: most large institutions now have technical support through single or cluster-based technicians. However, in order to ensure the widespread assimilation of learning platforms in the future, the support of learning technologists is essential to help produce online learning materials for use by parents and pupils. Although some 'off the shelf' resources are helpful, the value depends on whether they can be tailored to the needs of the learners and the teachers. From this point of view the tools must be labour-saving rather than requiring additional time and effort from the teacher.
- Provision of *formal CPD*: a preference was expressed for work-based learning that focused not only on using the technical aspects of a resource, but also the pedagogical implications of its use. Software developers might consider at the outset what types of learning and teaching their resources will support. The role of ICT coordinators in small schools is onerous, because of the continually changing, whole-school, technical and pedagogical environment, and the lack of peers in the same institution.
- Recognizing the importance of just-in-time sharing of ideas, informal networking and *informal CPD*: subject association support was considered important in knowledge sharing about future directions and problem-solving. Another source of potential progress was the informed parent who could drive technology use and innovation. In support of their own careers, some form of qualification might be appreciated by parents, in recognition of their efforts in supporting schools and teachers to move forward with technology.

Technology tools for the future: supporting the curriculum with respect to accountability and assessment

Formal assessment processes can drive or limit innovation and development in education systems. Statutory curriculum and assessment requirements are currently 'the elephant in the room' in discussions about digital solutions to assessment and accountability. Teachers contributing to the Education Futures research complained that present teaching styles and assessment practices are designed to restrict rather than inspire learners' responses. Technology developers' attention to assessment issues might help to change attitudes in this area, from an emphasis on gathering data on cohorts, to data that traces the achievements of individuals from a range of multimodal perspectives. Educators choosing measurement tools should look for tools which assess the whole child, including their social development – for example, learners' ability to be collaborative and cooperative, not just those areas that yield quantitative data. Assessment e-tools should credit what the learners are capable of doing rather than forcing them to provide evidence of learning in formats which are not appropriate for the needs and interests of the learners.

E-portfolios were seen to have significant potential, particularly as their design improves. There was a growing preference amongst the teachers for diagnostic/analytical tools rather than software that only permits the presentation and manipulation of cohort data. This trend to personalization might be reinforced if technology developers liaised more with learners, teachers and parents about what they want from education, as schools and colleges are likely otherwise to focus assessment on demands of existing external assessment requirements.

Further reinforcement of the trend towards personalization could be achieved by backing up parents' meetings with online systems for two-way communication with parents. As well as providing a means of presenting data, these systems, with learner access, should be a means by which the learners are able to demonstrate their capabilities. In this context assessment tools chosen for any learning platform should include e-portfolios and multimodal forms of assessment which go beyond assessing formal skills and knowledge. Online assessment could be available when the pupils are ready. Recording their achievements in an e-portfolio might include the use of automated tools that generate automatic emails to pupils who have not completed targets by deadlines, copied to tutors, parents and so on. Formative assessment tools that respond to learner activity and take account of learner voices are also important. Digitizing a paper-based system like Assessment of Pupil Progress (APP) might be worth considering.

Technology tools for the future, which support the curriculum with respect to assessment, need to take account of what is known to be effective

Effective assessment systems using technology should:

- be secure
- be accurate
- be reliable
- be portable
- be affordable
- be accessible
- be cross-platform
- be interoperable
- be usable across multiple contexts (home, school/college, other areas and international)
- take account of the learner's voice
- allow for lifelong learning achievements

- facilitate transition between phases, and
- be supported by professional networks managed by the profession in collaboration with the examination boards and university teachers to facilitate sharing of good practice.

Some school computerized *management systems* already support customization and allow schools and colleges to design the look and feel of the front page of their online management information system – that is, their own front-ends. Moving in the same direction, specifications for similar management systems of the future include open Application Program Interfaces (APIs) so that schools and colleges can create their own systems. Teachers should be empowered to structure data reports that are useful for them so that schools and colleges can take advantage of deeper professional insights. These systems should work on any kind of integrated device, fixed or mobile. Sufficient storage area per teacher was reported as vital. A development that the teachers expected to see more of in the future were applications like the Mentis verifier and Swift that display *holistic management thinking*. These empowering professional online school/college improvement systems support self-evaluation, school and college development plans and performance management – all in one. Swift, for example, connects information and documents across the system to aid school and college improvement and cut out duplicated work.

In the area of *accountability for e-safety*, tools that educate learners in the processes are recommended. Schools should all have e-safety policies, which will focus personal and social responsibility or undertaking policing (see also Chapter 7). Ways effective technology-based tools and digital resources can be used to help practitioners to do specific tasks well with respect to accountability and monitoring are set out in Table 8.1.

There are, however, risks accompanying the use of these technology tools:

- Previous reports on learners may adversely influence current responses to learners and current reports.
- If reports are open then it is difficult to include criticisms.
- Market leaders in software do not need to innovate at the speed that schools and colleges would wish.
- There are different approaches to assessment between primary and secondary schools and colleges, so data may look as if it is transferable across the academic year, but this is not always the case.

Increasingly, non-technology-based resources are being supplanted by technology-based systems, because of the sheer volume of assessment information being generated. However, digital systems are not always appropriate:

- Staggered pages in mark books are hard to replicate electronically and paper-based registers are still necessary where Management Information Systems (MIS) do not support online registration.

Table 8.1 Ways technology-based tools and digital resources support teachers in undertaking curriculum administration, accountability and monitoring (from Leask and Preston 2010)

Tasks supported by the tools	Ways tools support the undertaking of tasks
Monitoring learners' progress and their achievement against predictions	through progress tracking
Personalizing learning and planning	
Personalized learning through building on prior attainment	– checking learners previous achievement and teacher comments – providing information across subjects for 1–2–1 progress meetings – traffic lights acting as a starting point for discussion with parents and learners – more detailed information about learners being available
Collaboration through sharing knowledge	between primary and secondary with learners with parents
Time saving	everything in one place
Facilitating learner stakeholder voice	through anonymous feedback via online surveys and for use for monitoring quality of courses and programmes
Independent learning	through online materials
Assessment for learning	building on previous records
Managing parents' expectations	through reference to evidence
Capturing of data in different locations	using wi–fi and hand-helds inside and outside the school/college

- Some school and college systems are not robust enough to protect data from complete loss and unauthorized access.
- Some forms of assessment are quicker on paper and easier to work with: for example, Individual Learning Plans.
- Hard copy is better for longer pieces of work but, of course, not for work involving non-text media.
- There will always be a place for immediate face-to-face feedback to learners on their work and for group meetings and chat, which facilitates informal communication.

Table 8.2 summarizes characteristics of effective technology-based tools and digital resources used to support administration, accountability and monitoring (Leask and Preston 2010).

There is a clash between the impetus to innovate and the need to be professionally accountable, with aims to innovate technologies in schools often blocked by school policies. *Innovation* within schools and colleges needs to be actively managed if schools want to keep up-to-date. Institution-centred codes of conduct help teachers, school leaders and local authorities to integrate new technologies into the school and college systems. Recent examples include phones and social networking for

Table 8.2 Characteristics of effective technology-based tools for curriculum administration, accountability and monitoring

Characteristic	Tools should:
Pedagogical characteristics	• support formative assessment and improving learning rather than focusing on summative outcomes, that is, the technology should support the processes of learning rather than just recording the outcomes of learning • not just focus on target-led approaches and measurable outcomes • subject specific assessment tools should not be abstract but should include applications to the real world. • enable more generalized thinking and higher-order skills development • ensure exchange of data with a variety of devices by: 　– linking with e-portfolios – enabling teachers to easily record and monitor learners' progress, for example, in recording evidence for the six areas of achievement at the foundation stage; enabling learners to upload e-portfolio material 　– linking with PDAs which are used for recording learner progress data, for example, observation data 　– providing hyperlinks between assessment evidence and grades 　– dealing with digital data, for example, videos
Design characteristics	• support communication between stakeholders, by 　– being open to scrutiny by learners, teachers, parents and management 　– supporting blogging to engage and interact with parents and learners 　– being intuitive to use 　– being easily updatable by whole school/college workforce 　– sending alerts • be simple and strongly visual: e.g. outliers on graphs showing pupil achievement progress should be highlighted, using a traffic-light system when learners are falling behind or achieving well, to enable target setting and half-termly reporting • provide immediate access and updates, by 　– providing feedback to learners and teachers on demand 　– identifying irregular attendance patterns and communicating this to teachers and parents 　– being updatable quickly by the whole school/college workforce in response to events

(Continued)

Table 8.2 *(Continued)*

Characteristic	*Tools should:*
Technical characteristics	• provide one tool with multiple functions, and for multiple purposes, for example, Inspection, school/college, formative and summative needs. One teacher reported having to work with four different systems. • be comprehensive – provide management of all pupil data, for example, SEN, medical, child protection • be Web-based – access has to be Web-based for parents and whole-school/college workforce access • be robust – 'one crash and everyone loses faith' • be secure – 'one loss of privacy and everyone loses faith' • be flexible – with high standards of interoperability between commonly used packages: e.g. homework information on the learning platforms should be linked with homework returns by email and alerts about homework missed • allow staff appropriate access • there are different levels of access depending on 'need to know' • teachers need easy access to pupil/student data which is useful for lesson planning.

learners. These codes of conduct should manage the development of learner-focused and authored resources that make effective use of these devices and opportunities. Learners and teachers are using social networking sites, but this use is usually outside the formal school/college system and this carries risks for the school, the staff and learners.

Personalizing learning

Personalizing learning using digital media applies not just to pupils' learning, but also to teachers' learning. While privacy and security issues need to be addressed in schools/colleges, new tools and resources that are currently in the market place have considerable potential value for learning, and include:

- hand-held and laptop devices including fine-grained content and wi-fi connections
- hand-held and laptop devices linked to learning platforms
- podcasting (voice), vodcasting (video) and video conferencing
- email
- iChat (synchronous typed chat), backchannels (messaging), SMS and voice communication
- increasingly ubiquitous voice-operated software.

Schools and colleges already innovating with learner-choice have to confront significant issues of responsibility and trust in developing communications that involve people within and outside the institution. For example, the piloting of video used for performance review and mentoring raises ethical issues and the need for a Code of Conduct. Learners themselves need to know in which lessons recording will happen and how the information will be used. The use of web-cams is already controversial. Where a class web-cam is set up, teachers notice that learners are more reluctant to contribute or to volunteer when they think their parents might be watching (Leask and Preston 2010).

Pedagogical opportunities incorporating the use of mobile phones are extensive – learners are using them as cameras for taking before and after pictures in science, design technology and food technology, and as calculators, timers and for voice recording for projects. Multitasking e-activities that pupils indulge in socially should be encouraged in modern classrooms, but teachers need support in the pedagogical applications of these resources and in teaching learners how to mine information, assess its reliability, evaluate it and apply it with common sense. Applications that learners commonly use out of school and college which have pedagogical applications include: *multiuser, online 3-D virtual gaming*, a contested area where holographic projection is expected to be the next stage (Johnson et al. 2011). See Chapter 4 for further information on digital-games-based learning.

Mentoring and tutoring

There are opportunities for virtual tutoring via learning platforms linked to artificial intelligence software. Learners might also gain from being engaged in the technical tutoring of teachers and other learners – one 12 year old has posted a video on YouTube that explains how to use the iPhone. However, teachers themselves may not yet have much experience of social networking for professional practice.

Conclusions

The ideas here provide a wish list from teachers. Any school, department or teacher wanting to develop their own practice will need to map out their own path to development.

There is no shortage of ideas from teachers about how technologies can support personalized learning and assessment. So what are the barriers to having systems which teachers see as supporting the raising of individual achievement? This chapter and the other chapters in this book identify barriers as well as ways of overcoming them. However, changes in systems may require leadership and vision at the school, region and national level – leaders with the understanding of the potential of technologies to support improved learning outcomes are, however, more rare than one would hope given the technological advances made and sophistication of learner-owned devices, which is ever growing.

Further reading

Dawes, L. (2008) *The Essential Speaking and Listening*, London: Routledge.
Joyce, B., Calhoun, E. and Hopkins, D. (2008) *Models of learning – tools for teaching*, 2nd edn, Buckingham: Open University Press.

Useful websites

Teachmeets http://teachmeet.pbworks.com
A TeachMeet is an organized but informal meeting (in the style of an unconference) for teachers to share good practice, practical innovations and personal insights in teaching with technology.
Mirandanet http://www.mirandanet.ac.uk/mirandamods
The MirandaNet Fellowship, founded in 1992, is an e-community of practice for international technology policy-makers, teachers, teacher educators, researchers and commercial developers who are passionate about digital technology in teaching and learning and about using technologies to promote cultural understanding and democratic participation.

9 Resources: human capital, time and space for schools of the future

Overview

Innovative teachers expect schools and colleges of the future to embrace the concept of the 24 hour school or college – open to communities, parents and learners and co-learners crossing age groups and personalizing learning and that the pervading access to tools will create 'communities of knowledge' (Leask and Preston 2010).

The previous chapter outlined ways that digital tools can enable a more personalized learning approach inside and outside the institution. Teachers contributing to the Leask and Preston Education Futures research (2010) saw a future where each learner has one digital tool providing freedom from current space and time constraints. A tablet type tool is currently the closest to this specification. Realizing this vision requires, for most institutions, changes in material resourcing (in the use of time and space) and in the development and deployment of human resources.

Pause for a moment and consider what you would do if you were designing a school from scratch in this digital age. What hours would the school be open? What spaces would you have? How would you deploy staff? What pedagogical approaches would you employ? How, when and where would learners be working? What e-tools would you use? What human and material resources are needed?

Introduction and context

Some schools are considerably closer than others to implementing of the 24-hour school or college – open to communities, parents and learners and providing a mix of teaching and learning environments with personalized learning.

School leaders have two major resources to draw on in developing a school:

- material resources: funding for development and maintenance and buildings (including connectivity)
- human resources: staff, learners, parents and the community.

Material resources may place more constraints on imaginative school leaders, but much can be achieved through collaboration with communities through fundraising and with businesses sharing resources such as video-conferencing, IT help and staff mentoring learners to raise their aspirations.

Classroom designs need to be flexible to support different pedagogical approaches. In this context architects, developers and installers need to work with staff of schools and colleges, learners and parents. The scenarios in this book and this chapter present a range of challenges for education professionals who would have to manage such changes in schools, colleges and in communities. Teacher training too has to provide the teachers with the ability to meet the challenge of technology-supported learning.

The all-encompassing learning platforms that support the new approaches of innovative schools require a physical environment (time and space) that is fit for purpose and staff who have high levels of pedagogical understanding of how and why to use technologies to support learning.

Managing the human resources available is much more complex than any other challenge in the management of change. Creating a clear vision is a first step to engaging stakeholders in change and development, and the information in this text is intended to help the reader to develop a vision for their area of responsibility, whether they are an individual teacher, a leader of a curriculum area, a head of department or a senior school leader or policy-maker.

The vision does have to consider spaces and how they will be deployed, as the use of space affects the kinds of pedagogies which can be employed. For example, to what extent will open workspaces or 'productivity corners' become the norm with individuals and groups drawing on Web-based materials and working on personalized schedules and with teaching of core concepts to large groups, small groups or individuals organized as necessary to meet personal needs? Might walls be used as touch screens with wireless connectivity provided, inside and out. Will rooms such as the one in Emirates Stadium in London, which is designed with white slanted walls that can be written on and used as a desk, become the norm? These kinds of stimulating learning environments, both physical and virtual, are available in some schools now, but other schools and colleges are still working on a traditional didactic knowledge-transfer pedagogy producing, it is argued, young people more fitted for working in the nineteenth and twentieth centuries than the twenty-first.

Theory and research base

Anyone engaged in changing practice with large groups of people needs an understanding of management of change theory, which includes motivation theories. There is a plethora of advice on the Web as well as a major international industry of change consultants advising businesses on change management.

However, the principles are relatively simple:

- create a vision
- create and implement a strategy for realizing the vision

- take account of the human and material resources including time and space available
- assess the strengths and challenges these resources pose
- monitor the impact of the changes to ensure new goals are being met.

Each stage along the change path however requires decisions to be made which can have adverse impact on the outcomes.

In creating a vision, a decision has to be made about who contributes and what the impact of including or excluding particular stakeholders will be.

The vision needs to be based on an understanding of the benefits of making the change. In the case of integrating technologies into pedagogies, the Becta Harnessing Technology report (2008a) provides a useful foundation. It describes key pedagogic uses of technology tools and resources as being to:

- gather information
- analyse information
- support creativity
- solve problems
- individualize learning
- work with others.

To this list, teachers from the Leask and Preston (2010) research added three new categories. One relates to the learning of the individual:

- to support higher-order thinking.

The other two highlight the influence that digital technologies are having on how teachers interact with learners and on modes of learning where learners collaborate together inside and beyond schools and colleges:

- to change power relationships in learning contexts
- to enable the learner to make connections within and beyond the school/ college.

To realize these pedagogic goals requires prioritizing group work, personalized learning and collaborative problem-solving.

In engaging stakeholders, understanding the different motivations of individuals is essential in ensuring that their concerns are identified and needs are met. Figures 9.1 and 9.2 summarize key features of two well-known theories of motivation. Herzberg's two-factor theory (Figure 9.1) identifies factors which school leaders can influence in the work environment (hygiene factors) and personal motivation factors. Herzberg makes the point that the two sets of factors are not mutually dependent, and that preventing dissatisfaction can be as important as improving satisfaction.

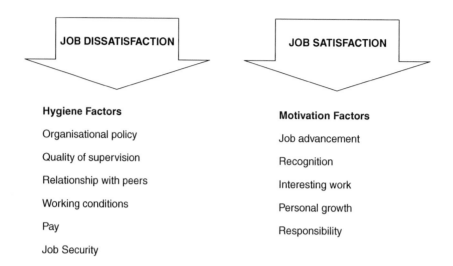

Figure 9.1 Herzberg's Dual Factor Theory of Motivation (1939 in Stello 2012). Summarized from: Christina M Stello's Integrative literature review by: Tafadzwa Gwarinda, University of Bedfordshire, UK.

Maslow's hierarchy of needs (Figure 9.2) looks at motivation from an individual perspective and suggests that, unless basic needs are satisfied for example for security, individuals will be less likely to be open to new ideas and change.

Other motivational theories include Stephen Reiss's 16 basic desires which provide intrinsic motivation: acceptance, power, independence, curiosity, order, saving (of things), honour, idealism, social contact, family, status, vengeance, romance, eating, physical exercise, and tranquillity (Reiss 2000). One of the lessons from the OECD ICT and whole-school improvement project (Kington et al. 2001) was that teachers who did not want to engage in innovation with technologies left the school as quickly as possible – applying Reiss's theory, they may have been seeking tranquillity or order and resisting change. However, regardless of the motivational factors causing staff to leave, when a school adopts new pedagogic approaches incorporating technology, staff turnover and the potential negative impact of that on the school function therefore has to be factored into any plans to manage the change.

The vision has to take account of the material resources including building structures and services available. While some school leaders will be able to design a new school, this will be the exception rather than the rule. Advice on good design is available and there are many examples of new types of pedagogical spaces available from expert sources in the UK. During 2007 to 2010, when there was a government initiative 'Building Schools of the Future', new designs for school were developed, often in consultation with children and communities. Following the termination of that programme by the UK Conservative and Liberal Democrat coalition Government (2010), a charity concerned with school design, the British Council for the School Environment, is now a key holder of knowledge on physical spaces for schooling.

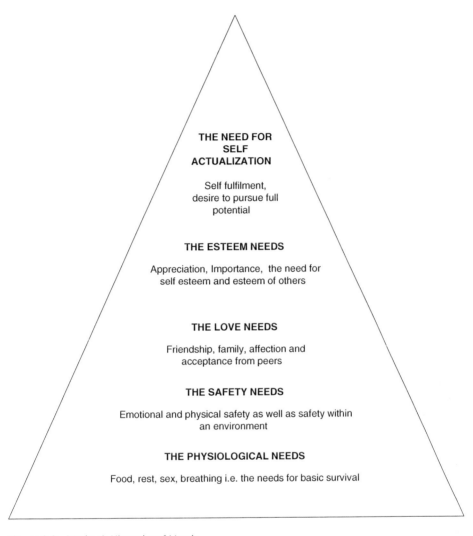

Figure 9.2 Maslow's Hierarchy of Needs.

Applications to practice

This chapter draws on views of innovative teachers contributing to the Leask and Preston (2010) Education Futures research. Teachers were asked specifically to envisage future schooling with ubiquitous technology tools and to consider the time-, space- and human resources-related issues which are likely to result. The chapter accordingly provides a framework for considering resourcing issues for technology-enhanced learning environments.

Educators usually have to adapt their pedagogy to the spaces available in their workplaces. Only rarely does the opportunity arise for the complete design of a new school. This section of the chapter considers the use of time and space for effective learning with e-tools. Some ideas will be beyond what is possible in some spaces but are perfectly feasible in others. Devices to be used and connectivity influence use as much as the physical space and the timetabling.

In terms of hardware, the most flexible approach is to have enough classroom laptops for a group to work together as well as a suite for whole-class, timetabled sessions. This feasibility allows technology to be embedded in everyday teaching (which mirrors the use of technologies in real life), but also allows for more intensive follow-up or the teaching of discrete skills in technology-suite-based lessons. Wireless access to the Internet supports experimental pedagogies but can be difficult to achieve cost-effectively in buildings of certain types.

Teaching spaces

There will always be a need for physical spaces such as individual classrooms, offices and libraries, but there is also a need for 'agile spaces' – big spaces for 'lectures' with teachers freed to support where appropriate with teaching approaches including the use of mobile devices and small flexible spaces for group work. Schools need to be designed for blended learning.

Having chosen the technologies to use, unexpected building-related issues can hinder implementation. Some older buildings are difficult to network (even wirelessly) and do not accommodate IWB technology easily. Some specific challenges in widening the scope of the school or college beyond the physical space the building inhabits are:

- overloads on the digital systems
- bans on teachers using the computers for personal uses in school or college
- the impact on initiatives when the innovator leaves (knowledge should not be held by one person).

Where will 24/7 learning take place?

The concept of the 24/7 school forces teachers to re-think their approach to teaching and learning and parents to consider what the role of the school is – are parents willing to support learners' working from home? Teachers contributing to the Education Futures research suggested schools of the future will dispense with timetables and encourage teachers to facilitate learners to learn as they wish, such as geography all day Monday, something else Tuesday. Some contributors to the research said this approach was unrealistic, but some schools are already experimenting with it and it also mirrors the pedagogical approaches of some schools independent of state control and of some home educators.

Solutions fell into four categories:

- *physical space*: building schools and colleges for learners from 3 to 16 so that all can benefit from bounded finance and resources
- *connectivity*: the use of 3G connection (QIK) phones that can be used to film and connect wirelessly to computers

Table 9.1   Characteristics of effective technology-based tools maximizing use of time and space (from Leask and Preston 2010)

Characteristic	Effective tools:
Pedagogical characteristics	• support for personalization so that learners are able to follow their personal interests in the way they access and use resources • support for collaboration between learners: e.g. through wikis and blogging • provide anywhere, anytime learning via remote access to learning platforms (but schools/colleges provide safe places for learners so offsite learning may be unsupervised) • are asynchronous – so that online learning potentially provides a platform for deeper learning with learners able to revisit material • give learners access to other countries: e.g. Google earth and webcams • allow parents to be easily involved
Design characteristics	• give anywhere anytime access • provide flexibility within online courses • are demonstrably time saving so it is apparent to staff why they should be used • tools help with mundane activities • provide learning platforms which are as attractive and whizzy as free social networking sites • make it easier to create course materials online through flexibility for customization
Technical characteristics	• use wireless networking • are accessible anywhere, anytime • support RSS integration to create personal learning environments

- *security issues*: adequate protection for equipment, learners' safety and sensitive data
- *professional attitudes*: the need for technology 'champions'.

Examples of pedagogical, design and technical characteristics of effective technology-based tools and digital resources used to maximize use of time and space are provided in Table 9.1.

Teachers contributing to the Education Futures research (Leask and Preston 2010) identified a number of issues to consider in building design. These include:

- positioning of power sockets in the floor and connections for network access – as these can affect pedagogical decisions
- how and when teachers will need to use digital tools and resources with learners for activities like IWB use, groups using a laptop or listening units, and learners using laptops with limited battery life

- checking ambient window light when IWBs and laptop screens need to be visible
- encouragement of 24-hour, open-access areas for the whole community
- allowing for learning outside the classroom
- the effect of more use of portable equipment such as wireless data loggers, PDAs and recording equipment flexibility
- the impact of more mobile equipment needing good battery life
- electronic tagging equipment to reduce the likelihood of devices being stolen
- health and safety issues like avoiding exposure to LCD projector beam for long periods of time by back projection or steeply angled projection
- reliability of electronic storage as opposed to paper storage in terms of space saving, printing and paper.

With respect to the use of staff time, sometimes the use of technology requires considerable commitment of time – for example, having to create online resources to support learning and teaching for blended learning requires more time and effort, and resources cannot be always reused, since a key feature of personalization is to match the resources to the needs of the learner.

While technology tools can support different forms of learning; unless teachers have the skills and knowledge to use e-tools in this way, the value of any investment will not be realized. Time for teachers to explore possibilities is critical through supported and sustained CPD. The effective use of tools needs confident and competent teachers as well as learners and an environment where teachers can learn from colleagues and learners about specific software. Table 9.2 summarizes the ways that digital tools can help practitioners use time and space effectively.

Teachers contributing to the Leask and Preston (2010) Education Futures research identified specific benefits related to time issues for teachers and learners such as:

- administrative gains for teachers: auto-recording of meeting minutes and automatic registering of learner attendance
- 'just in time' learning: flexibility of schooling for learners aged over 14 years; allowing 14–16 in employment and 16+ return to formal schooling.

These were in addition to specific benefits relating to *space* such as:

- electronic storage for school or college records
- new technical configurations like 'thin clients', rather than desktop PC
- resources accessed from multimedia servers, rather than on local machines
- individual devices reducing the need for computer rooms, referred to BYOD (Bring Your Own Device)
- local authorities and government devolving autonomy of tool choices to learners and teachers to suit their use of space
- tools that are adaptable for different pedagogical uses.

Table 9.2 How effective digital tools and resources help teachers use time and space well (from Leask and Preston 2010)

How tools help	Effective tools and resources:
Support for learning	• support anywhere, anytime access: learners can continue working outside the school/college on tasks which they have started in school/college. However, learners working at home may miss out on social interaction • encourage learning outside school/college which can have a knock-on effect to the wider community • enable events to be recorded so those not there can access them • develop the traditional model of distance learning • support personalization which is particularly useful for learners who are disaffected • provide wikis and blogging so that learners' collaboration can be sustained beyond the time and place and the engagement of individuals can be traced potentially providing evidence of sustained shared thinking. Discussion can be more important in assembling skills and capabilities • enable learners in small institutions to access broad curriculum delivered elsewhere via synchronous and asynchronous tutorial software • support tablets in the classroom so they can be used naturally to support work on a needs basis. Restricting access to IT on a timetable – the suite, the laptop trolley – means the resources are used less flexibly and less naturally • enable materials for supply teachers to be pre-recorded: e.g. introduction to lessons • support 'webquests' – gathering information not just from the Web but also from the locality, using GPS • connect learners across the world in ways which encourage learning.

The scenario of the 24/7 school presents a range of challenges for the profession that pertain to the management of change in schools/colleges and in communities. Issues teachers will need to resolve are:

1. *School leadership*
   • how can professional leadership and management teams become familiar with technology issues?
   • what is the best way to work within a school/college climate that encourages change?
   • how can digital evangelists be supported and encouraged?

- how can the social system be reconfigured to support an 'open school/ college' model?
- who needs to consider the privacy issues raised by the implementation of new technologies in open schools/colleges?

2. *CPD*
   - what is appropriate training for education professionals?
3. *Families*
- is there a need to educate the families as well as the child?
- what kinds of support do families require in an open school/college system?
- how to work with parents who are not motivated to have their children learning at home
- how to work with parents whose use of technologies is adversely influenced by issues of culture, ethnicity and religion?

The teachers contributing to the Leask and Preston (2010) research estimated that currently only a small percentage of the teaching profession understand how the future might unfold with respect to technology and teaching and learning. Given the difficulties of teachers in schools accessing CPD, exchanging examples of practice through national collaborative professional networks was seen as a cost-effective form of CPD. See chapter 10 for further information about this approach.

Developing teachers so they can use technology to support the curriculum and subject teaching

The quality of teachers, their vision and their capabilities require investment, challenge and management. Earlier research (Kington et al. 2001) found that staff who were not comfortable with technologies moved to schools which were less demanding. The polarization of the teaching professional into those who use technology and those who do not has to be recognized by school & college leaders wanting to create an ethos where technology is embedded in everyday practice. The following section provides a framework for teachers to use in developing appropriate software and pedagogical approaches for their subject areas.

Table 9.3 summarizes the characteristics of effective technology-based tools and digital resources for subject teaching. Ideas are grouped around three characteristics: *pedagogical*, *design* and *technical*. Some characteristics may appear to conflict, because their application will depend on the age of the learner, the skill of the subject teacher and the subject matter of the package.

Teachers contributing to the Education Futures research who worked with 16+ learners stressed that the design of materials and tools on learning platforms should enable the role of the learner to change with maturity. This might be because older learners are expected to be more autonomous than is the case with younger learners.

Table 9.3 The characteristics of effective technology-based tools and digital resources for subject teaching

Characteristic	Effective technology-based tools and digital resources are those which:
Pedagogical characteristics	• have tasks which are realistic and authentic: e.g. tasks use credible circumstances and are related to local environments where possible • are designed for teachers by teachers where appropriate • provide extra learning power for conventional tasks: e.g. through additional links to activities and resources • are adaptable for different purposes including SEN • are open-ended, creative, flexible, engaging • allow teachers and users to control the pace and direction of learning
Design characteristics	• have explicit pedagogical models underpinning their design • are intuitive, easy to use, modify and update and easy to return to sometime later: i.e. 'save' facilities are available • support a quick start but also allow for growth • protect work held on the school learning platform so this cannot be wiped including by the service provider • have updates which are quickly and easily accessible • have a sensible licensing or subscription model • are flexibly structured • provide a single clear focus • demonstrate value for money and added value wherever possible • include additional follow-up activities and resources • allow student authors to own their work on the school learning platform
Technical characteristics	• are multi-platform • are economic on bandwidth • are safe and secure • provide a good, rapid-response back-up service • integrate with and are compatible with other systems including home systems and are interoperable with other tools • put technical quality and robustness first before price

These teachers described two kinds of use of online learning environments: virtual learning environments (or learning platforms) and personal learning environments:

- *Virtual Learning Environments* (learning platforms) are class-teacher-institution-focused (push) and use a delivery model: resources are structured and organized.
- *Personal Learning Environments* are person-focused (pull) and use a personalized learning model: the learner is free to select, choose, control resources and learning experiences.

Teachers conceived the online learning platform as a tool that served and linked two learning phases:

- In *phase 1* the Virtual Learning Environment (learning platform) builds independent learning in the first phase of learner use and generates familiarization with the wider collaborative features of online learning.
- In *phase 2* the Personal Learning Environment emerges out of the learner's initial VLE experience and enables the learner to draw together the resources and materials relevant to them.

To achieve this transition, these teachers of older learners emphasized that the most important lesson for the learner is 'learning how to learn' in the earliest stages of education – '*[Learners] need to know what each tool does and how to use it*'. They also emphasized the changing role of the teacher – from the director of learning to the facilitator of learning – the teacher's role being not only to teach subject content, but also to teach learners how to learn, to encourage lifelong learning and to support the learning process.

The introduction of a learning platform that promotes independence was recognized as a challenge to teachers who are still questioning the need to change their role from teacher to facilitator. Because this shift is uncomfortable for some, they argued that teachers need tools to support that change in role. Consequently, both for teachers and learners the design for learning approach to the learning platform should emphasize less 'push' and more 'on demand' resources.

Learning platforms need then to be designed for teachers as expert learners with provision for a continuum of learning and flexible pedagogy. Teachers contributing to the Education Futures research conceptualized the platform as a framework to hang tools and resources from: a virtual learning kiosk where teachers know what to expect of the products available. In this learning environment teachers and learners needed to be able to identify which tools will support their purposes.

As primary schools do not have the same levels of technical support as secondary schools and colleges, tools must be easy to use. Teachers do not have time to read a manual. Software that was simple to use and had a strong pedagogical underpinning was highly praised by primary and secondary teachers.

Teachers' views on Interactive Whiteboards (IWBs)

Teachers contributing to the Leask and Preston research (2010) complained about Interactive Whiteboard (IWB) software suites that major on resources that promote mechanistic, behaviourist approaches – for example, testing knowledge instead of constructing it. This kind of testing approach has limited application and is over-represented in software available to schools. It has some value for checking on progress from time to time, but little value in concept development for the individual learner.

The teachers recommended IWB resources that have a sound pedagogical base and which can be used to develop thinking skills, such as the mind-mapping tools that already exist, and resources for sorting and classifying or for logging experiences in an immediate and representative way. The best IWB products were considered to be generic tools rather than those that provide specific one-off resources. In order to master specific one-off resources, a teacher has to carry around a lot of information about what might be used just once for a particular job – whereas tools that can be adapted to meet a range of needs are more likely to be used. Teachers in some subjects said there was little software available to support work in their specific subjects. To maximize the adoption and embedding of new practice, many teachers need exemplars which are explicit about pedagogic issues. Descriptions and case studies in which pedagogic approaches are implicit are not sufficient. See chapter 3 for a filler discussion on IWBs.

Developments of LOGO-type control programming were praised because they have developed the original product so that the same program can be used without an interface to begin with, but teachers can then move on to the control of external devices with the older learners – hence they can be used with a range of age groups.

In terms of costs teachers prefer robustness to cheap and easy availability, such as low-quality, digital still cameras. Teachers become disenchanted when equipment breaks easily and cannot be repaired. However, designers needed to be alert to issues like telephone costs. One idea to be explored is that laptops for learners, loaded with all the textbooks, might be cheaper than printed books if the copyright issues can be agreed. Further points to consider in choosing digital resources are summarized in Table 9.4.

Any investment in education should be linked to learning gains. If the case can't be made that learning gains result, then the plans are not sufficiently formed. Table 9.5 summarizes general questions to use in evaluating resources.

When the teachers contributing to the Education Futures research (Leask and Preston 2010) compared digital with non-digital tools and resources, they commented on the greater teaching power they now have with digital tools and resources at their fingertips. They pointed out that, while there are some experiences that cannot be replaced by technology (such as handwriting, music and sport), even these activities and learning experiences can be both supported and enhanced by technology – for example, the use of video to demonstrate and analyse performance.

The shift in school and college purchasing practice in the UK from the position of teachers purchasing individual packages to suit their teaching to a central model of purchasing materials to use via the learning platform has implications not only for industry and for licensing arrangements, but also for innovative teachers who may be

Table 9.4 Choosing digital resources: points to consider

Support for learning: *Do the digital resources:*

Help learners to explore ethical and moral issues in a practical context through the need to deal with inappropriate sites	Facilitate interactions between teachers and learner as well as between learners	Help learners gain a range of perspectives through monitoring multiple channels of communication
Provide a range of learning routes	Help with demonstrations	Support planning via use of hyperlinks
Provide opportunities to share learning, collaboratively edit and add to work	Provide access to school/ college systems from anywhere	Offer innovative ways of communicating though music and sport
Support communication and collaboration via cameras, podcasts, wikis	Provide time to think and apply knowledge instead of taking notes because the lesson can be printed	Help teachers to keep abreast of current specialisms like Assessing Pupil Progress (QCA booklet)
Provide a means of publishing samples of good work	Provide quick recording of data from class discussion	Support learning by backchannel chat around main activity
Help very young children and children with writing difficulties to record and publish their work	Provide opportunities for pupils to personalize their own learning	

Communications support – *technology-based tools and digital resources:*

Via video conferencing and other tools connect people, teachers, learners across distances: e.g. for global collaboration	Help to involve parents via learning platforms in the home	Provide access to a broad curriculum through links with learners elsewhere and support anywhere anytime learning – learners no longer limited to being in school/college
Provide business sites for the community	Provide professional presentation of resources	

prevented from developing leading practice because institutional processes prevent innovation. Even where teachers are willing to adopt new practices, keeping up to date can be difficult, and school leaders as part of their vision for the school will need to plan for ways of supporting teachers in keeping abreast of progress.

How do teachers find out about new tools and resources?

Teachers contributing to the Education Futures research (Leask and Preston 2010) were asked how they keep up to date and find out about new tools and resources.

Table 9.5 Examples of general evaluation questions teachers might use in choosing software

• evidence for the improvement of teaching and learning and that the technology makes the learning easier	• appropriateness
	• piloting opportunities
	• the availability of the resource: e.g. 24/7
• compatibility and flexibility – can generic tools from other suppliers be added: e.g. to the learning platform	• storage capacity required
• access for parents, teachers, learners outside of school/college/institution context	

Social networking was one of the ways teachers reported they are using to keep up to date. Subject groups currently meet in face-to face-conferences, whereas social networking software supports collaboration between meetings as well as providing the chance for those in remote areas to obtain information live when professionals are meeting. Different kinds of collective learning behaviour are emerging in professional networks (Leask and Younie 2001a; Leask 2011). One solution emerging to teachers' hesitation in changing pedagogic approaches to use technology tools would be formal and informal CPD designed to promote social and professional networking to encourage collaborative learning between professionals. Teachers could have access to knowledgeable advisers, experts and peers during this learning episode for knowledge exchange and sharing practice. Teachers should be experiencing joint projects and just-in-time learning themselves using these new media. This requires professional networking tools that provide ways for teachers with the same interests to locate each other, such as the European Union e-twinning project. This enables professionals to find 'people who know' and share projects. Collaboration is also possible with industry and local stakeholders through Web 2.0 technologies, but requirements for police safety checks can prevent activities engaging volunteers. Teachmeets (http://teachmeet.pbworks.com) and Mirandanet mods (http://www.mirandanet.ac.uk/mirandamods/) provide new forms of CPD knowledge sharing using innovative knowledge management and webinar tools.

Solutions to the challenges of providing CPD for teachers which minimize the costs of removing teachers from the school setting include:

- maximizing online collaboration tools
- providing CPD through networking and access to experts and establishing sustainable models to support the efforts of cross-curricula and subject associations. (Current networks depend on considerable volunteer effort – are these sustainable? What other models exist?)
- creating CPD, giving time for play and space to develop pedagogy for new technology tools – for example, through local authority roadshows
- avoiding the CPD cascade model – 'Chinese whispers do not work'
- increasing the use of online and video conferences and new ways of working described as 'unconferences'

- creating a collaborative environment with e-facilitators that is open and international. How can fragmentation be overcome? How can links between networks be made? The exclusivity of some current networks prevents effective exchange of knowledge
- developing more people to people connections and e-twinning opportunities.

Importantly, ethical and intellectual property issues need to be resolved as teachers work more online, sharing knowledge and resources, and there is a need to develop a common code of conduct for such work. Any sites supporting professional networking will normally have terms and conditions with protocols for codes of conduct which include:

- How can listeners in the e-forums be identified?
- What ethical code do contributors subscribe to?
- Who owns the ideas and the content posted by teachers?

Teachers report using a very wide variety of sources to gain information about new tools and resources. These include:

- *personal contacts*: learners, friends, colleagues, parents
- *professional contacts*: peers, subject coordinators, in-school/college specialists (providing demonstrations), staff in other schools/colleges
- *professional networking*: various professional associations
- *examination boards*: especially for moderators
- *reviews*: magazines and specialist sections of newspapers: for example, the *TES, Guardian*
- *exhibitions*
- *local authorities*: through advisory teachers and teachers' centres or virtual teachers' centres where ideas can be pooled and shared
- *reputable software providers*
- *associated universities*
- *technicians who work across schools and colleges*: these are reported as becoming a conduit for the sharing of knowledge, because they see what staff in other schools and colleges are doing and can judge what works. A suggestion from teachers contributing to the Education Futures research was that technicians should be trained to understand pedagogy as well as technology. In addition, a cluster of schools and colleges could have a roaming e-learning technologist as well as a team of technicians.
- *well-designed CPD programmes* providing examples of pedagogical applications and giving time to play, test out and evaluate. Teachers contributing to the Education Futures research said the best CPD programmes are not just about 'what' the product can do but also about 'how' a digital tool or resource can be used. This recommendation was made because staff will not always see the relevance or potential of a piece of kit or software unless it is linked to the curriculum. Decontextualized technical training was not considered useful unless

it was accompanied by realistic and usable ideas for how a resource can be used in a real classroom with real teachers and real children.

- The teachers did appreciate some *intervention from external agencies* to avoid the reinventing of old ideas. Advisory teachers were particularly useful, particularly for passing on information through their re-visiting of schools and colleges to support and then to provide follow-up ideas. Top-down regional advisory meetings that focus on policy were considered to be far less useful than opportunities for teachers to share their ideas. One view was that the coffee-time chat was often more productive than the formal input. Workshops should model for teachers the constructivist learning contexts they are expected to provide for learners.
- FE staff and primary specialist staff find it particularly difficult to find networks of peers and experts who are working in the same areas.
- CPD programmes should not just be available online as this can result in professional isolation. However, Web 2.0 technologies provide new CPD opportunities through social and professional networking.

Conclusions

The most significant factors limiting or supporting change are the attitudes and understanding of the individuals who collectively make up the school community and whether institutional processes support of inhibit innovation and development. The aim of this chapter has been to provide frameworks and rationales to help decision-making about the adoption of technology-enhanced pedagogies, but any successful change will depend on the knowledge and competence of staff, and the vision of school leaders and their ability to motivate staff to change.

Further reading

Bolam, R. and Weindling, D. (2006) *Synthesis of research and evaluation projects concerned with capacity-building through teachers' professional development: Full research report*, London: General Teaching Council for England.

Pickering, J., Daly, C. and Pachler, N. (eds) (2007) *New Designs for Teachers' Professional Learning*, Bedford Way Papers, London: Institute of Education, University of London.

Useful websites

British Council for the School Environment www.bcse.uk.net

National College – Managing school resources. This advice is from the website of the government-funded National College for school leaders in England.

http://www.nationalcollege.org.uk/index/leadershiplibrary/leadingschools/leading-an-effective-organization/managing-schools/manage-resources.htm

10 Twenty-first-century educational practice: research, evidence and knowledge management

Overview

The challenges facing education systems and teachers continue to intensify. In modern knowledge-based economies, where the demand for high-level skills will continue to grow substantially, the task in many countries is to transform traditional models of schooling . . . into customised learning systems that identify and develop the talents of all students. This will require the creation of 'knowledge-rich', evidence-based education systems, in which school leaders and teachers act as a professional community with the authority to act, the necessary information to do so wisely, and the access to effective support systems to assist them in implementing change . . . in many countries, education is still far from being a knowledge industry in the sense that its own practices are not yet being transformed by knowledge about the efficacy of those practices.

(OECD 2009a: 3)

Given the importance of the education system to any national economy, the OECD findings that education systems are not 'knowledge-rich' or 'evidence-based' is surely an astonishing state of affairs. The McKinsey Report (2007) *How the world's best performing schools come out on top* asserts that teacher quality is the single most important issue to be addressed in systems which wish to improve. A comparison of knowledge-management practice between the education sector and the medical profession, comparing the adoption of technologies to support international collaboration in the synthesis of evidence and the collaborative building and testing of knowledge to disseminate evidence to inform practice (see for example the Cochrane collaboration), shows that the education sector is still in the dark ages.

This chapter makes the case for national education systems to adopt tried and tested knowledge management and Web 2.0 tools used by other sectors. It examines the problem of the quality and extent of the evidence base underpinning teachers' practice, which is often unacknowledged. In the twenty-first century, through the use of technology, the research and evidence base underpinning teachers' practice could be made accessible to all. This lack of research-based professional knowledge is a particular problem for subject specialist issues and is further compounded by the fact that research published in journals is not generally designed around questions teachers want answered; yet this is rarely if ever acknowledged in the discourse about school and system improvement. This chapter proposes new ways of working using technology to meet these challenges.

Introduction and context

The findings from OECD's Teaching and Learning International Survey (OECD 2009a) set out the global challenges facing education sectors worldwide. This OECD research

> ... challenges national systems to consider the processes in place for building and accessing the knowledge base for educational practice and policy making and to consider the quality of key levers for change in the system, i.e. the quality and extent of the knowledge base and the quality and training of teacher educators.
>
> (Leask 2011: 2)

This chapter examines ways in which the education sector might become a 'knowledge industry', and how it might support knowledge transfer, collaborative knowledge building and knowledge sharing within education sectors in individual countries as well as worldwide.

The McKinsey report's (2007: 2) key finding that the quality of teaching is the single most important factor in improving learner outcomes might seem to be stating the obvious, yet in the research around improving quality in education, the quality of the professional knowledge base – for example, how teachers know how to teach and whether they are basing their practice on up-to-date knowledge, information and resources, or indeed research and evidence – is largely ignored. Against the evidence, governments in a number of countries are encouraging graduates to 'Teach First', placing them on accelerated training schemes and often deploying them in schools in deprived areas where logic might suggest that this is where more experienced teachers with proven track records should be placed.

We argue that improvements in quality of teaching will come if practice is underpinned by an evidence base for practice which is easily accessible to teachers anywhere at any time. There is an opportunity for those concerned with improving the quality of education to provide a national infrastructure of e-tools and e-resources which will enable educators, academics, researchers and teachers:

- to keep up to date through accessing the evidence-based knowledge they need to improve practice, at the time they need it and in the form they need it

- to work collaboratively with peers and experts to co-construct new knowledge as changing circumstances require
- to be engaged in collaborative research projects which produce outcomes substantial enough to warrant changes in practice.

The argument is made that the provision of a national online community network linking academics, teachers and researchers can support low-cost yet effective ways of building and sharing knowledge about effective educational practice. This chapter outlines specific examples for improving e-communications for school-based educational research. The core challenges about developing appropriate e-connectivity and new ways of working, fit for a twenty-first-century context need to focus on:

1. The importance of knowledge management and evidence-based practice in the context of international competition and drives for improvement at the national level
2. Improving the quality of research – challenges and roles including levers for change
3. How twenty-first-century technologies might be harnessed to improve the quality, relevance and timeliness of educational research
4. Knowledge Management tools utilizing Web 2.0 technologies need to be developed, but knowledge management is not widely understood in the education sector.

Theory and research base

The importance of knowledge management and evidence-based practice

International comparative studies of learner outcomes from school-based education systems such as PIRLS, TIMMS and PISA show the relative positions of different countries on a range of measures and spur countries to invest to improve the quality of the education system (OECD 2003, 2009, 2007b,c; http://timss.bc.edu/; www.pisa.oecd.org). However, improving education systems is an elusive goal with teacher quality being identified as more important than financial investment in raising attainment levels (OECD 2009; McKinsey 2007). One aspect of the goal of improving teacher quality is improving the research and evidence base underpinning practice (OECD 2003).

Improving the quality of teaching is stated as a high priority in the documentation from different countries (see for example the Australian government DEST 2005, DEEW 2007, 2010; Indian government NCTE 2010a, b; China Education and Research Network 2000; Ming-yuan 2006; OECD 2003, 2007a, b; UNESCO 2010 a,b.; US Department of Education 2006; UK DCSF 2006; Proton Europe 2007; Cochran-Smith and Zeichner 2005). Examples of statements made in this respect are as follows:

> Teacher status and education are considered fundamental for the improvement of educational quality. This is the commitment of UNESCO State Members . . . .
>
> (UNESCO 2010a: 1)

Teacher quality is essential for student achievement. In this modern era of global economic competitiveness, what teachers know and do to improve student achievement is of critical importance for maintaining America's economic strength.'

(US Department for Education 2006: 1)

Teacher education is the manufacturing machine for the Chinese education undertaking.

(China Education and Research Network 2000: 1)

However, in these reports from many countries little analysis is undertaken of how teacher quality is to be improved. Research in the UK undertaken by the General Teaching Council in England (GTCE 2007, 2006; Bolam and Weindling 2006) pinpoints collaboration and networking as key features of effective teacher development – both of which can be supported in a variety of ways through a national e-infrastructure and acknowledgement of the role of knowledge management in the twenty-first century.

Specifically missing from these reports is how the research and evidence base underpinning practice is built by research producers and accessed by research users. There are some notable exceptions and the OECD reviews (2003) which include examination of the research evidence base underpinning practice provide some detail of specific initiatives in different countries.

A number of national e-communications tools and environments can be identified, such as the Scottish Glow project, the Australian Ultranet project, the European Schoolnet (Leask and Younie 2001), the Regional Broadband consortia in the UK, the various e-communication tools used in universities (Blackboard; WebCT), as well as the e-communication tools used by ministries of education and subject associations. For the most part these tools and ways of working are either not focused on sharing and building research-based knowledge or are only available for closed communities and fail to connect up the various research producers and users in any systematic way. This latter point applies particularly to the free e-tools on the Internet – without some formal coordination these do not provide the kind of e-infrastructure to support research-based educational practice.

These developments, it is argued, while worthy enough within their own context, are by their disparate and unconnected nature not contributing effectively to developing 'education as a knowledge industry' and to the challenge of building evidence-based practice and providing access to this to education practitioners and research users.

E-systems and knowledge management (KM) tools now have a key role to play in cost-effective knowledge transfer in the private sector and in branches of the public sector outside education (Henley 2008a, 2008b; IDeA 2008, 2009; Collison and Parcell 2006; and Davenport and Prusak 1998). Yet, in the reports on the quality of education mentioned earlier, which identify the quality of teaching and teacher education as critical to improving quality outcomes, there is little recognition of the opportunities provided through e-systems to support these desired changes. The quality and content of the professional knowledge base underpinning educational practice

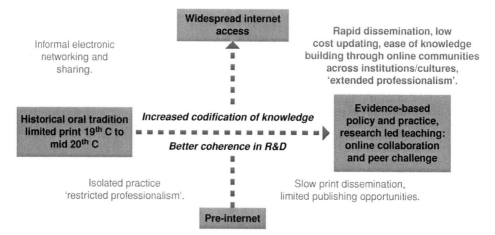

Figure 10.1 Increased codification of knowledge – moving from 19th C to 21st C professional practice.

and teacher education, and the knowledge and training of teacher educators and the ways that knowledge transfer takes place, are taken as unproblematic. However, in a number of countries policy documents set out an expectation that practice and policy will be evidence-based (OECD 2007b, 2007c). There are of course many websites and documents giving teaching tips and advice to teachers (though few giving advice to teacher educators). However, a scrutiny of such advice as often as not reveals a lack of citation of any evidence.

Detailed examination of how research is generated in education in the UK context shows that there is little investment in subject-specialist research in pedagogy (TDA 2002), that government funding is principally spent in evaluating policy, and that much research is undertaken on a small-scale basis and is unfunded except through an individual staff member's time. This is hardly a recipe for the production of research of such quality and depth that it could impact on national and international policy and practice.

Figure 10.1 (from Leask and White 2004) illustrates how rapidly the context in which research is generated and published has moved on, from a situation in the 1980s where publication was costly, slow and based on individual endeavour, to one where publication is rapid using online resources and can be collaborative. Twenty-first-century Web 2.0 tools support online publication and low-cost updating of publications, year on year as more research and evidence becomes available, but brings the problem of volume and quality.

Arguably, effective e-support for these new ways of working and updating the evidence base requires a national and international e-infrastructure if maximum benefit is to be gained by utilizing existing resources in the system. There are several emerging models which illustrate these points and the potential for new ways of working to be adopted, which will improve research quality, relevance and timeliness.

Improving the quality of educational research: challenges and roles

For whom is educational research undertaken? The answer to the question is not straightforward. There are probably two major sorts of research report – one being a major report commissioned by a funder, the second the traditional academic journal article which is subject to peer review, with peers being academic researchers.

An associated issue is the variation of quality of reporting in research articles. An analysis of this variation led to the production of guidance in the writing of research articles, which was drawn to the attention of journal editors by the education ministry in the UK (Newman et al. 2004). For the period of the Labour government (1997–2010) there was considerable central government investment in the development of one particular process for systematic review (see www.eppi.ioe.ac.uk) in an attempt to synthesize research findings, following a not dissimilar model established for medicine from the Cochrane reviews (www.cochranecollaboration.org), but without the success of the Cochrane collaboration. However, the Campbell Collaboration work is acknowledged as having the potential to provide an international lead for education in synthesis.

One direct consequence of the availability of the Internet is to make available educational research which previously might have been difficult to find. This creates an unmanageable volume of potentially relevant material for the user who wishes to build on the evidence base of what has happened before. Take, for example, modern foreign languages (MFL) teaching: when MFL was being introduced into the primary curriculum by the UK government in 2003, over 5000 research articles covering relevant elements of pedagogy were found to produce guidance about the evidence base for practice; these needed to be read, synthesized and the relevant information extracted to produce an effective evidence base for practice.

It would be unrealistic to expect any teacher, practitioner, research user or research generator to become familiar with such a volume of material. In any case many of the articles were not sufficiently well constructed nor did they report the research in sufficient depth for users to be confident about changing personal or national practice on the basis of their findings. In addition, the cost of the production of such material in staff time alone must have been in the region of many millions of dollars. This one example represents a waste of resources in the system, and the volume of articles is replicated across the major areas of educational practice. However, research into fine-grained aspects of educational practice is missing or very difficult to find. Take, for example, research into barriers that learners have to overcome in understanding concepts in many subject areas.

Currently e-resources supporting knowledge management in education are scattered, inaccessible and incoherent. Clearly, responsibility needs to be taken at the national and international levels for the development of an e-infrastructure to provide signposts, validation of content and meeting places for education practitioners dedicated to the development of professional knowledge. In gathering evidence for the parliamentary select committee, Leask and Younie (2009) found that for teachers, access to much of this up-to-date knowledge is patchy. In addition, further research conducted with practitioners (from across primary, secondary and FE) Leask and Preston (2010) identified that UK teachers wanted an e-infrastructure to provide access to validated knowledge and the means of collaborative creation of new knowledge. This is clearly possible with the widespread availability of Web 2.0

technologies for communication, collaboration, knowledge creation and knowledge management.

Applications to practice

How twenty-first-century technologies might be harnessed to improve the quality, relevance and timeliness of educational research

As discussed, the issue of the sheer volume of small-scale research made available through Web 1.0 technologies (read-only) is apparent. Web 2.0 technologies (read and write) provide opportunities for collaborative knowledge building and peer challenge which previously simply did not exist. Publishing is swift, so timeliness is assured. Review and challenge by users and research generators is facilitated through online tools supporting asynchronous dialogue.

The Internet has revolutionized knowledge sharing and knowledge building and there is potential for these ways of online working to improve the quality of access to knowledge. Figure 10.2 shows the front page of a prototype low-cost and open national knowledge sharing and building environment using Web 2.0 technologies (Education communities www.educationcommunities.org). There are a growing number of communities of practice listed, and through a 'people finder' the professional profiles of people across the education sector can be viewed. The software allows for the creation of multiple interlinked communities, which may be open or closed and for the profiles of all professionals registered on the site to be searchable.

Figure 10.2 National online communities of practice for professional networking and knowledge management in the UK for local government.

Figure 10.3   National online communities of practice for professional networking and knowledge management in the UK for education.

This provides a powerful knowledge base for educational practitioners and the opportunity for low-cost collaboration. This is a clone of a successful Web 2.0 environment for local government in the UK (IDeA 2008) (Figure 10.3).

It is our contention that there is a role for a national e-infrastructure in each country to support knowledge building and knowledge sharing across a vast range of areas in order to gain maximum benefit nationally and internationally from the intellectual capital held in a particular discipline area. However, such a resource requires coordination and a commitment to ongoing funding.

Knowledge management and examples from other sectors

Knowledge management is an emerging discipline (Henley 2008a,b; IDeA 2006, 2008, 2009) and in the UK a Knowledge Management Council for central government to complement the Information Management Council has been established. Staff in organizations with effective knowledge-management strategies can be expected to demonstrate five characteristics in that they find and use research-based knowledge, create and share knowledge as well as manage knowledge to ensure their work is based on the latest knowledge of effective practice.

Figure 10.4 sets out these characteristics and provides examples of the tools necessary in a research environment to ensure effective knowledge management. These tools include:

- the linking of research databases so they are cross-searchable (see for example www.eep.ac.uk)
- an expectation that practitioners and policy-makers will use research (as demonstrated through appraisal procedures)

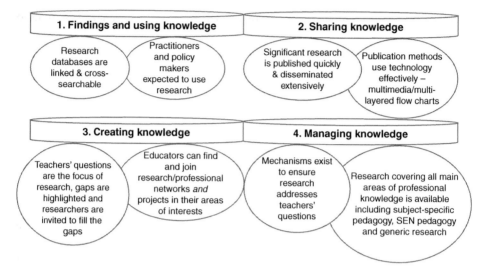

Figure 10.4 National knowledge management tools for education.

- mechanisms for quickly publishing and disseminating significant research – to improve timeliness
- the use of publication mechanisms which include multimedia and are not just restricted to text (see the flow chart example of map of medicine health-guides www.mapofmedicine.com) – to allow easy access to the knowledge needed at the time of need and easy identification of gaps in knowledge
- mechanisms for identifying the research questions that users need answering and providing access to these of research generators – to improve relevance
- easy access to research networks – in order to support collaborative working
- access to list of ongoing projects – in order to minimize duplication
- a listing of invitations to join projects – in an attempt to limit the proliferation of small-scale research projects
- a research and evidence base which addresses fine-grained policy and practice issues as well as more generic issues
- the presence of online community-of-practice workspaces which provide appropriate functionality and e-tools.

Knowledge management (KM) tools need to be provided nationally so that teachers and researchers can *find* and *use* knowledge to build next practice and *create, share* and *manage* knowledge for the benefit of the education sector.

In comparison with health and local government, for example, the Cochrane Collaboration (www.cochrane.org) and IDeA (www.communities.idea.gov.uk) the education sector is considerably behind in harnessing the power of technology to support ongoing professional development, knowledge sharing and evidence building. In local government in the UK, as part of a national knowledge-management strategy for the local government sector, a national e-infrastructure to support professional networking has been developed to encourage sharing of both 'tacit' as well as 'explicit' knowledge across the whole of the UK. In a sample of more than 1300 employees, key benefits were identified as:

- value through saving time
- keeping up to date with current thinking
- innovations
- sharing *good practice* and avoiding duplication of work
- developing ideas
- carbon footprint reduction and other environmental savings
- induction to new roles and staff development
- relationship building. (IDeA November 2009: 5)

In education, to change teachers', academics' and researchers' professional practice is not a task to be undertaken lightly, yet the benefits (for countries which can forge new ways of working) will be significant. Many practitioners and research generators will be members of professional communities. Improving the knowledge base of such professional communities may improve professional practice across a whole sector. Such collaboration would require the development of mutual trust and shared objectives in improving the quality of the knowledge and evidence base.

Conclusions

Web 2.0 technologies and knowledge-management approaches provide opportunities to develop more effective ways of undertaking educational research, publishing research and creative opportunities for new ways of working between practitioners, academics and policy-makers. Using Web 2.0 technologies for online networking and knowledge management (finding, using, sharing, creating and managing knowledge), teachers could easily access relevant research evidence to inform their practice.

In the UK, depressingly, major national knowledge-management initiatives undertaken by the numerous education agencies in the UK have resulted in a plethora of small networks with significant management and development costs, a lack of sustainability as the networks are linked with time-limited projects, and fragmentation of energies. Without any coherent, joined-up 'portal' to access such networks, the result is a fragmentation of what is available and lack of inter-operability. This means that the potential of e-networking to improve professional practice is not realized. This could be easily redressed by providing a 'one point of entry' approach.

Figure 10.4 referred to earlier provides a minimum specification for an e-infrastructure to improve the quality of educational research, its relevance and timeliness. To realize this vision requires the allocation of resources, coupled with the devolution of the management of such an e-infrastructure to professional networks in order to ensure freedom of speech and open discussion and exchange of ideas. The online Education Communities solution (Figures 10.2 and 10.3) shows new ways of working. The next step in improving the quality, relevance and timeliness of educational research really does require some central coordination at national levels. Developing individual country systems, which could be linked up internationally, would require the work of a group of visionaries, but the benefits for teachers, research generators and research users the world over are likely to be substantial and sustainable. Such an initiative however would have to sit independently of government systems so as to be credible.

Further reading

Davies, H., Nutley, S. and Smith, P. (eds) (2000) *What works? Evidence-based policy and practice in public services*, Bristol, UK: The Policy Press.
Wenger, E., McDermott, R. and Snyder, W. (2002) *Cultivating communities of practice: a guide to managing knowledge*, Cambridge, Mass: Harvard Business School.

Useful websites

Education communities - http://www.educationcommunities.org
This is a Web 2.0 site for educators that shows the power of interconnecting Web 2.0 environments with a people and community finder which supports knowledge sharing and building across individual interest groups. It mirrors the successful local government facebook for education sites (see Figures 10.2 and 10.3).
http://www.idea.gov.uk/idk/core/page.do?pageId=8152457
Knowledge management – for local government. This site contains advice about knowledge management for local authorities.

References

360° Safe (2010) *School E-Safety Self Review Tool*, http://www.360safe.org.uk/Manual Uploads/ School-E-SafetyV3.pdf (accessed 2 March 2012).

Abbott, C. (2001) *ICT: Changing Education*, London and New York: RoutledgeFalmer.

Agalianos, A., Noss, R. and Whitty, G. (2001) LOGO in Mainstream Schools: The Struggle Over the Soul of an Educational Innovation, *British Journal of Sociology of Education*, 22(4): 479–500.

Anderson, J. and Page, M. (2004) Richard Fothergill: Educationalists who put computers in schools, *The Guardian*, 15 November 2004. www.guardian.co.uk/news/2004/nov/15/ guardianobituaries.obituaries (accessed 25 March 2012).

Arkes, H.R. and Garske, J.P. (1977) *Psychological Theories of Motivation*, California: Brooks/ Cole Pub. Co.

Aspden, L. and Pountney, R. (2002) Community and Constructivism: implicit pedagogical models in virtual learning, in M. Driscoll and T. Reeves (eds), *Proceedings of World Conference on E-Learning in Corporate, Government, Healthcare, and Higher Education:* 2043–2046, Chesapeake, VA.

Atherton, J.S. (2011) *Learning and Teaching; Conversational learning theory, Pask and Laurillard.* http://www.learningandteaching.info/learning/pask.htm (accessed 15 March 2012).

Australian Government (2007) *Quality Teaching*, Curriculum Corporation, Canberra, Australia, http://www.deewr.gov.au/Schooling/QualityTeaching/AGQTP/Documents/Quality Teachers.pdf (accessed 25 March 2012).

Australian Government DEEW (Department of Education, Employment and Workplace relations) (2010) *Quality Teaching*, Canberra, Australia.

Australian Government DEST (Department of Education, Science and Training) (2005) *The emerging business of knowledge transfer: creating value from intellectual products and services*, Canberra, Australia.

Bandura, A. (1994) Self-Efficacy, in *Encyclopedia of Human Behaviour*, New York: Academic Press.

Barnett, R. (1997) *Higher Education: A Critical Business*, Buckingham: Society for Research into Higher Education and Open University Press.

Barrow, C. and Heywood-Everett, G. (2005) *E-safety: the experience in English educational establishments*, Coventry: Becta.

Beard, C. and Wilson, J. (2006) *Experiential Learning: a best practice handbook for educators and trainers*, London: Kogan Page.

Becker, H.J. (1994) How Exemplary Computer-Using Teachers Differ From Other Teachers: Implications for Realising the Potential of Computers in Schools, *Journal of Research on Computing in Education*, 26(3): 291–321.

Becta (1998) *Multimedia Portables for Teachers Pilot Project Report*, Coventry: Becta.

Becta (2001) *NGfL Pathfinders: Preliminary Report on the Roll-out of the NGfL Programme in Ten Pathfinder LEAs,* London: DfEE/Becta.

Becta (2003) *The Benefits of an Interactive Whiteboard,* Coventry: Becta.

Becta (2004) *ICT in Schools Survey,* Coventry: Becta.

Becta (2006) *Learning Platform Functional Requirements,* Coventry: Becta.

Becta (2008a) *Harnessing Technology Review 2008: The role of technology and its impact on education,* Coventry: Becta. http://dera.ioe.ac.uk/1422/1/becta_2009_htreview_report.pdf (accessed 25 March 2012).

Becta (2008b) *Multimedia Analysis: handheld games consoles in education,* Coventry: Becta.

Becta (2009a) *Enabling Next Generation Learning: enhancing learning through technology,* Coventry: Becta.

Becta (2009b) *Making Learning Personal: how are you making Next Generation Learning personal?* Coventry: Becta.

Becta (2009c) *Harnessing Technology for Next Generation Learning: Becta at work: a progress report 2008,* Coventry: Becta.

Becta (2009d) *Inspire Parental Engagement: How are you engaging parents in Next Generation Learning?* Coventry: Becta.

Becta (2009e) *Harnessing Technology for Next Generation Learning: children, schools and families,* Coventry: Becta.

Becta (2009f) *Safeguarding Children Online: How e-safe are your school and your learners? Safetynet,* Coventry: Becta.

Becta (2010a) *The Impact of Technology: value added classroom practice final report,* Coventry: Becta.

Becta (2010b), *Safetynet,* Coventry: Becta.

Becta/Pittard, V. (2005) *Research and the 'Harnessing Technology Strategy',* Becta's Annual Research Conference: Towards an ICT Research Agenda, National Motorcycle Museum, Solihull, 10 June 2005.

Beetham, H. and Sharpe, R. (2007) *Rethinking Pedagogy for a Digital Age: Designing and delivering e-learning,* London: Routledge.

Bell, B. and Gilbert, J. (1994) Teacher Development as Professional, Personal and Social Development, *Teaching and Teacher Education,* 10(5): 483–97.

Bennett, R. and Leask, M. (2005) Using ICT for professional purposes: an introduction, in Capel, S., Leask, M. and Turner, T. (2009) (eds) *Learning to Teach in the Secondary School: A companion to school experience* (5th edn), London and New York: Routledge.

Bentley, T. (1998) *Learning Beyond the Classroom: Education for a changing world,* London: Routledge.

Berlyne, D.E. (1960) *Conflict, Arousal and Curiosity,* New York: McGraw-Hill.

Bijker, W.E. (1997) *Of Bicycles, Bakelite and Bulbs: Towards a theory of sociotechnological change,* Cambridge, MA.

Black, P. and Wiliam, D. (2009) Developing the theory of formative assessment, *Educational Assessment, Evaluation and Accountability,* 21: 5–31.

Bloom, B.S. (ed.) (1956) Taxonomy of Educational Objectives, the classification of educational goals – Handbook I, *Cognitive Domain,* New York: McKay.

Bolam, R. and Weindling, D. (2006) *Synthesis of Research and Evaluation Projects Concerned with Capacity-Building through Teachers' Professional Development*, London: General Teaching Council.

Bourdieu, P. (1974) The school as a Conservative Force: Scholastic and cultural inequalities, in J. Egglestone (ed.) *Contemporary Research in the Sociology of Education*, London: Methuen and Co. Ltd.

Bowles, C. (1999) *Improving Teacher Competence in ICT*, MA Thesis, School of Education, Leicester University.

Boys, J., Ryan, S., Younie, S. and Ebbrell, D. (2001) Pedagogic Assumptions and Student Affordances: A Case Study of Reusable Educational Software, in *ALT-C Changing Learning Environments, proceedings of ALT-C: Association for Learning Technology, 8th International Conference*, Oxford: Information Press.

Brown, P. and Lauder, H. (1997) Education, Globalisation and Economic Development, in A.H. Halsey, H. Lauder, P. Brown and A.S. Wells (eds) *Education, Culture, Economy and Society*, Oxford: Oxford University Press, pp. 172–92.

Brundrett, M., Comber, C., Sommefeldt, D., McEune, R. and Burton, N. (2002) *Strategic Leadership in ICT Programme: Interim Report*, Unpublished Evaluation Report, Nottingham: National College of School Leadership.

Bruner, J.S. (1960) *The Process of Education*, Cambridge, MA: Harvard University Press.

Bruner, J.S. (1966) *Toward a Theory of Instruction*, Cambridge, MA: Harvard University Press.

Buckingham, D. (2007) Selling childhood? Children and consumer culture, *Journal of Children and Media*, 1(1): 15–24.

Byron, T. (2008) *Safer Children in a Digital World*, The Report of the Byron Review, London: DCSF.

Byron, T. (2010) *Do we have safer children in a digital world?* – A review of progress since the 2008 Byron Review, London: DCSF.

Cameron, R. (2006) Towards an integrated framework for designing effective ICT-supported learning environments: the challenge to better link technology and pedagogy, *Technology, Pedagogy and Education*, 15(2): 39–255.

Capel, S., Leask, M. and Turner, T. (2009) (eds) *Learning to Teach in the Secondary School: A companion to school experience* (5th edn), London and New York: Routledge.

Casey, P. (1996) Computing as Educational Innovation: A Model of Distributed Expertise, *Journal of Information Technology for Teacher Education*, 5(1 and 2): 13–23.

CEOP (Child Exploitation and Online Protection Centre), Annual Review 2007–2008. http://ceop.police.uk/Documents/ceopannualreview2008.pdf (accessed 29 August 2012).

China Education and Research Network (2000) *Teacher Education In China(II)Remarkable Results of Reform and Development Of Teacher Education*, http://www.edu.cn/20010101/21924.shtml (accessed 25 May 2012).

Clarke, K. (2003) Using self-directed learning communities to bridge the digital divide, *British Journal of Education Technology*, 34(5): 663–5.

Cochran-Smith, M. and Zeichner, K. (2005) *Studying Teacher Education: the Report of the AERA panel on research and teacher education*, Washington D.C.: American Educational Research Association in conjunction with Lawrence Erlbaum Associates, Mahwah, New Jersey.

Collison, C. and Parcell, G. (2006) *Learning to Fly*, London: Wiley.

Comber, C. and Hingley, P. (2004) The Strategic Leadership of ICT Programme: A Model for Professional Development? *British Educational Research Association Annual Conference,* UMIST University, Manchester, 16–18 September 2004.

Comber, C., Lawson, T. and Hargreaves, L. (1998) From Familiarisation to Adaptation: Teachers' Responses to the Introduction of Communications Technology into the Classroom, *Proceedings of the European Conference on the Educational Uses of the Internet and Identity Construction (IN-TELE),* Strasbourg.

Cooper, M., Jones, C., Davies, P. and Fletcher, M. (2010) *Getting 14–19 commissioning right,* London: InfoGroup/Orc International. http://www.orc.co.uk/pdfs/getting-14-19-commissioning-right.pdf (accessed 5 April 2012).

Cox, M., Webb, M., Abbott, C., Blakeley, B., Beauchamp, T. and Rhoades, V. (2003) *ICT and pedagogy, a review of the research literature, A report to the DfES.* London: DfES.

Cox, M.J. (1993) Information Technology Resourcing and Use, in Watson, D.M. (ed.) *Impact: An evaluation of the Impact of the Information Technology on Children's Achievements in Primary and Secondary Schools,* London: King's College.

Crook, C.K. and Lewthwaite, S. (2010) Technologies for formal and informal learning, in K. Littleton, C. Wood and J.K. Staarman (eds) *International Handbook of Psychology in Education,* Emerald, pp. 435–61.

Csíkszentmihályi, M. (1975) *Beyond Boredom and Anxiety,* San Francisco, CA: Jossey-Bass.

Csíkszentmihályi, M. (1990) *Flow: The psychology of optimal experience,* New York: Harper Collins.

Culp, K., Honey, M. and Mandinach, E. (2003) *A Retrospective on 20 years of Educational Policy,* Washington, DC: USA Department of Education.

Cuthell, J.P. (2003) Virtual Learning, in Kirjonen, J. (ed.) *Knowledge Work and Occupational Competence,* Jyvaskyla, Finland: Institute for Educational Research, pp. 23–37.

Cuthell, J.P. (2006) Steering the Supertanker: Changing Teaching and Learning, in C. Maddux, and C. Binghamton (eds) *Computers in the Schools: Technology Applications in Education,* New York: The Howarth Press.

Daanen, H. and Facer, K. (2007) *2020 and Beyond: Future scenarios for education in the age of new technologies,* Bristol: Futurelab.

Davenport, T. and Prusak, L. (1998) *Working Knowledge,* Boston, Mass: Harvard Business School Press.

Davies, H., Nutley, S. and Smith, P. (eds) (2000) *What Works? Evidence-based policy and practice in public services,* Bristol, UK: The Policy Press.

Davis, N.E. (2008) How may teacher learning be promoted for educational renewal with IT? in Joke Voogt and Gerald Knezek (eds) *International Handbook of Information Technology in Education,* Amsterdam: Kluwer Press.

Dawes, L. (1999) Chalky and the Interactive Whiteboard: Media Representation of Teachers and Technology, *Proceedings of the British Educational Research Association Annual Conference,* Brighton: University of Sussex.

Dawes, L. (2001) *The National Grid for Learning and the Professional Development of Teachers: Outcomes of an Opportunity for Change,* Ph.D. Thesis, Leicester: De Montfort University.

Dawes, L. (2008) *The Essential Speaking and Listening,* London: David Fulton.

DCSF (2006) *2020 Vision: Report of the Teaching and Learning in 2020 Review Group,* London: DCSF.

De Freitas, S. and Jameson, J. (2006) Collaborative e-support for lifelong learning, *British Journal of Educational Technology*, 37: 817–24.

Deal, T. (1999) Reframing Reform: Educational Leadership, in B. Sheppard, and J. Brown (eds) *Overcoming Barriers to Innovation in Schools Through Organisational Learning*, Budapest: European Distance Education Network.

Delwiche, A. (2006) Massively multiplayer online games (MMOs) in the new media classroom, *Educational Technology and Society*, 9(3): 160–72.

DES (1989) *Discipline in Schools: The Elton Report*, London: DES.

Desforges, C. (1995) *An Introduction to Teaching: Psychological Perspectives*, Oxford: Blackwell.

Dewey, J. (1916) *Democracy and Education. An introduction to the philosophy of education*, (1966 edn), New York: Free Press.

Dewey, J. (1933) *How We Think*, New York: Houghton Mifflin Company.

Dewey, J. (1938) *Education and Experience, The Kappa Delta Pi Lecture Series*, New York: Macmillan.

Dewey, J. (1966) *Lectures in the Philosophy of Education*. New York: Random House.

DfE (2011) *The Framework for the National Curriculum. A Report by the Expert Panel for the National Curriculum Review*, London: Department for Education.

DfEE (1997) *Connecting the Learning Society: National Grid for Learning; the Government's Consultation Paper*, London: DfEE.

DfEE (1998a) *Open for Learning, Open for Business*, London: DfEE.

DfEE (1998b) *Connecting Schools, Networking People: ICT Planning, Purchasing and Good Practice for the National Grid for Learning*, London: DfES/Becta.

DfEE (1998c) *Teaching: High Status, High Standards. Requirements for Courses of Initial Teacher Training*. Annex B: Initial Teacher Training National Curriculum for the Use of Information and Communications Technology in Subject Teaching. Circular 4/98, pp. 17–31. London: DfEE/TTA.

DfEE (1999) *The National Numeracy Strategy, Framework for Teaching Mathematics from Reception to Year 6*, London: DfEE.

DfES (2002) *ImpaCT2 – The Impact of ICT on Pupil Learning and Attainment*, London: DfES/Becta.

DfES (2002b) *Transforming the Way We Learn: A Vision for the Future of ICT in Schools*, London: DfES.

DfES (2003) *Fulfilling the Potential: Transforming Teaching and Learning Through ICT in Schools*, London: DfES.

DfES (2004) *Interactive Whiteboards: Frequently asked questions*, London: DfES.

DfES (2005a) *Harnessing Technology: Transforming Learning and Children's Services*, London: DfES.

DfES (2005b) *Higher Standards, Better Schools for All – more choice for parents and pupils*, London: DfES.

Douch, R., Attewell, J. and Dawson, D. (2010) *Games Technologies for Learning: More than just toys*, London: LSN.

Doughty, R. (2006) The State of ICT in Schools: The Story so Far, *Education Guardian*, London, 1–7.

Doyle, W. and Ponder, G. (1977) The Practicality Ethic in Teacher Decision-Making, *Interchange*, 8: 1–12.

Dupagne, M. and Krendle, K.A. (1992) Teachers' Attitudes Towards Computers: A Review Of The Literature, *Journal of Research on Computing in Education*, 24(3): 420–29.

Dwyer, D.C., Ringstaff, C. and Sandholtz, J.H. (1991) Changes in Teachers' Beliefs and Practices in Technology Rich Classrooms, *Educational Leadership*, 48(8): 45–52.

Dymoke, S. and Harrison, J. (2008) *Reflective Teaching & Learning*, London: Sage.

Earley, P., Evans, J., Collarbone, P., Gold, A. and Halpin, D. (2002) *Establishing the Current State of School Leadership in England*, London: DFES.

Eckhardt, B. (1995) I.T. – The Hidden Agenda, *Computer Education*, 81: 31–2.

EDSI Report (1997) *Preparing for the Information Age: Synoptic Report of the Education Departments' Superhighways Initiative (EDSI)*, Coventry: NCET.

Egenfeldt-Nielsen, S. (2007) *Educational Potential of Computer Games*, London, New York: Continuum International Publishing Group.

Eraut, M. (1994) *Developing Professional Knowledge and Competence*, London: RoutledgeFalmer.

Evans, L. (2002) What is Teacher Development? *Oxford Review of Education*, 28(1): 123–37.

Facer, K., Joiner, R., Stanton, D., Reid, J., Hull, R. and Kirk, D. (2004) Savannah: mobile gaming and learning? *Journal of Computer Assisted Learning*, 20: 399–409.

Fisher, R. (1995) *Teaching Children to Learn*, London: Stanley Thornes.

Fraser, J. (2011) The city as the learning environment: making change happen in Leicester's schools, *Keynote at ALT-C Thriving in a colder and more challenging environment, proceedings of ALT-C: Association for Learning Technology, 18th International conference*, University of Leeds.

Fredrickson, B.L. and Joiner, T. (2002) Positive Emotions Trigger Upward Spirals Toward Emotional Wellbeing, *Psychological Science*, 13(2): 172–75.

Fullan, M. (1993) *Change Force: Probing the Depths of Educational Reforms*, London: Falmer Press.

Fullan, M. (1991) *The New Meaning of Educational Change*, New York: Teachers College Press.

Fullan, M. and Hargreaves, A. (eds) (1992) *Teacher Development and Educational Change*, London: Falmer Press.

Gardner, H. (1983) *Frames of mind: the theory of multiple intelligences*, New York: Basic Books.

Gardner, H. (1993) *Multiple Intelligences: The theory in practice*, New York: Basic Books.

Gardner, H. (2006) *The Development and Education of the Mind: The selected works of Howard Gardner*, London: Routledge.

Gee, J.P. (2003) *What Video Games Have To Teach Us About Learning and Literacy*, New York: Palgrave Macmillan.

Gee, J.P. (2005) What would a state-of-the-art instructional video game look like? *Innovate*, 1.

Ghergulescu, I. and Muntean, C.H. (2010) Assessment of Motivation in Gaming Based E-Learning, *Proceedings of IADIS International Conference on Cognition and Exploratory Learning in Digital Age*.

Gibson, J.J. (1979) *The Ecological Approach to Visual Perception*, Boston: Houghton Mifflin.

Glover, D. and Miller, D.J. (2001) Running with Technology: the pedagogic impact of the large-scale introduction of interactive whiteboards in one secondary school, *Journal of Information Technology for Teacher Education*, 10(3): 257–75.

Glover, D. and Miller, D.J. (2002) The Introduction of Interactive Whiteboards into Schools in the United Kingdom: Leaders, Led, and the Management of Pedagogic and Technological Change, in *International Electronic Journal for Leadership in Learning*, 6 (24): University of Calgary Press. http://www.ucalgary.ca/iejll/glover_miller (accessed 2 April 2012).

Glover, D., Miller, D.J. and Averis, D. (2003) The Impact of Interactive Whiteboards on Classroom Practice: Examples drawn from the teaching of mathematics in secondary schools in England. The Mathematics Education into the 21st Century Project, *Proceedings of the International Conference The Decidable and the Undecidable in Mathematics Education*, Brno, Czech Republic, http://dipmat.math.unipa.it/~grim/21_project/21_brno03_Miller-Averis.pdf (accessed 5 October 2011).

Glover, D., Miller, D.J., Averis, D. and Door, V. (2004) Leadership implications of using interactive whiteboards: linking technology and pedagogy in the management of change, *Management in Education*, 18: 27–30.

Glover, D., Miller, D.J., Averis, D. and Door, V. (2007) The evolution of an effective pedagogy for teachers using the interactive whiteboard in mathematics and modern languages: an empirical analysis from the secondary sector, *Learning, Media and Technology*, 32(1): 5–20.

Goddard, D. and Leask, M. (1992) *The Search for Quality: Planning for improvement and managing change*, London: Paul Chapman.

Goleman, D. (1996) *Emotional Intelligence: Why it can matter more than IQ*, London: Bloomsbury.

Goodson, I.F. and Mangan, J.M. (1995) Subject Cultures and the Introduction of Classroom Computers, *British Educational Research Journal*, 21(5): 613–28.

Gordon, P. and Lawton, D. (2003) *Dictionary of British Education*, London: Woburn Press.

Gross, R. (2001) *Psychology: The Science of Mind and Behaviour* (4th edn), London: Hodder and Stoughton.

GTCE (General Teaching Council for England) (2007) *Making CPD better – Bringing Together Research about CPD*, Leaflet produced by R. Bolam and D. Weindling from the full report, London: GTCE.

Hadley, M. and Sheingold, K. (1993) Commonalities and Distinctive Patterns in Teachers' Integration of Computers, *American Journal of Education*, 101(3): 261–315.

Hall, G.E. (1979) The Concerns-Based Approach for Facilitating Change, *Educational Horizons*, 57: 202–8.

Hall, G.E. and Hord, S.M. (1987) *Change in Schools: Facilitating the process*. Albany, NY: State University of New York Press.

Hall, I. and Higgins, S. (2005) Primary school students' perceptions of interactive whiteboards, *Journal of Computer Assisted Learning*, 21: 102–17.

Ham, V. (2010) Technology as a Trojan Horse: a 'generation' of information technology practice, policy and research in schools, in A. McDougall, J. Murnane, A. Jones and N. Reynolds (eds) *Researching IT in Education: Theory, Practice and Future Directions*, London: Routledge.

Ham, V., Toubat, H. and Williamson-Leadley, S. (2006) National Trends in the ICT CPD School Clusters Programme 2003–2005. A Report to the New Zealand Ministry. http://www.educationcounts.govt.nz/publications/ict/49515/9 (accessed 26 August 2012).

Hammond, M. (2010) What is an affordance and can it help us understand the use of ICT in education? *Education and Information Technologies*, 15(3): 205–17.

Hammond, M., Younie, S., Woollard, J., Cartwright, V. and Benzie, D. (2009) *What does our past involvement with computers in education tell us? A view from the research community*, Coventry: Warwick University Press and ITTE.

Hargreaves, A. (2003*) Teaching in the Knowledge Society: Education in the age of insecurity*, New York: Teachers College Press.

Hargreaves, D.H. and Hopkins, D. (1991) *The Empowered Schools: The management and practice of development planning*, London: Cassell.

Harrison, C., Comber, C., Fisher, T., Haw, K., Lewin, C., Lunzer, E., McFarlane, A., Mavers, D., Scrimshaw, P., Somekh, B. and Watling, R. (2002), *Impact2: The impact of information and communication technologies on pupil learning and attainment*, Coventry: Becta.

Hawkridge, D. (1983) *New Information Technology in Education*, London: Croom Helm.

Henley Knowledge Management Forum (2008a) Building and sustaining communities of practice, *Knowledge in Action,* (7), Henley, UK: Henley Management College.

Henley Knowledge Management Forum (2008b) Sharing knowledge with other organizations, *Knowledge in Action,* (8), Henley, UK: Henley Management College.

Hennessy, S. (2011) The role of digital artefacts on the interactive whiteboard, *Journal of Computer Assisted Learning,* 27(6): 463–89.

Hennessy, S. and Warwick, P. (eds) (2010) Research into School Teaching and Learning with Whole-Class Interactive Technologies, *Technology, Pedagogy and Education* (Special Edition) 19(2): 127–31.

Hennessy, S., Deaney, R. and Ruthven, K. (2003) *Pedagogic Strategies for Using ICT to Support Subject Teaching and Learning: an analysis across 15 case studies.* Research Report 03/1. Cambridge: University of Cambridge.

Hennessy, S., Deaney, R. and Ruthven, K. (2005) *Developing pedagogical expertise for integrating use of the interactive whiteboard in secondary science*, Glamorgan, UK: British Educational Research Association.

Hennessy, S., Deaney, R., Ruthven, K. and Winterbottom, M. (2007) Pedagogical strategies for using the interactive whiteboard to foster learner participation in school science, *Learning Media and Technology,* 32(3): 283–301.

Hennessy, S., Ruthven, K. and Brindley, S. (2002) Teacher Perspectives on Integrating ICT into Subject Teaching: Commitment, Constraints, Caution and Change, *Journal of Curriculum Studies,* 37(2): 25–63.

Hennessy, S., Warwick, P. and Mercer, N. (2011) A dialogic inquiry approach to working with teachers in developing classroom dialogue, *Teachers College Record,* 113(9): 1906–59.

Hennessy, S., Warwick, P., Mercer, N., Brown, L., Neale, C. and Rawlins, D. (2010) Using the interactive whiteboard to support classroom dialogue, in J. Douglas (ed.) *The Ultimate Guide to Interactive Whiteboards,* Melbourne, Australia and New Zealand: Dataworks Australia and Engage Learning, pp. 12–16.

Hertz, J.C. (1997) *Joystick Nation*, Boston: Little, Brown and Co.

Higgins, S., Beauchamp, G. and Miller, D. (2007) Reviewing the literature on interactive whiteboards, *Learning, Media and Technology,* 32(3): 213–35.

Higgins, S., Falzon, C., Hall, I., Moseley, D., Smith, F., Smith, H. and Wall, K. (2005) *Embedding ICT in the Literacy and Numeracy Strategies: Final Report*, Newcastle: Newcastle University.

Holmes, B., Tangney, B., Fitzgibbon, A., Savage, T. and Mehan, S. (2001) Communal Constructivism: Students Constructing Learning For as Well as With Others, in J. Price, D. Willis, N.E Davis and J. Willis (eds) *Proceedings of the 12th International Conference of the Society for Information Technology in Education*: 3114–19.

Holt, J. (1967) *How Children Learn*, New York: Pitman Publishing Corporation.

Hooper, S. and Rieber, L.P. (1995) Teaching with technology, in A.C. Ornstein (ed.) *Teaching: Theory into Practice*, Needham Heights, MA: Allyn and Bacon, 154–70.

Howard, J. (2005) Knowledge exchange networks in Australia's innovation system: overview and strategic analysis, A report to department of Education, *Science and Training* (6), Canberra: Howard Partners, 1–32.

Howe, M.J. A. (1984) *A Teacher's Guide to the Psychology of Learning*, Oxford: Blackwell.

Hromek, R. and Roffey, S. (2009) 'Promoting Social and Emotional Learning with Games: 'it's fun and we learn things,' *Simulation and Gaming*, 40(5): 626–44.

Hunt, M., Parsons, A. and Fleming, A. (2003) *A Review of the Research Literature on the Use of Managed Learning Environments and Virtual Learning Environments in Education and a Consideration of the Implications for Schools in the United Kingdom*, Coventry: Becta.

Hutchins, E. (1995) *Cognition in the Wild*, Cambridge, MA: MIT Press.

IDeA (UK: Improvement and Development Agency for Local Government) (2008) Knowledge Management Tools and Techniques: helping you find the right knowledge at the right time, London: IDeA.

IDeA (UK: Improvement and Development Agency for local government) (2009) *Communities of Practice*: Internal Research Report, London: IDeA.

IDeA (UK: Improvement and Development Agency for local government) (2006) *Knowledge Management Strategy: board paper,* IDeA internal document, London: IDeA.

Indian Government National Council for teacher education: a statutory body of the government of India (2010a). http://www.ncte-india.org/ (accessed 26 March 2012).

Indian Government National Council for Teacher Education: a statutory body of the government of India (2010b) *Awards to teacher educators in India*. http://www.ncte-india. org/teacheraward.htm (accessed 26 March 2012).

Jarvis, P.J. (ed.) (2002) *The Theory and Practice of Teaching*, London: RoutledgeFalmer.

Jewitt, C., Hadjithoma-Garstka, C., Clark, W., Banaji, S. and Selwyn, N. (2010) *School Use of Learning Platforms and Associated Technologies*, Coventry: Becta.

Johnson, L., Smith, R., Willis, H., Levine, A. and Haywood, K. (2011) *The 2011 Horizon Report*, Austin, Texas: The New Media Consortium.

Jones, A. (2004) *A Review of the Research Literature on Barriers to the Uptake of ICT by Teachers*, Coventry: Becta.

Joyce, B., Calhoun, E. and Hopkins, D. (2002) *Models of Learning – Tools for Teaching* (2nd edn), Buckingham: Open University Press.

Ke, F. (2008) A case study of computer gaming for math: engaged learning from gameplay? *Computers and Education*, 51: 1609–20.

Kemmis, S., with Atkins, R. and Wright, E. (1977) *How Do Students Learn? Working Papers on Computer Assisted Learning*, Occasional Publication No. 5, Centre for Applied Research in Education, University of East Anglia: 450.

Kennewell, S. (2001) Using affordances and constraints to evaluate the use of information and communications technology in teaching and learning, *Journal of Information Technology for Teacher Education*, 10(1–2): 101–16.

Kennewell, S. (2004) Researching the influence of interactive presentation tools on teacher pedagogy, *Proceedings of the British Educational Research Association Conference*, UMIST, Manchester. http://www.leeds.ac.uk/educol/documents/151717.doc (accessed 30 March 2012).

Kennewell, S. (2005) Interactive teaching with interactive technology, *Proceedings of the World Conference in Computer Education*, Stellenbosch, South Africa.

Kennewell, S. (2006) Reflections on the interactive whiteboard phenomenon: a synthesis of research, *Proceedings of the British Educational Research Association Conference*, University of Warwick.

Kennewell, S. and Beauchamp, G. (2007) The features of interactive whiteboards and their influence on learning, *Learning Media and Technology*, 32(3): 227–41.

Kennewell, S., Parkinson, J. and Tanner, H. (eds) (2003) *Learning to teach ICT in the secondary school*, London: Routledge Falmer.

Kennewell, S., Connell, A., Edwards, A., Hammond, M. and Wickens, C. (2007) *A Practical Guide to Teaching ICT in the Secondary School*, London: Routledge.

Kerr, S.T. (1991) Lever and Fulcrum: Educational Technology in Teachers' Thought and Practice, *Teachers College Record*, 93(1): 114–36.

Kington, A., Harris, S., Lee, B. and Leask, M. (2001) Information and communications technology and whole school improvement: case studies of organisational change, *Education-Line*, September: 1–16, http://www.leeds.ac.uk/educol/documents/00001905.htm (accessed 29 March 2012).

Kirkwood, M., Van Der Kuyl, T., Parton, N. and Grant, R. (2000) The New Opportunities Fund (NOF) ICT Training for Teachers Programme: Designing a Powerful Online Learning Environment, *Proceedings of the European Conference on Educational Research*, University of Edinburgh.

Kirriemuir, J. and McFarlane, A. (2004) *Literature Review in Games and Learning*, Bristol: Futurelab.

Kitchen, S., Dixon, J., McFarlane, A., Roche, N. and Finch, S. (2006) *Curriculum Online Evaluation: Final Report*, Coventry: Becta.

Knight, S. (2009) *Effective Practice in a Digital Age: a guide to technology enhanced learning and teaching*, Bristol: JISC.

Koehler, M.J. and Mishra, P. (2005) What happens when teachers design educational technology? The development of technological pedagogical content knowledge, *Journal of Educational Computing Research*, 32(2): 131–52.

Koenraad, A.L.M. (2008) *Interactive Whiteboards in Educational Practice: the research literature reviewed*, Netherlands: Hogeschool Utrecht University.

Kolb, D. (1984) *Experiential Learning*, Englewood Cliffs, New Jersey: Prentice Hall.

Laudrillard, D. (1998) Multimedia and the learner's experience of narrative, *Computers & Education*, 31(2): 229–42.

Laudrillard, D. (1993) *Rethinking University Teaching*, London: Routledge.

Lave, J. and Wenger, E. (1991) *Situated Learning: legitimate peripheral participation*, Cambridge. Cambridge University Press.

Lawson, T. and Comber, C. (1999) Superhighways Technology: Personnel Factors Leading to Successful Integration of ICT in Schools and Colleges, *Journal of Information Technology for Teacher Education*, 8(1): 41–53.

Lawson, T. and Comber, C. (2000) Introducing Information and Communications Technologies into Schools: The Blurring of Boundaries, *British Journal of Sociology of Education*, 21(3): 419–33.

Lawson, T. and Comber, C. (2004) School Leadership and ICT: Training for Integration, in M. Brundrett and I. Terrell (eds) *Learning to Lead in the Secondary School*, London: Routledge Falmer.

Leask, M. (1987) *TVEI Internal Evaluation*, London: London Borough of Enfield.

Leask, M. (2002) *Evaluation of New Opportunities Fund ICT Training for Teachers and Librarians*, London: Training and Development Agency for Schools.

Leask, M. (2004a) Using research and evidence to improve teaching and learning in the training of professionals – an example from teacher training in England, *Proceedings of the British Educational Research Association Conference*, University of Manchester.

Leask, M. (2004b) Accumulating the evidence base for educational practice: our respective responsibilities, *Proceedings of the British Educational Research Association Conference*, University of Manchester.

Leask, M. (2010a) *A national and international model for scaling up small scale educational research: country wide HEI/school Collaborative Research Networks?* Occasional paper No. 8, London: Brunel University.

Leask, M. (2010b) Improving education through improving research quality, relevance and timeliness: new ways of working through a national e-infrastructure which connects research producers with users, *Proceedings of the Higher Education in a world changed utterly: doing more with less*, Paris: OECD/IMHE Conference.

Leask, M. (ed.) (2001) *Issues in Teaching Using ICT*, London: RoutledgeFalmer.

Leask, M. and Meadows, J. (eds) (2000) *Learning to Teach with ICT in the Primary School*, London: Routledge.

Leask, M. and Pachler, N. (1997) The Background and Rationale for the TeacherNet UK Initiative – harnessing the potential of the Internet for improving teachers' professional development and pupil learning, *Proceedings of the Open Classroom II Conference*, Athens: European Distance Education Network/Lambrakis Foundation.

Leask, M. and Pachler, N. (2005) *Learning to Teach Using ICT in the Secondary School: A Companion to School Experience* (2nd edn), London: Routledge.

Leask, M. and Preston, C. (2010) *ICT Tools for Future Teachers*: Becta: Coventry. http://www.beds.ac.uk/__data/assets/pdf_file/0010/19459/ict-tools2009.pdf (accessed 18 June 2012).

Leask, M. and White, C. (2004) Initial Teacher Training (ITT) Professional Resource Networks (IPRNs) – rationale and development, *Proceedings of the British Educational Research Association Conference*, University of Manchester.

Leask, M. and Williams, L. (2005) Whole school approaches: integrating ICT across the curriculum, in M. Leask and N. Pachler (eds) (2005) *Learning to Teach Using ICT in the Secondary School: A Companion to School Experience* (2nd edn), London: Routledge.

Leask, M. and Younie, S. (2000) *The EUN Learning School Project Final Report: The integration of the EUN into classroom practice: the dynamics of change*, Brussels: European Commission.

Leask, M. and Younie, S. (2001a) Communal Constructivist Theory: information and communications technology, pedagogy and internationalisation of the curriculum, *Journal of Information Technology for Teacher Education*, 10(1 and 2): 117–34.

Leask, M. and Younie, S. (2001b) The European Schoolnet. An Online European Community for Teachers: A Valuable Professional Resource? *Journal for Teacher Development*, 5(2): 157–75.

Leask, M. and Younie, S. (2009) *Parliamentary Select Committee Inquiry into Initial Teacher Training and CPD Report:* submission of written evidence to House of Commons, London.

Leask, M. (2011) Improving the Professional Knowledge Base for Education: using knowledge management and Web 2.0 tools, *Policy Futures in Education*, 9(5): 644–60. http://dx.doi.org/10.2304/pfie.2011.9.5.644 (accessed 18 June 2012).

Lewin, C., Mavers, D. and Somekh, B. (2003) Broadening access to the curriculum through using technology to link home and school: a critical analysis of reforms intended to improve students' educations attainment, *The Curriculum Journal*, 14(1): 23–5.

Lewin, K. (1951) *Field Theory in the Social Sciences,* New York: Harper and Row.

Livingstone, I. and Hope, A. (2011) *Next Gen. Report*, London: NESTA.

Livingstone, S. and Bober, M. (2005) *UK children go online: Final report of key project findings,* London: LSE Research Online. Available at: http://eprints.lse.ac.uk/399/ (accessed 26 March 2012).

Longman, D. and Hughes, M. (2006) Whole class teaching strategies and interactive technology: towards a connectionist classroom, *Proceedings of British Educational Research Association Conference*, University of Warwick.

Loucks, S.F., Newlove, B.W. and Hall, G.E. (1998) *Measuring levels of use of the innovation: a manual for trainers, interviewers and raters*, Austin, Texas: Southwest Educational Development Laboratory.

Louks-Horsley, S. Hewson, P., Love, N. and Stiles, K. (1998) *Designing professional development for teachers of science and mathematics,* Thousand Oaks, CA: Corwin Press.

Loveless, A. (2001) *The Interaction Between Primary Teachers' Perceptions of Information and Communication Technology (ICT) and Their Pedagogy,* PhD Thesis, Brighton: Brighton University.

Loveless, A. (2005) Challenge and Change with Information Technology in Education: Do We Really Mean It? *Technology, Pedagogy and Education*, 13(3): 277–81.

Loveless, A. and Stevens, V. (2002) *Evaluation of East Sussex Portables for Teachers Scheme Phase 3,* East Sussex County Council.

LSN (2008) *Measuring e-maturity in Further Education*, Coventry: Becta.

Lyotard, J.F. (1984) *The Postmodern Condition: A Report on Knowledge*, Minneapolis: University of Minnesota Press.

Maslow, A.H. (1943) A Theory of Human Motivation, Originally Published in *Psychological Review*, 50, 370–96. Now reproduced by Christopher D. Green, York University, Toronto, Ontario http://psychclassics.yorku.ca/Maslow/motivation.htm (accessed 2 March 2012).

Mayes, T. and De Freitas, S. (2004) *Review of e-learning theories, frameworks and models. Stage 2 of the e-learning models desk study*, Bristol: JISC.

McCormick, R. and Scrimshaw, P. (2001) Information and Communications Technology, Knowledge and Pedagogy, *Education, Communication and Information,* 1(1): 37–57.

McDougall, A., Murnane, J., Jones, A. and Reynolds, N. (eds) (2010) *Researching IT in Education: Theory, Practice and Future Directions,* London: Routledge.

McKinsey (1997) *The Future of Information Technology in UK Schools,* London: McKinsey and Company.

McKinsey (2007) *How the World's Best-Performing School Systems Came Out on Top,* report produced by Barber, M. and Mourshed, M. http://www.mckinsey.com/clientservice/ Social_Sector/our_practices/Education/Knowledge_Highlights/Best_performing_ school.aspx (accessed 26 March 2012).

McMordie, R. (undated) *The BBC Computer Literacy Project – The BBC Micro (1981)* http:// www.mcmordie.co.uk/acornhistory/bbchist.shtml (accessed 26 May 2012).

Mead, G.H. (1934) *Mind, Self, and Society,* Chicago: University of Chicago Press.

Meadows, M.S. (2008) *I, Avatar,* Berkeley, US: New Riders.

Mercer, N. (2000) *Words and Minds: How we use language to think together,* London: Routledge.

Mercer, N., Hennessy, S. and Warwick, P. (2010) Using interactive whiteboards to orchestrate classroom dialogue, *Technology, Pedagogy and Education (themed issue on interactive whole class technologies),* 19(2): 195–209.

Mercer, N., Warwick, P., Kershner, R. and Kleine Staarman, J. (2010) Can the interactive whiteboard provide 'dialogic space' for children's collaborative activity? *Language and Education,* 24(4): 1–18.

Miller, D.J. and Robertson, D.P. (2009) Using a games-console in the primary classroom: effects of 'Brain Training' programme on computation and self-esteem, *British Journal of Educational Technology,* 41(2): 242–55.

Miller, D.J. and Robertson, D.P. (2010), Educational benefits of using game consoles in a primary classroom: A randomised controlled trial, *British Journal of Educational Technology,* 42: 850–64.

Miller, D.J. and Glover, D. (2006) *Interactive whiteboard evaluation for the secondary national strategy: Developing the use of interactive whiteboards in mathematics, Final Report for the Secondary National Strategy,* London: DfES. http://www.standards.dfes.gov.uk/keystage3/ downloads/ma_iaw_eval_rpt.pdf (accessed 3 October 2011).

Miller, D.J., Glover, D. and Averis, D. (2004) Matching Technology and Pedagogy in Teaching Mathematics: Understanding Fractions using a 'Virtual Manipulative' Fraction Wall, *British Educational Research Association,* Manchester. http://bit.ly/fractions04bera (accessed 4 October 2011).

Millwood, R. (2009) *A short history off-line,* Coventry: Becta.

Ming-yuan, G. (2006) *The Reform and Development in Teacher Education in China,* Beijing Normal University. http://www.icte.ecnu.edu.cn/EN/show.asp?id=547 (accessed 26 April 2012).

Mishra, P. and Koehler, M.J. (2006) Technological Pedagogical Content Knowledge: A Framework for Teacher Knowledge, *Teachers College Record,* 108(6): 1017–54.

Moffatt, A. (2009) *Technology in Education: an examination of the transformative nature of ICT,* MA Thesis Education, De Montfort University, Leicester.

MoLeNET (2010) *Games Technologies for Learning: more than just toys,* London: LSN.

Morris, D. (2010) E-confidence or incompetence: Are teachers ready to teach in the 23rd century? *World Journal on Educational Technology,* 2(2): 141–54.

Moseley, D., Higgins, S. and Newton, L. (1999) *Ways Forward with ICT: Effective Pedagogy Using Information and Communications Technology for Literacy and Numeracy in Primary Schools,* Newcastle: University of Newcastle.

Moss, G., Jewitt, C., Levaãiç, R., Armstrong, V., Cardini, A. and Castle, F. (2007) *The interactive whiteboards, pedagogy and pupil performance evaluation: an evaluation of the Schools Whiteboard Expansion (SWE) Project: London Challenge.* DfES Research Report 816, London: DfES.

Mumtaz, S. (2000) Factors affecting teachers' use of information and communications technology: a review of the literature, *Journal of Information Technology for Teacher Education,* 9(3): 319–41.

Murray, W.E. (2006) *Geographies of Globalization,* London: Routledge.

NAACE (2001) *The Impact of ICT on Schooling,* Nottingham: National Association for Advisors for Computers in Education.

NCET (1995) *How ICT helps learners learn mathematics,* Coventry: NCET.

NCET (1997) Highways for Learning – The Internet for Schools and Colleges – Towards an Evaluation, *Net Magazine,* March: 118.

Newman, F. and Holzman, L. (1997) *The End of Knowing,* London: Routledge.

Newman, M., Elbourne, D. and Leask, M. (2004) Improving the usability of educational research: guidelines for the reporting of empirical primary research studies in education, *Proceedings of the 5th Annual Conference of the Teaching and Learning Research Programme,* Cardiff.

NFER (2008) *Harnessing Technology: Schools Survey,* Coventry: Becta.

Novello, M. (1989) *The Changing Role of the Teacher,* London: Routledge.

Oakley, A. (2003) Research Evidence, Knowledge Management and Educational Practice: early lessons from a systematic approach, *London Review of Education,* 1(1): 21–34.

OECD (2002) *ICT and whole school improvement reports.* Paris: Ceri.

OECD (2003) *New Challenges for Educational Research.* This report has two of the five reviews of educational R&D which CERI conducted in five countries: New Zealand, England, Mexico, Denmark and Switzerland.

OECD (2007a) *Taking Stock of Educational R&D*: Joint OECD-CORECHED International Expert Meeting http://www.oecd.org/document/36/0,3343,en_2649_35845581_39379876_1_1_1_1,00.html (accessed 3 January 2012).

OECD (2007b) *Evidence in Education: Linking Research and Policy,* http://www.oecd.org/document/56/0,3343,en_2649_35845581_38796344_1_1_1_1,00.html (accessed 3 January 2012).

OECD (2009a) *Creating Effective Teaching and Learning Environments: First Results from Teaching and Learning international Survey (TALIS)* http://www.oecd.org/document/54/0,3343,en_2649_39263231_42980662_1_1_1_1,00.html (accessed 1 February 2012).

Ofsted (2001) *ICT in Schools: The Impact of Government Initiatives: An Interim Report,* London: Ofsted.

Ofsted (2004) *ICT in Schools: The Impact of Government Initiatives Five Years On,* London: Ofsted.

Ofsted (2009) *Virtual Learning Environments: an evaluation of their development in a sample of educational settings,* London: Ofsted.

Ofsted (2009a) *The importance of ICT: Information and communication technology in primary and secondary schools, 2005–2008,* London: Ofsted.

Ofsted (2009b) *Identifying good practice: a survey of college provision in information and communication technology*, London: Ofsted.

Ofsted (2010) *The Safe Use of New Technologies*, Manchester: Ofsted. http://www.ofsted.gov.uk/resources/safe-use-of-new-technologies (accessed 29 Feb 2012).

Ofsted (2012*) Staying Safe online*, Manchester: Ofsted. http://www.ofsted.gov.uk/news/staying-safe-online (accessed 29 Feb 2012).

Opie, C. and Fukuyo, K. (2000) A Tale of Two National Curriculums: Issues in Implementing the National Curriculum for Information and Communications Technology in Initial Teacher Training, *Journal of Information Technology for Teacher Education*, 9(1): 79–95.

Owen, M. (2004) *The Myth of the Digital Native*, Bristol: Futurelab.

Pachler, N., Preston, C., Cuthell, J., Allen, A. and Torres, P. (2011) *The ICT CPD Landscape in England*, Coventry: Becta.

Passey, D., Rogers, C., Machell, J. and Mchugh, G. (2004) *The motivational effect of ICT on pupils*, Lancaster: Lancaster University, Dept. of Educational Research. DfES: 1–78.

Pavlov, I.P. (1927) *Conditioned Reflexes*, London: Oxford University Press.

Pearson, M., Haldane, M. and Somekh, B. (2004) *St Thomas of Aquin's Interactive Whiteboard pilot*, Manchester: Manchester Metropolitan University.

Pelgrum, W.J. (2001) Obstacles to the Integration of ICT in Education: Results from a Worldwide Assessment, *Computers and Education*, 37: 163–78.

Piaget, J. (1951) *Play, Dreams and Imitation in Children*, London: RKP.

Piaget, J. (1963) *The Origins of Intelligence in Children*, New York: Norton.

Piaget, J. (1973) *The Child's Conception of the World*, London: Paladin.

Piore, M. (1986) Perspectives on Labour Market Flexibility, *Industrial Relations*, 45(2).

Pittard, V. (2005) Research and the 'Harnessing Technology Strategy', *Proceedings of Becta's Annual Research Conference: Towards an ICT Research Agenda*, Solihull.

Plomp, T. and Pelgrum, W.J. (1991) *The Use of Computers in Education Worldwide*, Oxford: Pergamon Press.

Plowden, P. (1967) *Children and their Primary Schools* (the Plowden Report), London: HMSO.

Prensky, M. (2001) *Digital Game-Based Learning*, New York: McGraw Hill.

Prensky, M. (2006) *Don't Bother Me Mom-I'm Learning!* Minnesota: Paragon House.

Prensky, M. (2009) H. Sapiens Digital: From Digital Immigrants and Digital Natives to Digital Wisdom, *Innovate*, 5(3): 0–9.

Preston, C. (2004) *The Full Evaluation of the English NOF ICT Teacher Training Programme (1999–2003)*, London: MirandaNet.

Preston, C., Cox, M. and Cox, C. (2000) *Teachers as Innovators: an Evaluation of the Motivation of Teachers to Use ICT*, London: MirandaNet.

Proton Europe (2007) *Experiences on the US knowledge transfer and innovation system*, Proton Europe Innovation from Public Research, http://www.proinno-europe.eu/NWEV/uploaded_documents/US-knowledge-transfer-innovation-system.pdf (accessed 26 January 2012).

Ravenscroft, A. (2007) Promoting Thinking and Conceptual Change with Digital Dialogue Games, *Journal of Computer Assisted Learning*, 23(6): 453–65.

Reiss, S. (2000) *Who Am I? The 16 Basic Desires That Motivate Our Action and Define Our Personalities*, US: Tarcher/Putnam.

Rhodes, V. (1989) *Barriers to Innovation: A Seminar Report.* Lancaster (England): ESRC.

Roffey, S. (2004) *The New Teacher's Survival Guide to Behaviour*, London: Sage.

Rogers, E.M. (2003) *Diffusion of Innovations* (5th edn), New York: Free Press.

Rogers, E.M. and Shoemaker, F. (1971) *Communication of Innovations*, New York: MacMillan Free Press.

Rosen, L.D. and Weil, M.M. (1995) Computer Availability, Computer Experience and Technophobia among Public School Teachers, *Computers in Human Behaviour*, 11(1): 9–31.

Ruben, B.D. (1999) Simulations, Games and Experience-Based Learning: the quest for a new paradigm for teaching and learning, *Simulation and Gaming*, 30(4): 498–505.

Rudd, T. (2007) *Interactive whiteboards in the classroom*, Bristol: Futurelab.

Russell, B. (1995) *Autobiography*, London: Routledge.

Ryan, R. and Deci, E.L. (2000) Self-Determination Theory and the Facilitation of Intrinsic Motivation, Social Development, and Well-Being, *American Psychologist*, 55(1): 68–78.

Rylands, T. (2010) Using Myst to develop literacy skills, *Key Note, Proceedings of the ITTE Conference*, Liverpool Hope University, Liverpool.

Sabel, C. (1982) *Work and Politics: The Division of Labour in Industry*, Cambridge: Cambridge University Press.

Salovey, P. and Mayer, J.D. (1990) Emotional Intelligence, *Imagination, Cognition and Personality*, 9: 185–211.

Sandford, R., Ulicsak, M., Facer, K. and Rudd, T. (2006) *Teaching with Games: using commercial off-the-shelf-computer games in formal education*, Bristol: Futurelab.

Sandholtz, J.H., Ringstaff, C. and Dwyer, D.C. (1997) *Teaching with Technology: Creating Student-Centered Classrooms*, New York: Teachers College Press.

Savin-Baden, M. (2007) *A Practical Guide to Problem-Based Learning Online*, London: Routledge.

SCAA (1997) *Information Technology, Communications and the Future Curriculum*, London: SCAA (School Curriculum and Assessment Authority).

Scaife, J. and Wellington, J. (1993) *Information Technology in Science and Technology Education*, Buckingham: Open University Press.

Schon, D. (1983) *Educating the Reflective Practitioner: Towards a New Design for Teaching and Learning in the Professions*, San Francisco: Jossey-Bass Publishers.

Schon, D. (1987) *The Reflective Practitioner: How Professionals Think in Action*, New York: Basic Books.

Schwab, J.J. (1964) The structure of the disciplines: meanings and significance, in G. Ford, and L. Purgo (eds) *The Structure of Knowledge and the Curriculum*, Chicago: Rand McNally.

Scrimshaw, P. (1997) *Preparing for the Information Age: Synoptic Report of the Education Departments' Superhighways Initiative (EDSI)*, Coventry: NCET.

Scrimshaw, P. (2003) ICT in European Schools: Emerging Issues From the ValNet Project, *The Curriculum Journal*, 14(1): 85–104.

Scrimshaw, P. (2004) *Enabling Teachers to Make Successful Use of ICT*, Coventry: Becta.

Selinger, M. (1996) Beginning Teachers Using I.T: The Open University Model, *Journal of Information Technology for Teacher Education*, 5(3): 253–70.

Selwyn, N. (1998) A grid for learning or a grid for earning? the significance of the Learning Grid initiative in UK education, *Journal of Education Policy*, 13(3): 423–31.

Selwyn, N. (1999a) Differences in Educational Computer Use: The Influence of Subject Cultures, *Curriculum Journal*, 10(1): 29–48.

Selwyn, N. (1999b) Why the Computer is not Dominating Schools: A Failure of Policy or a Failure of Practice? *Cambridge Journal of Education*, 29(1): 77–91.

Selwyn, N. (2002) *Telling tales on technology: qualitative studies of technology and education,* Aldershot: Ashgate.

Selwyn, N. (2011) *Schools and Schooling in the Digital Age: A critical analysis,* London: Routledge.

Shaffer, D.W., Squire, K.D., Halverson, R. and Gee, J.P. (2005) Video games and the future of learning, *Phi Delta Kappan,* 87(2), 104–11.

Shaffer, D.W. (2006) *How Computer Games Help Children Learn,* New York: Palgrave Macmillan.

Shaffer, D.W., Squire, K.R., Halverson, R. and Gee, J.P. (2004) Video games and the future of learning, *Phi Delta Kappan,* 87(2): 105–11.

Sheingold, K. and Hadley, M. (1990) *Accomplished Teachers: Integrating Computers into Classroom Practice,* New York: Centre for Technology in Education.

Sherry, L. and Gibson, D. (2002) The Path to Teacher Leadership in Educational Technology, *Contemporary Issues in Technology and Teacher Education,* 2(2), http://www.citejournal. org/vol2/iss2/general/article2.cfm (accessed 27 March 2012).

Shulman, L. (1987) Knowledge and teaching: Foundations of the new reform, *Harvard Educational Review,* 57(1): 1–22.

Skinner, B.F. (1953) *Science and Human Behaviour,* New York: Macmillan.

Smith, F., Hardman, F. and Higgins, S. (2006) The impact of interactive whiteboards on teacher-pupil interaction in the national literacy and numeracy strategies, *British Educational Research Journal,* 31(3): 443–57.

Smith, H.J., Higgins, S., Wall, K. and Miller, J. (2005) Interactive whiteboards: boon or bandwagon? A critical review of the literature, *Journal of Computer Assisted Learning,* 21: 91–101.

Smith, P., Rudd, P. and Coghlan, M. (2008) *Harnessing Technology: Schools Survey 2008 Report 1, Analysis,* Coventry: Becta.

Snoeyink, R. and Ertmer, P. (2001) Thrust Into Technology: How veteran teachers respond, *Journal of Educational Technology Systems,* 30(1): 85–111.

Somekh, B. (1991) Pupil autonomy in learning with microcomputers: rhetoric or reality? An action research study, *Cambridge Journal of Education,* 21(1): 47–64.

Somekh, B. (2000) New Technology and Learning: Policy and Practice in the UK, 1980–2010, *Education and Information Technologies,* 5(1): 19–37.

Somekh, B. (2007) *Pedagogy and Learning with ICT: Researching the art of innovation,* London and New York: Routledge.

Somekh, B. (2010) The practical power of theoretically informed research into innovation, in A. McDougall, J. Murnane, A. Jones and N. Reynolds (eds) *Researching IT in Education: Theory, Practice and Future Directions*: 129–41.

Somekh, B. and Davis, N. (1997) (eds) *Using IT effectively in teaching and learning: studies in pre-service and in-service teacher education,* London and New York: Routledge.

Somekh, B. and Haldane, M. (2006) How can interactive whiteboards contribute to pedagogic change? Learning from case studies in English primary schools, *Proceedings of IFIP Conference,* Ålesund, Norway.

Somekh, B. and Underwood, J. (2006) *Evaluation of the ICT Test Bed Project,* Nottingham: Nottingham Trent University.

Somekh, B. et al. (2005) *Interim Report to the Department for Education and Skills,* Unpublished report from the SWEEP project, London: DCSF.

Somekh, B., Lewin, C., Mavers, D., Scrimshaw, P., Haldane, A., Levin, C. and Robinson, J. (2003) *Evaluation of the GridClub Educational Service: Final Report to the Department for Education and Skills,* Manchester: Manchester Metropolitan University.

Somekh, B., Haldane, M., Jones, K., Lewin, C., Steadman, S., Scrimshaw, P. et al. (2007) *Evaluation of the Primary Schools Whiteboard Expansion Project (SWEEP): Report to the Department for Education and Skills,* London: DCSF.

Spring-Keller, F. (2010) The Enjoyment of Learning – digital environments, in A. McDougall, J. Murnane, A. Jones, and N. Reynolds (eds) *Researching IT in Education: Theory, Practice and Future Direction,* London: Routledge, 79–87.

Stager, G.S. (1995) Laptop schools lead the way in professional development, *Educational Leadership,* 53(2): 78–81.

Stello, C. (2012) *Herzberg's Two-Factor Theory of Job Satisfaction: An Integrative Literature Review Department of Organizational Leadership, Policy, and Development,* College of Education and Human Development, University of Minnesota, http://www.cehd.umn. edu/olpd/research/StudentConf/papers/StelloHerzberg.pdf (accessed 29 March 2012).

Stenhouse, L. (1975) *An Introduction to Curriculum Research and Development,* London: Heinemann Educational Books.

Stevenson, D. (1997) *The Independent ICT in Schools Commission. Information and Communications Technology in UK Schools: An independent inquiry,* London: HMSO.

Stronach, I., Corbin, B., McNamara, O., Stark, S. and Warne, T. (2002) Towards an uncertain politics of professionalism: teacher and nurse identities, *Journal of Education Policy,* 17(1):109–38.

Struppert, A. (2010) 'It's a whole new fun different way to learn.' Students' perceptions of learning with an electronic simulation: selected results from three case studies in an Australian, an American and a Swiss middle school, *The International Journal of Learning,* 17(9): 363–75.

Tagg, B. (1995) The Impact of Government Initiatives on IT Education in UK Schools, *Computer Education,* 81: 5–9.

Tanner, H., Jones, S., Kennewell, S. and Beauchamp, G. (2005) Interactive whiteboards and pedagogies of whole class teaching, in P. Clarkson, A. Downton, D. Gronn, M. Horne, A. McDonough, R. Pierce and A. Roche (eds) *Building Connections: Research, Theory and Practice* "Proceedings of the 28th annual conference of the Mathematics Education Research Group of Australasia, Melbourne," Sydney: MERGA, pp. 720–7.

TDA (2002) *Evaluation of New Opportunities Fund ICT training for teachers and librarians.* Report produced by Leask, M., London: TDA.

TeachersTV (2010) *E-safety – Five Whole-School Tips.* http://www.teachers.tv/videos/ e-safety-five-whole-school-tips (accessed 26 March 2012).

TTA (1998) *Initial Teacher Training National Curriculum for the Use of Information and Communications Technology in Subject Teaching (Annex E),* London: TDA.

TTA (2002) *The New Opportunities Fund: Training for Teachers and School Librarians in the Use of ICT; Progress Review and Lessons Learned Through the Central Quality Assurance Process in England,* London: TDA.

Twining, P. (2000) The computer practice framework: a tool to help identify the impact in educational practice of investments in information and communication technology, *in ALT-C Changing Learning Environments, proceedings of ALT-C: Association for Learning Technology, 8th International Conference,* Oxford: Information Press. http://kn.open. ac.uk/public/document.cfm?docid=1652 (accessed 12 September 2012).

Twining, P. (2005) *DICTateEd: Discussing ICT, Aspirations and Targets for Education.* http:// www.med8.info/dictated/rationales.htm (accessed 12 September 2012).

U.S. Department of Education (2006) *The Secretary's Fifth Annual Report on Teacher Quality: A Highly Qualified Teacher in Every Classroom*, Washington DC: U.S. Department of Education. http://www.ed.gov/about/reports/annual/teachprep/index.html (accessed 26 March 2012).

UK Council for Child Internet Safety (2009) *Click Clever Click Safe: The first UK Child Internet Safety Strategy*, London: UKCCIS.

Underwood, J., Banyard, P., Baguley, T., Dillion, G., Farrington Flint, L., Hayes, M., Le Geyt, G., Murphy, J. and Selwood, I. (2010) *Understanding the Impact of Technology: Learner and School Level Factors*, Coventry: Becta.

UNESCO (1996) *Learning, the treasure within*, report for the International Commission on Education for the Twenty-first Century, Paris: UNESCO.

UNESCO (2010a) *Qualifying and training teachers in Brazil*. http://www.unesco.org/en/brasilia/education/other-education-themes/teacher-education-and-training/ (accessed 26 March 2012).

UNESCO (2010b) *The Teacher Training Initiative for Sub-Saharan Africa (TTISSA)*. http://www.unesco.org/en/teacher-education/ (accessed 26 March 2012).

Valcke, M., Schellens, T., Van Keer, H. and Gerarts, M. (2006) Primary school children's safe and unsafe use of the Internet at home and at school: An exploratory study, *Computers in Human Behaviour*, 23(6): 2838–50.

Van Eck, R. (2006) Digital game-based learning: It's not just the digital natives who are restless, invited cover story for *Educause Review*, 41(2).

Veen, W. (1993) How Teachers Use Computers in Instructional Practice: Four Case Studies in a Dutch secondary school, *Computers and Education*, 2(1): 1–8.

Veen, W. and Vrakking, B. (2006) *Homo Zappiens: Growing up in a Digital Age*, London: Network Continuum.

Vygotsky L.S. (1978) *Mind and Society*, Cambridge MA: Harvard University Press.

Vygotsky, L.S. (1986) *Thought and Language*, (tr and ed) A.Kozulin, Cambridge, MA: MIT Press.

Warwick, P. and Kershner, R. (2008) Primary teachers' understanding of the interactive whiteboard as a tool for children's collaborative learning and knowledge-building, *Learning, Media and Technology*, 33(4): 269–87.

Warwick, P., Hennessy, S. and Mercer, N. (2011) Promoting teacher and school development through co-enquiry: developing interactive whiteboard use in a 'dialogic classroom', *Teachers and Teaching: theory and practice*, 17(3): 303–24.

Warwick, P., Mercer, N., Kershner, R. and Kleine Staarman, J. (2010) In the mind and in the technology: The vicarious presence of the teacher in pupils' learning of science in collaborative group activity at the interactive whiteboard, *Computers and Education*, 55(2): 350–62.

Watkins, C. (2005) *Classrooms as Learning Communities: What's in it for schools?* London: Routledge.

Watson, D.M. (1993) *The ImpacT Report: An Evaluation of the Impact of Information Technology on Children's Achievements in Primary and Secondary Schools*, DfE, London: Kings College, University of London.

Watson, J.B. (1924) *Behaviourism*, New York: J.B. Lippincott.

Webb, M.E. (2002) Pedagogical reasoning: issues and solutions for the teaching and learning of ICT in secondary schools. *Education and Information Technologies*, 7(3): 237–55.

Webb, M.E., and Cox, M.J. (2004) A review of Pedagogy related to ICT, *Technology, Pedagogy and Education,* 13(3): 235–86.

Webb M. (2005) Affordances of ICT in science learning; implications for an integrated pedagogy, *International Journal of Science Education,* 27(6) 705–35.

Webb, M.E (2010) Models for exploring and characterising pedagogy with information technology, in A. McDougall (ed.) *Researching IT in Education: theory, practice and future directions,* , London: Routledge, 91–111.

Wenger, E. (1998) *Communities of Practice: Learning, Meaning, and Identity,* Cambridge, MA: Cambridge University Press.

Wenger, E., McDermott, R. and Snyder, W. (2002) *Cultivating Communities of Practice: a guide to managing knowledge,* Cambridge, MA: Harvard Business School.

West Burnham, J. (2007) Understanding learning, *Leadership Development and Personal Effectiveness,* Nottingham: NCSL.

Williamson, B. and Facer, K. (2003) More than just a game: the implications for children's computer games communities, *Education, Communication and Information,* 4(2/3): 253–68.

Williamson, B. and Payton, S. (2009) *Curriculum and Teaching Innovation,* Bristol: Futurelab. http://archive.futurelab.org.uk/resources/documents/handbooks/curriculum_and_teaching_innovation2.pdf (accessed 26 May 2012).

Willoughby, T. and Wood, E. (eds) (2008*) Children's Learning in a Digital World,* Oxford: Blackwell.

Winnans, C. and Brown, D.S. (1992) Some Factors Affecting Elementary Teachers' Use of the Computer, *Computers and Education,* 18(4): 301–9.

Woollard, J. (2007) *Learning and Teaching Using ICT in Secondary Schools* (Achieving QTS). Exeter, UK: Learning Matters Ltd.

Woollard, J., Pickford, T. and Younie, S. (2010) Evaluation of e-safety materials for initial teacher training; meeting the needs of primary phase trainees, *Proceedings of The Association of Information Technology in Teacher Education (ITTE) Annual Conference,* Liverpool: Liverpool Hope University.

Wragg, E.C. (ed.) (2004) *The RoutledgeFalmer Reader in Teaching and Learning,* London: RoutledgeFalmer.

Wright, D. (2001) *Mathematics and IT – A Pupil's Entitlement.* Keele: Keele University.

Youngman, M. and Harrison, C. (1998) *Multimedia Portables for Teachers Pilot Project Report,* Coventry: Becta.

Younie, S. (2002) Situating Government Policy on ICT in Education in the Context of Post-Fordism: Economic Efficiency and Learning Gains – Conflating Agendas? *Proceedings of the Information Technology in Teacher Education, Research Conference,* University of Cambridge.

Younie, S. (2006) Implementing Government Policy on ICT in Education: Lessons Learnt, *Education and Information Technologies,* 11(3–4): 385–400.

Younie, S. (2007) *The Integration of Information and Communications Technology into Teachers' Professional Practice: the cultural dynamics of change,* Phd Thesis, De Montfort University, Leicester.

Younie, S. and Leask, M. (2009) *Use of Learning Platforms to Support Continuing Professional Development in HEIs and Schools.* Coventry: Becta.

Younie, S. and Leask, M. (forthcoming 2013) Implementing learning platforms in schools and universities: lessons from England and Wales, *Technology, Pedagogy and Education.*

Appendix 1 Glossary of terms, acronyms and abbreviations

Becta	**British Educational Communications and Technology Agency:** A government agency assigned with responsibility for overseeing the implementation of technology policy initiatives in schools and further education (FE) colleges. Becta was an agency of the Labour government, for three terms of office from 1998–2010.
Blog	**web log:** Online reflective journal that other internet users can also post comments on; allows collaborative publishing.
CD-ROM	**Computer Disc-Read Only Memory:** A computer disc that stores information that is 'read only'.
Community of practice	Groups of people who share a common concern and have knowledge and skills to share. For example, a subject association network or a network of teachers working on solving a particular problem.
Core subjects	**Foundation** subjects, which are taught at both KS3 and KS4 comprising English, ICT, mathematics and science in the National Curriculum for England (from 2000 – 2014). Thereafter, ICT is to become a 'basic' subject in the national curriculum.
CPD	**Continuing Professional Development:** The term given to serving teachers' training needs.
Department for Education (DfE)	**DES** Department of Education and Science in England (became DfE in 1992). **DfE** Department for Education (previously **DES**) became **DfEE** in 1995. **DfEE** Department for Education and Employment (previously **DfE**) became **DfES** in 2001. **DfES** Department for Education and Skills (previously **DfEE**) (became **DCSF** in 2007). **DCSF** Department for Children, Schools and Families (previously **DfES**) became **DfE** in 2010. **DfE** Department for Education (previously **DCSF**) from 2010.
Digital camera	A camera that stores photographs in digital format.
EDSL	**European Computer Driving Licence:** An internationally accredited computer training qualification.

Foundation subjects	Subjects that **state-maintained schools** are required by law to teach. In England four **Foundation subjects** are designated **Core subjects** (q.v.) in the national curriculum (until 2014). Different subjects are compulsory at different Key Stages in England.
Hardware	A general term for referring to computers and, often, other peripheral devices such as printers that connect to computers.
ICT	**Information and Communications Technology:** includes a range of tools and techniques relating to computer-based hardware and software. For example, word-processing, databases, graphics and spread-sheet applications; Internet access that supports other communication activities, such as email, video-conferencing.
IT	**Information Technology:** methods of gaining, storing and retrieving information through microprocessors. Often encompassed within Information and Communications Technology (ICT), a compulsory subject in the National Curriculum for England.
IWB	**Interactive whiteboard:** a large, touch-sensitive board which is connected to a digital projector and a computer.
Internet	The worldwide 'network of networks' connected by telephone communication systems; enables the transfer of information such as text, pictures, databases and email, and provides publishing and networking opportunities.
ITT	Initial Teacher Training (ITT) provides accredited programmes that lead to QTS (Qualified Teacher Status) and these are conducted in universities and colleges throughout the UK.
Key Stage (KS)	The periods in each pupil's education to which the elements of the National Curriculum apply. There are four Key Stages, normally related to the age of the majority of the pupils in a teaching group. They are: Key Stage 1, beginning of compulsory education to age 7 (Foundation stage, Years 1 and 2); Key Stage 2, ages 7–11 (Years 3–6); Key Stage 3, ages 11–14 (Years 7–9); Key Stage 4, 14 to end of compulsory education (Years 10 and 11). Post-16 is a further Key Stage.
Local Authority (LA)	Local Authority – have a statutory duty to provide education in their geographical area; each LA is a government designated regional area in the UK.
Learning Outcomes	These are specific statements, which set out what pupils are expected to learn from a particular lesson in a way that allows teachers to identify if learning has occurred. These specify the expected pupil outputs.
MMOs	**Massively Multiplayer Online** computer games.

NCET	**National Council for Educational Technology**: The government agency assigned with responsibility for educational technology in schools, superseded by Becta from April 1998.
NGfL	**National Grid for Learning**: Launched in March 1998, this was the government's key initiative for improving ICT provision in schools, developing a wide range of digital resources for teaching and learning and equipping teachers to be effective users of ICT.
NOF	**New Opportunity Fund**: The funding body, which provided a national 'ICT Training' programme for serving teachers and librarians, launched in April 1998.
Pedagogic knowledge	The skills to transform subject knowledge into suitable learning activities for a particular group of pupils.
Ofsted	Office for Standards in Education. Non-Ministerial government department established under the Education (schools) Act (1992) to take responsibility for the inspection of schools in England.
Scaffolding	Scaffolding learning refers to the process of building pupils learning on the foundation of their existing knowledge, skills, capabilities and attitudes.
Software	The applications (or programs) which run on computers.
Social software	Software tools that allow users to interact and share information/data with other users over the Internet.
Statutory order	A statutory instrument which is regarded as an extension of an Act, enabling provisions of the Act to be augmented or updated.
TDA	Training and Development Agency for Schools: In 2005 the TDA superseded the TTA (Teacher Training Agency) with an extended remit for overseeing standards and qualifications across the school workforce. This has now become the TAC (Teaching Agency) part of the DFE from 2012.
Web 2.0	Web 2.0 technologies refers to online collaborative tools and services; these include social networking sites like Facebook, media-sharing sites like flickr and YouTube, collaborative publishing using blogs and wikis, social bookmarking like del.iciou.us.
wiki	Series of Web pages that multiple users can edit, add to and re/publish; these can be open and public, or private and password protected; allows for collaborative publishing. For example, Wikipedia, the free online encyclopedia that any one can edit, which is built collaboratively using wiki software.

Appendix 2 Research and evaluation underpinning this book led by Leask and/or Younie 1984–2012

Date/funding body	International and national research and development and evaluation reports
2011 University of Bedfordshire and LMD Learning Solutions	Education Pathways: this approach supports Chapter 10, item 2.2 in Figure 10.4.
2012 HEA/JISC	Digital Literacy and Creativity: this approach supports Chapter 10, item 4.2 in Figure 10.4.
2011 University of Bedfordshire and Core Education	Web 2.0 online education communities' project mirroring the local government project IDeA (qv). This approach supports Chapter 10, items 2.1 and 3.2 in Figure 10.4 and could support items 3.1, 3.3 and 4.1.
2010 Becta	'ICT Tools for Future teachers' with Christina Preston, Mirandanet fellows and teachers. The views of innovative practitioners in this research from this contributed to the formation of the model in Figure 10.4 and underpins the work in Chapters 8 and 9.
2010 TDA	'Developing E-Safety resources for primary trainees in initial teacher education'. The findings from this project underpin the e-safety advice in Chapter 7.
2010 JISC	'Transition and support for non-traditional learners using online tools'. The findings from this project underpin the work in Chapter 8 on personalized learning.
2009 ITTE (IT in Teacher Education) and Brunel University	**Parliamentary Select Committee Inquiry** into Initial Teacher Training and CPD: submission of written evidence. The findings from this project about the knowledge base for teacher training underpin the advice in this text about the use of the Web to support professional development. This research informs Chapter 5 on teachers CPD and Chapter 10 on knowledge management.

2009 Becta	'Use of Learning Platforms to support Continuing Professional Development in HEIs and Schools'. The findings from this show the unrealized potential of an initiative such as the 2006–2008 IDeA 'online tools for local government professional networking' and how this can be developed for the education sector. This research informs Chapter 10.
2009 TDA UK Training and Development Agency for schools	SEN Portal Development: this development provided the sort of evidence-based professional online resource bank as envisaged in Chapter 10, Figure 10.4 item 4.2. These sites were archived by the 2010 Conservative Liberal Coalition government in the UK.
2006–2008 IDeA development phase – now ongoing (IDeA is the UK Improvement and Development Agency for local government)	See Figure 10.2 Development and implementation of online communities of practice for local government (www.communities.idea.gov.uk) using Web 2.0 technologies and allowing local government officers to create online workspaces for working with colleagues across local authorities. See the education version in Chapter 10, item 2.1 in Figure 10.4.
2006–2008 ITTE	IT in Teacher Education: the 'voices' project, which was published as, 'What does our past in involvement with computers in education tell us? a view from the research community'. The findings from this project underpin the history of technology as outlined in Chapter 1.
2002 TDA UK Training and Development Agency for Schools	Evaluation of the New Opportunities fund for the ICT training of teachers and librarians. This research revealed the difficulties of sharing expert knowledge across a national system, the lack of CPD support for schools and the isolation of teachers wishing to adopt new ways of working with technologies, which informs Chapter 5. Web 2.0 tools can support the rapid knowledge building and sharing needed for a society to develop educational practice quickly, which informs Chapter 10.
2002 NOF (TCT)	Evaluation of the Technology Colleges Trust (TCT) New Opportunities Fund (NOF) ICT Training for Teachers. The findings from this project underpin the work in Chapter 2 on policy and technology training for teachers, and underpin the work in Chapter 5 on teachers' professional development.

2002 EU European Commission, Socrates Programme	EU 'Web @ Classroom' 'Integrating ICT into the Curriculum: investigating teaching and learning outcomes in the permanently connected classroom' Final Report. (Socrates ODL 87866) **International Innovation Award**: 'ICT Best Practice in European Education'. The findings from this international research project underpin the work throughout the text, which examines how teachers incorporate technology into their professional practice; the factors supporting and hindering change. This informs an understanding of how policy at a national level effects change; those countries in the project with a central technology policy drive were more advanced than those without.
2002–2006 TDA UK Training and Development Agency for schools	The development and implementation of: **Teacher Training Resource Bank** concept www.ttrb.ac.uk; associated subject specific websites; **SEN portal**; **Multiverse** and **Behaviour for Learning** sites. Providing access to the research evidence base for the teaching profession, specifically teacher training. This development provided the sort of evidence-based professional online resource bank as envisaged in Figure 10.4 item 4.2. These sites were archived by the 2010 Conservative Liberal Coalition government in the UK.
2002–2006 eep	**Education Evidence Portal (www.eep.ac.uk)** – providing a search tool to search across high quality sources and research – see Chapter 10, Figure 10.4, item 1.1. Eep was funded initially by a range of government agencies.
2002 British Council	**ICT in Education in Mexico; ICT in Education in Hong Kong.** The findings compared practice in the use of technologies in classrooms in these countries with the UK. The findings from this research underpin the work on policy in the text. In particular, this informs an understanding of how policy at a national level effects change in the school education system of a country.
2000–2002 DFID	ICT for non-formal education (CERP project). This research informs an understanding of the uses of technology that promote learning outside the classroom.

2000–2001 IEA/SITES	**The Second Information Technology in Education Study** (SITES). The study focused on innovative practice using technology at classroom level across a number of countries and the findings on innovative practice provided an analytical framework for reviewing innovative pedagogies in schools. This research informs the work in the text on policy and pedagogy.
2000–2001 DCSF funded	**OECD ICT and School Improvement** UK: the findings from this project showed the power of Rogers' (1993) Diffusion of Innovations model, which was used to provide the theoretical underpinning for the national 2002 TDA and 2006 IDeA projects (qv) and the author's academic writings and ideas discussed in this text.
1999–2000 EU European Commission, Socrates Programme	EU **'European Knowledge Centre'** part of the European Schoolnet Multi Media Project: 'Developing the teacher-researcher interface on the European Schoolnet web site' Final Report (Socrates ODL 71511). The findings from this project provided the theoretical framework for the 2002 TDA research and development initiatives (qv) and the author's academic writings and ideas discussed in this text.
1999 TLTP	**Teaching and Learning Technology Programme 3** 'SOURCE: Software Use, Reuse and Customisation in Education'. The findings from this research informed the work on pedagogy, discussed in Chapter 5.
1998–2000 EU funded by ministries of EU countries plus the European Commission Socrates Programme	EU **'The Learning School Project'** part of the European Schoolnet Multi Media Project: 'Researching effective practice with ICT in schools across Europe' Final Report (MM1010). The findings from this research into how schools were adopting new technologies and new ways of working online to create and build knowledge provided the foundation on which many of the projects above were built. This project established the European Schoolnet and continues. The E-twinning project connects 5% of the teachers and pupils across Europe in online collaborative projects.
1997–1999 British Council	New Images project: this project developed new ways of working with the Web to support transnational knowledge sharing and informed the projects above and the vision expressed in Chapter 10 on knowledge building for the teaching profession at a national and international level.

1995–2002 DCSF Department for Children Schools and Families, companies such as Oracle, Sun Microsystems and De Montfort University Bedford

Development of **TeacherNet** concept www.teachernet. gov.uk. This project brought together expert educators, policy-makers and companies across the UK to explore the potential of the Internet to support teacher professional development. It led to the establishing of the DFE TeacherNet site 2000–2010. These sites were archived by the 2010 Conservative Liberal Coalition government in the UK.

1994–1997 De Montfort University Bedford with various companies

Project Connect: this project was focused on innovative schools and their experiences with connecting to the Internet and developing innovative pedagogies using technologies. This research informs the work **throughout the text, which examines how teachers incorporate emergent technologies into their professional practice.**

1984–1989 London Borough of Enfield/ Manpower Services Commission

TVEI: evaluation of the Technical Vocational Education Initiative. The Evaluation Reports for this initiative addressed the adoption of new technologies in schools and curriculum change. This research informs the work in Chapter 1 on History and Chapter 2 on Policy.

Index